WHAT ARE YOU WITHOUT GOD?

WHAT ARE YOU WITHOUT GOD?

HOW TO DISCREDIT RELIGIOUS THOUGHT AND REBUILD YOUR IDENTITY

Christopher Krzeminski

CEK Books

ISBN-13: 978-0615789453
ISBN-10: 0615789455

Dedicated to

My cousins, John Krzeminski, Jr. and Joey Deitch, Jr.

and

My friends, Lester Aaron Finuf and Sarah Gillie

Table of Contents

Preface

Taking a new step, uttering a new word, is what people fear most.
— Fyodor Dostoyevsky

For most of my life, I believed that there was a god. He was not particularly in the front of my mind on a daily basis, but I thought that the fact that he existed was basically well-settled. I did not think that he was directly affecting my life or interfering in the world on my behalf, but I had a misty hunch that there was some cosmic plan of his design that I was acting out each and every day. I had deep respect for people who devoted their lives to their religions. I understood that the wrongs of the world would be corrected in some other place and time. I expected my deeds to be assessed for their merit, tallied, and revisited upon me in an ultimate judgment whenever it was that I closed my eyes for good. Now, I do none of these things, and I only vaguely remember the person who I have just described.

The cracks in religious thought began as I proceeded through higher education, a stage of intellectual disciplining that the staunchest religious believers correctly fear and attack to protect the integrity of their ethos. Before my higher schooling, I had never taken a class or met a person who had challenged religious thought, and even if I had had such an experience, I likely would not have been receptive to the stance. As a student majoring in mathematics who was also encountering a host of other ideas in his curriculum however, the poetic musings of religious thought had to give way to the crushing pressure of analysis and critical thinking, and I became a lapsed believer. I say "lapsed" because I had not yet done the work to squarely confront and discredit religious thought.

Instead, it became a quaint curiosity to me, a strange yet familiar stowaway in the cargo of my reasoning. For the next seven or eight years, I lingered in an uncomfortable place with respect to religious thought in that I could not see its realistic accuracy with respect to the world, but a part of me was afraid not to believe it. After acquiring a graduate degree and more years of emotional maturity, I figured it out, and I write this book to complete the circle. This book is a gift to my former self, a memento from the future of what I would have needed to solve the puzzles that once trapped me. If you feel similarly caught in the web of religious thought, I hope that it will serve the same purpose for you.

I have met several young people in various forums debating this topic who have asked me questions about how I have arrived at my conclusions regarding the existence of gods, how I have informed my family of those conclusions, what life means to me without a god, and countless others. These people have been a main inspiration for this work as they have brought home to me the urgency of what is at stake. I see the patterns of my life recur in theirs. I can tell that they have heard the grating screech of religion's hull raking across the iceberg of science and logic, I recognize their alarm at seeing the often-profane behavior of those who are fervently religious, and I remember the secret horror and isolation of not understanding why anyone else seemed to sense the same.

These young individuals and their cleverness in the face of a world that is failing to prepare them to address these ideas have been another motivation for this work and have made me aware of the need to deliver a resource that can enable their safe passage through the morass of religious thought. If left to reconcile these ideas alone, perhaps many of them would have reached correct conclusions on the subject, but the problem is that time is a factor. When one abandons religious thought, that point becomes all too clear.

Personally, I did not expect my departure from religious thought to be a positive one, and I am convinced that many people feel similarly. The emotional relief that washed over me when I had completed my approach towards the conclusion that gods do not exist was a surprise, but it ought not to be. Many books about atheism concentrate their criticism on theism's intellectual failures, which are ample, but we will proceed beyond purely intellectual treatment of the topic and explore how it has adversely tampered with our emotional development as well.

Surely, the most decisive arguments against religious thought arise from its logical and evidentiary bankruptcy, but it also does not deserve to be able to claim the high ground on emotional matters either. Presently, many people who would not tolerate the practice of religion on its rational merits do so because they have come to view it as an institution that is good for one's emotions, and that is an unacceptable result, causing the emotional stagnation of countless people who engage it.

My goal in this book is to provide a complete refutation of religious thought and its associated conclusion of theism while simultaneously demonstrating the intellectual and emotional benefits of reason-based thinking and its associated conclusion of atheism. In Part One, we will discredit religious thought from the ground up by systematically attacking its terms and assumptions in order to collapse its conclusions. In Part Two, we will fill the void left both in our intellects and emotions after the discrediting of religious thought with consistent extensions implied by reason-based thinking.

We are destroying and then rebuilding; we are removing a faulty circuit and replacing it with a new, functional one. What we will discover as we proceed through the debate over the existence of gods is that both religious thought and reason-based thinking are nothing more than sets of assumptions about reality with associated methods of acquiring knowledge about it.

As we will further discover, these sets of assumptions cannot tolerate each other, i.e., they are diametrically opposed and mutually exclusive.

At no point in this book do I reference the specific name of any religion, and the reason is that they are all the same when it comes to the minimum assumptions to which one must subscribe in order to participate. Their common characteristic is what I refer to as "religious thought", which is any set of ideas or practices rooted in the religious assumptions that we will review in Chapter 2. That religions have generated quizzical oddities peculiar to the cultures in which they have developed is interesting from an anthropological standpoint but ultimately irrelevant for our discussion.

Regardless of the set of customs for any given religion, those quirks will not save any of them from an analysis that discredits their essential core, which will be where our pressure is applied. In this manner, the religious definitions and terminology employed in Part One will not engage the endless meanderings of any given religion and will instead capture the crux of religious thought, on which all religions are built. In other words, the form in which a culture has institutionalized religious thought is not at issue; the substance of its belief is what is at hand.

For the record, I do not particularly care to refer to myself as an atheist because that term merely represents my conclusion, not my analysis. I tolerate labeling myself as such only to demonstrate my opposition to religious thought for the benefit of fence-sitters who may have never met someone willing to engage the social taboo that protects religions from questioning. All I am is a person who consistently adheres to standards of analysis when assessing information that purports to establish knowledge about objective reality. Those standards of analysis have been derived from mathematical, scientific, and logical techniques that have yielded humanity unprecedented predictive capability in its surrounding environment, and there is no compelling reason to abandon them on the question of the existence of a god. Indeed, they are needed the most when the question at issue inflames one's emotions to distracting proportions.

Due to the nature of the debate, we will at some points wade into deep water when it comes to the nature of human behavior, society, and knowledge itself, and I have endeavored to minimize the theoretical musings on these topics. This is not to say that our discussions will shy away from heavy, philosophical considerations but rather that such issues will be nestled closely to practical sensibilities. For a line of argumentation to be truly convincing, both theory and practice must unify, and our discussions will place a high value on practicality.

I have debated hundreds of religious believers by now, and I have learned that the clever ones attempt to suck the conversation into a totally theoretical world because, once safely ensconced there, they earn substantial latitude to spin up objectively bizarre propositions, free from any cumbersome links to reality. I doubt that this is a technique to which most believers consciously resort, but they employ it to cling to the notion that the existence of a god is indeed possible, which is a proposition that I will not contest. After all, anything is possible, but not all things are probable or likely.

Finally, our discussion regarding one's framework for his new worldview based on reason-based thinking will be limited to momentous concepts about either the internal self or external reality that sit unexplained after the removal of religious thought from one's perspective. To engage smaller concepts that emerge from the forfeiture of religious thought is presumptuous and goes beyond the scope of this book's minimalistic goals. What one determines about the staggering complexity of humans and their nuanced interactions is his decision, hopefully arrived at after a high order of moral and rational deliberation.

When it comes to economics, politics, and other momentous areas of debate, one will find atheists all over the map. All that unifies atheists is their desire to see reliable evidence and sound logic constitute the underpinning of an opinion. Beyond that, all bets are off. Besides, one would likely never leave or have left religious thought in the first place if he still needed conformity of opinion imposed on his thinking from an external source.

With that, we are ready to begin. I hope you feel nervous anticipation. What lies before you is a great opportunity for intellectual relief and emotional maturation. As you will come to realize, the coming pages will not provide a skeleton key to unlock the doors to the prison in which you may find yourself. Instead, they will provide you with a new perspective to realize that the door to your cell is and always has been wide open. The only thing keeping you inside is you.

Always,
Chris

PART ONE

DISCREDITING
RELIGIOUS THOUGHT

1 – Terminology

Most controversies would soon be ended, if those engaged in them would first accurately define their terms, and then adhere to their definitions.
— Tryon Edwards

So much of the problem when it comes to understanding and dissecting religious thought arises from its poorly-defined terminology that enables looping, contradictory reasoning. The inertia of its vagueness must be thwarted with some preliminary work to clarify exactly what is at issue, and the first step will be elucidating the key terms needed for the debate. After all, one cannot rationally say whether he believes in a god unless he obtains some understanding of what the word itself means. Although the key terms of religious thought need discussion in order to achieve minimal clarity, it is impossible to define them such that they are reasonably specific. Indeed, religious thought unapologetically claims that its secrets are impenetrable to the human brain. Fortunately, the opaqueness of that proposition will not operate to stymie the present discussion.

In addition to the definition of religious terminology, later sections will engage basic concepts in both scientific and legal terminology. Unlike religious terminology, these concepts enjoy a reasonable level of precision, and they will be defined because their implementation will be advantageous in future discussions with respect to scientific knowledge and commentary regarding the state of the evidence for the places and beings posited by religious thought to exist in objective reality.

Religious Terminology

In light of the hazy nature of religious thought and its terminology, all that needs to be accomplished is the articulation of its key concepts with minimal precision and parsimony. By carving out their minimum, necessary scope, any extra aspects that have not been included will be moot if the terms render logical contradictions on the basis of their indispensable characteristics. To analogize, the fact that the branches of a tree are still attached will not keep the whole tree from falling if its trunk is severed. By concentrating on the essential nature of religious thought's terminology, the focus is on the trunk of its tree, and if that trunk can be decisively cut, then the entirety of religious thought will collapse.

God

Gods do not carry the same meaning or attributes across the entire gamut of religions, and their personality traits often vary from person to person. Some religions have one theistic god (monotheism), some believe in many gods simultaneously (polytheism), and others use the word as a description of a non-being like love or nature. There are multiple incarnations of what the word "god" means to people, but the more exotic and unusual formulations are unnecessary to consider. The overwhelming majority of religious believers accept three main characteristics of a god.

God – An immortal being that is omnipotent and benevolent.

Ordinarily, gods are also claimed to be omniscient, but one could hardly be said to be omnipotent if there are things that he does not know, which would hinder his ability to truly be all-powerful. In other words, the quality of omniscience is fairly implied by that of omnipotence and need not be independently mentioned.

So, gods have three necessary qualities: 1) immortality, 2) omnipotence, and 3) benevolence. Without any one of these traits, they would cease to have the necessary lifespan, power, or care for humanity to merit worship. On that note, recognize that the necessary characteristics of gods constitute the core of what makes a person care whether they exist. Consider what a god would look like if he were to lose any one of these three characteristics.

If there were an immortal being that merely cared deeply for humanity but was powerless to help man either in life or death, his existence would likely be met with general indifference. Worshiping him would be fruitless, and living one's life according to his will would pay no dividends. Such a being is only a pleasant thought. If there were an immortal being that was omnipotent but not benevolent towards mankind, why would a person waste his time worshiping something that is either indifferent to or openly hates him? He will not help man in the struggles of his life or death and may even be the source of what ails him in the first place. Such a being is a nightmare. If there once existed a being that was both omnipotent and benevolent but is now dead, then he is gone and has no use for worship. Such a being is simply a memory.

Gods matter to people because they are alleged to exist today, to be capable of intervening in the world in any manner, and to care about what happens to mankind or his believers. This is the nature of what makes gods relevant in people's lives from the perspective of investing time worshiping them and divining what their wishes are.

There are smaller philosophies that slightly tweak some of the characteristics of gods in such a manner as to render their worship pointless. One such philosophy takes the position that its god has all or most of the three qualities as defined above but that he does not intervene in the world, i.e., he created the world and then left. As a consequence of this belief, the adherents to such a philosophy do not have rituals or meetings to commune with their god, do not follow any holy instructions on how to live a life that pleases him, and do not believe that miracles occur.

In other words, such an entity is *de minimis* in a person's life, i.e., the effort put into the belief is so small that it is unlikely to affect his emotional stability, rational coherence, or moral decision-making. The point of this aside is that the definition of "god" created above has been tailored for accuracy first and foremost but also to capture a practical issue, namely, to focus on the version of gods that people are substantially altering their reasoning or lives in order to accommodate.

Faith

Faith does heavy duty in religious thought. Unfortunately, it is also the most malleable of its terms, prone to subtle misunderstandings about its meaning. "Faith" can mean "to believe in god's existence and benevolence" when the question is whether a god exists, "to trust that god will intervene" when the question is whether one will survive a trying ordeal, or even a shorthand way of saying "one's religion". Despite its confounding, alternative usage, the concept of faith as religious thought requires it has tremendous importance.

Faith – The acceptance of the truth of an assertion in the absence of both empirical evidence and sound logic to reasonably establish it.

Would one ever expect to hear a religion talk about what a blessing faith was if it had evidence or logic to reasonably establish what it claimed? Indeed, faith is the Alamo of reasoning, the place of final retreat for an argument that has seen its empirical and logical positions overrun. The merits of faith are so pivotal to the debate over the existence of gods that the entirety of Chapter 5 is dedicated to the topic.

While the definition provided suggests that faith is an action that one takes in the absence of reasonably convincing evidence and logic, it also includes the acceptance of the truth of assertions that are contradicted by the bulk of evidence and logic. In this manner, faith is simply accepting assertions without a reasonable, rational basis.

For practical purposes, decisions that operate on faith are often based on emotional hunches, which is a troubling mismatch of tools when the issue to be determined is a question of fact with respect to objective reality. However, the definition provided does not need to speculate into the tools that a person is bringing to bear on his decision to accept the truth of an asserted matter. For the purposes of this discussion, it suffices to understand only what he forgoes, namely, reasonably appealing evidence and logic.

This is a good spot to take a short but important digression on the confounding of the meaning of faith by its colloquial usage. The word "faith" has entered the standard lexicon, which sadly gives undeserved legitimacy to the version of the concept employed by religious thought. For example, everyone has said things to an old friend like, "No need to make any promises; I have faith in you." Of course, what such a comment really means is, "We have known each other for a long time, and I have reasonable evidence based on our past experiences with each other that you will do what you say you will, especially with respect to me."

Another example that stretches the level of personal contact a bit more would be a statement such as, "I have faith in humanity." Again, this is colloquial shorthand for, "I have known and experienced many members of the human race as well as their propensities for decency and profanity, and based on that evidence, I find it likely that our decency trumps our viciousness on average." People simply do not speak in this verbose manner because what they intend to convey is understood in at least a cursory way by their listeners. The point is that neither of these statements has anything to do with accepting the truth of assertions without a reasonable basis in either evidence or logic; they are examples of the same word being used to express concepts of different substance.

Religious believers often use the concept of faith as both a shield and a sword, i.e., they utilize it both to insulate their positions from rational inquiry as well as to attack the integrity of competing methods of thinking as also containing elements of faith. While this schizophrenic treatment of the term will be addressed later, it is imperative to realize that the concept of faith is accustomed to regular abuse due to its having bled into many different colloquial uses. When faith is discussed in this book, it means something specific, and its definition will not change as it often does in casual discussions.

As will be demonstrated, faith occupies a rather suspicious role in religious thought. Most of the time, religions are quite comfortable to explain their belief systems in an orderly, logical fashion. When religious thought gets into a bind however, faith always seems to be smeared on its logical cracks like putty, designed to preserve a veneer of consistency, and due to this role, faith is the nerve center of religious thought.

The Metaphysical

The metaphysical has many different names across religions, e.g., the transcendent, the other-worldly, *et. al.* The metaphysical is a concept that intentionally flouts human knowledge. Considering that all that humans can taste, smell, hear, see, and touch is physical by definition, there is no knowledge with which to engage the metaphysical other than to describe it by what it is not.

The Metaphysical – A realm existing beyond physical nature and incapable of being sensed with the body's five senses.

This definition is redundant because if something exists beyond nature, it cannot by definition be sensed with the five senses. However, the complete uselessness of man's senses when it comes to assessing the metaphysical has been explicitly included in the definition because it is too important to leave implied, as will be seen in discussing the concept of the metaphysical in the next chapter.

The significance of this definition will become clear in the juxtaposition of religious thought with reason-based thinking, but there are some initial nuances to consider. On the question of what can be sensed with man's five senses, sometimes tools are employed to augment the senses as with a microscope. Simply because one requires such a tool to sense a thing does not mean that it is metaphysical but rather that it is a physical object that the senses require amplification in order to perceive. In locating anything metaphysical, the senses are completely incongruent to the task. If something is defined to exist outside of physical nature, then the body's senses are of no use whatsoever in capturing it.

As a corollary, realize that if something crosses the boundary from the metaphysical into the physical world, then it becomes physical and ceases to be metaphysical, i.e., one cannot have empirical proof of the existence of the metaphysical by definition. Indeed, the metaphysical and the physical constitute a game of mutually exclusive definitions, which is the main point to remember when the time comes to utilize the concept.

The Soul

The concept of the soul will not come up frequently, but when it does, it will be useful to have some specificity in its definition. Doubtlessly, the concepts of god, faith, and the metaphysical are the most important terms in the debate, but the soul has unique significance. In religious thought, the soul is the concept that personalizes the infinite ramifications of its other aspects.

Indeed, a strong argument could be made that the existence of the soul is more important than the existence of a god on the question of a person's interest level in his religion. If a person's consciousness ends at death, he would be considerably less inclined to spend his meager time in life appeasing a god that has limited time to exercise his power upon him.

The Soul – The immortal seat of a person's consciousness.

The bottom line for what makes the concept of the soul relevant to a person is that it is a bypass of physical death. A person's physical body will die, but the soul is supposed to survive that event and preserve a person's personality, memories, and emotions.

Presently, few religions now suggest that the soul is a part of the physical body, which suggests that it is a metaphysical entity. Nevertheless, its definition need not contain such a qualification. Whatever the soul may be in terms of its other properties, its nature as the immortal vehicle of a person's most valued thoughts and feelings is all that is required for the present purpose.

Religion

Ironically, the word "religion" will not be a focal point of the effort to discredit religious thought, and the reason is that religion is the practical embodiment of religious thought, which entails additional complexities regarding human interaction that are irrelevant in assessing the merits of the ideology that supports the institution. The term is defined here for the sake of completeness as well as for its main use in Part Three.

Religion – A system of belief that 1) utilizes religious thought and practices 2) rituals and 3) meetings in order to commune with or worship a god or gods.

A ritual is a symbolic action performed in accordance with religious custom, e.g. prayer, and meetings are the coming together of religious believers into a group for the purposes stated in the definition. Most people that believe in a god have a religion, which is not to say that that is the only manner in which a person can exercise his belief in gods. Of course, there are less costly systems of belief, and they will be systematically explored in Chapter 10.

The three requirements in the definition must all exist together in order for a system of belief to be a religion. In other words, the definition of religion here models what one might colloquially call "organized religion". Religions take many shapes, ranging from tiny to global, but their specific qualities cannot change the nature of their foundations, i.e., religious thought. As mentioned earlier, the formalistic appearance of a group or its behavior means nothing as long as it is substantively engaged in religious thought, which is the mandatory cornerstone of any religion.

*   *   *

With that, the necessary concepts to discuss and assess the reliability and soundness of religious thought have been assembled. Returning to the tree metaphor at the beginning of the chapter, the terms of god, faith, the metaphysical, and the soul constitute the trunk of the tree of religious thought, which will bring down the entire worldview that it posits if they do not stand on their own merits.

Secondary and tertiary concepts like devils, sin, prayer, heaven, and hell do not have the same import. They occupy the upper branches of the system, and to discredit any or all of them does not succeed in ending the legitimacy of religious thought by logical necessity. If prayer is proven useless or illogical, that does not mean that the justice system of a religion is defunct, and if neither heaven nor hell exists, that does not mean that gods cannot find some place to put one's soul in order to revisit what that individual has done to displease them.

At times, these non-essential concepts may come up for casual reflection or to demonstrate a stark inconsistency, but they will not be a focus. After all, the key terms of religious thought put on a show by themselves. If gods and the soul are its main characters, the metaphysical realm is the stage on which they perform, and faith is the ticket with which one gains access to the theater.

Scientific Terminology

Unfortunately, some of science's most basic terminology has confounding uses in common parlance. Most notably, the word "theory" means something very different in ordinary language than it does in scientific jargon. As delving into nuances of scientific methodology is beyond the scope of this book, the only necessary items will be those that establish the essential elements for the assumptions of reason-based thinking as well as those that enable proper understanding of the current state of the art with respect to well-established scientific explanations.

Scientific Hypothesis

The acceptable formulation of a scientific hypothesis is a crucial step in the scientific method. As will be discussed in Chapter 3, a scientific hypothesis is appropriate to test assertions regarding questions of fact in objective reality.

Scientific Hypothesis – A proposed explanation of a natural phenomenon that utilizes sufficiently well-defined terms and is both testable and falsifiable.

The clause of "utilizes sufficiently well-defined terms" is fairly implied in the requirement that the proposition be falsifiable since one cannot prove a statement false if its terms refuse sufficient definition. The problem of terms purporting to make statements regarding questions of fact in objective reality while refusing to be sufficiently well-defined as to permit being expressed in a scientific hypothesis will recur in later chapters, most notably, Chapter 8.

For now, it suffices to understand that science is a controlled method of tracing causality through nature's systems, and the entrance point to the scientific method is the scientific hypothesis. Without formulating a hypothesis conducive to experimentation with terms that possess a reasonably sufficient level of testable specificity, scientific analysis cannot occur.

The requirement that a scientific hypothesis be falsifiable is significant. If one were to create a proposition for investigation without realizing that no set of results from experimentation could reasonably falsify it, then he leaves himself open to cognitive errors that could result in his tending to find his hypothesis corroborated, even though it may have a high level of probability of being an inaccurate portrayal of objective reality. In other words, confirmation biases become a problem in such situations.

Confirmation biases are routine and appealing errors of human cognition, which the refinement of the scientific method has attempted to counter by requiring that a hypothesis be falsifiable. When a person or belief system makes statements regarding the existence of places and beings asserted to exist in objective reality, the scientific method is the best tool for that investigation as its methodology acts to ensure reliability in what the senses perceive.

Scientific Theory

This term has been done great harm by the colloquial use of the word "theory" in ordinary language. A "scientific theory" is a term of art with a specific definition, expressing a much higher level of certainty in what it asserts than a person does when speaking of a theory in casual conversation.

Scientific Theory – An accepted explanation of a natural phenomenon that is well-substantiated by repeated experimental results and observations.

A scientific theory is not a speculative guess; it is the highest level of certainty that science has to offer. When a scientific hypothesis reaches a significant level of examination and corroboration, it becomes a scientific theory, at which point the accuracy of its predictions and strength of its explanatory power have both been accepted.

Of course, scientific theories are always subject to revision or modification upon the introduction of contradictory results or information, but their assertions are based on the best available evidence and constitute an explanation of causality in nature that enjoys overwhelming corroborative evidence and logical force. Tragically, many religious believers discard the scientific theory of evolution on no basis other than seeing the word "theory" and moving to dismiss what it asserts as flimsy and unproven.

Scientific theories do not necessarily enjoy feelings of utter unanimity in their fields. Many studies attempt to undercut the methodology of previous experiments and to challenge their assumptions, regardless of the level of scientific consensus on the matter. A scientific hypothesis becomes a scientific theory when its explanation of a natural phenomenon is so far beyond reasonable questioning in the state of the art that the vast majority of the scientific community considers the phenomenon accurately explained, but unanimity is never required. Any one researcher may disagree with the conclusion due to his own assumptions that the rest of the community does not accept as logical.

Dissent and disagreement are natural occurrences in scientific communities, especially when theoretical disciplines come into conflict with empirical ones, and the intensity of the debate is intentional and desired. The highest likelihood of rendering reliable causal connections in objective reality is achieved when ideas are challenging each other freely such that the best rises to the top by the force of its argument and accuracy of its predictions.

Evidentiary Terminology

These two final concepts will only be of use in Chapter 6 where types of evidence for the existence of gods will be assessed by utilizing elementary legal terminology in order to categorize characteristics of religions' evidentiary portfolios. Generally, the concept of evidence means anything that has relevance on the establishment of a fact, i.e., anything that tends to prove or disprove a matter.

Circumstantial (Indirect) Evidence

Circumstantial evidence is a term that is thrown around a lot in common parlance, and people intuit its definition with reasonable accuracy. Since the use of the concept in this setting will be a little strange however, a rigorous definition of what it means is preferable.

Circumstantial Evidence – Evidence that requires at least one inference to establish a fact.

Suppose that I witness Mack fire a gun at and shoot John. If believed as credible, my eyewitness testimony of that action is direct evidence on the question of whether Mack shot John. If I instead see Mack chase John around a corner, hear gunshots, and then run to find John shot dead, my eyewitness testimony to those events is circumstantial evidence that Mack shot and killed John because it requires an additional inference on the part of the person hearing the testimony in order to conclude that Mack did in fact kill John. One such inference would be that no one else was there with a gun when the two men ran around the corner out of my sight, and another inference is that

Mack even had a gun, which my testimony would be unable to establish.

In this situation, my testimony is strong circumstantial evidence that Mack has killed John, but it is still circumstantial by definition. This is not to say that circumstantial evidence on its own is never enough to reasonably establish a fact because it often is if there is enough of it in terms of quality and quantity. In order to make such a determination, the probative value and likely authenticity of the circumstantial evidence must both be weighed to determine the likelihood that it reasonably establishes the fact at issue.

Direct Evidence

Direct evidence is easier to spot than circumstantial evidence, but it is also far rarer. When it comes to the question of the existence of a being, direct evidence would be things like a photograph, a fingerprint, or eyewitness testimony.

Direct Evidence – Evidence that establishes a fact without an additional inference.

Imagine that investigators are trying to determine whether Kyle was ever in a given apartment in a building where a murder was committed. If a photograph emerges of him smiling for the camera at an earlier point while in the room, then that constitutes direct evidence that he had in fact once been there, i.e., the picture establishes the fact in question without the need for an additional inference. Likewise, eyewitness testimony from a neighbor who saw Kyle once leave the apartment and close the door behind him also constitutes direct evidence on the matter.

As with circumstantial evidence, direct evidence can always be attacked based on doubts with respect to its authenticity, but as far as what the evidence suggests without questioning its reliability and authenticity, it does not require any additional inferences to establish the question at issue. As will be seen in Chapter 6 when these evidentiary concepts are employed, the evidentiary portfolio of any given religion is both lacking on its own merits and of dubious authenticity.

*   *   *

Capturing both the generally understood meaning of terms as well as giving them reasonable precision is not a trifling matter. In fact, the routine failure to do so when it comes to religious thought is the central reason why people find it so impenetrable and mysterious. It is always tempting to fly headlong into the debate, but deliberate, circumspect construction of the playing field will yield more stable and convincing results. The purpose of language is to convey ideas, and if language is changeable and undefined, the ideas that it expresses will lack traction.

As one progresses through this book, regular consultation of this chapter to refresh one's memory of exactly what certain words mean is warranted. Sadly, some of the key terms defined here have alternate definitions or outright misconceptions with respect to their meaning, and it is important that those issues not be permitted to jumble the definitions created here. As will become apparent, thinking with clarity and precision is not a bonus with respect to reason-based thinking; it is the price of admission.

2 – The Two Assumptions of Religious Thought

It is easier to resist at the beginning than at the end.
— Leonardo da Vinci

Having delivered minimum specificity to the key terms of religious thought, it is now time to tackle the other problem that it poses for inquiring minds, namely, that it is not inclined to provide easy access into its assertions. Religious thought touts an air of mystery, which can make it feel impregnable from a deliberate, rational assault. Indeed, the exact location where it grounds its explanations for the human experience is safe from investigation because it has been defined outside human understanding. Nevertheless, religious thought must leave some loose ends in the realm of human knowledge if it is to be more than a set of fantastical discussions that bear no connection whatsoever to objective reality.

While certainly not without logical flaws, religions are not altogether logically inconsistent from an internal standpoint, and to the extent that they contain fatal errors, they will be located in their assumptions about the world, on which their internal logic is built. The required assumptions of religious thought have subtle elegance in that they are remarkably simple, yet produce the power to speak on a limitless range of events. So, what are the minimum assumptions about existence that one must accept in order for the remainder of the structure of religious thought to logically follow?

The First Assumption
The metaphysical exists in objective reality.

One does not have to investigate religious thought with much zeal to get the message that the world is literally not enough from its perspective. Religious thought has a strong aversion to classifying anything, especially man, along physical or material lines, mainly because it needs to generate an infinite existence for its audience, and it does so by alleging that an individual's consciousness will survive its doomed physical body. This is possible because of the concept of the soul, which is a time capsule in which the dearest parts of a person are protected from the meddling of life until uncorked and released by death in their perennial, unadulterated form.

But where is a person's soul located? To date, countless surgeons and anatomists have opened the human body, and no one has ever found the soul, i.e., there is no anatomic reason to believe that it exists. The same question applies to gods. Where are these beings? In order to escape the confines of empirical evidence in this respect, religious thought concludes that there is another realm of existence that humans are incapable of sensing, i.e., the realm of the metaphysical, which is the venue of religious thought, and it must convince its followers to accept its existence in objective reality in order for the rest of its commentary to have relevance.

It would be wonderful to speak with more depth and precision on what the metaphysical actually is, but the nature of the concept itself precludes the possibility. After all, one cannot reliably convey information about a place that has been defined around his perception, and in this manner, the bizarreness of religious thought operates to obscure its assumptions. As one wrestles with what does not add up about religion, he may ask questions about gods and the soul and why neither can be located, but people usually fail to bring such inquiries to fruition due to their failure to use suspicion instead of wonder with respect to the concept of the metaphysical.

The problem is that the assumption that the metaphysical exists in objective reality leaves a person without recourse to independently review the validity of further propositions delivered by religious thought. Unsurprisingly, people struggle to challenge their religion's assertions because they are often sourced in the metaphysical, which is an unassailable intellectual bastion once one concedes that it exists anywhere outside the imagination.

The existence of the metaphysical in objective reality is an assumption with substantial mileage when one reflects on its implications, and the additional wrinkles that any given religion can choose to incorporate on the basis of its existence are endless. For example, can what occurs in the metaphysical directly alter what happens in the physical world, i.e., can a cause in the metaphysical world have an effect in the physical? To what extent do the physical and metaphysical worlds interact? The answers to such questions depend on the strength of the assumption that a given religion chooses to employ.

The spectrum of positions on the causality interaction between the metaphysical and the physical runs the gamut. On one extreme, some religions portray the metaphysical as a passive warehouse for key beings like gods and the soul, i.e., there is limited or no causality between the realms. On the other extreme, the metaphysical is in routine control of everything physical, i.e., total causality exists with the metaphysical being the cause of all physical effects.

Of course, the extent to which a given religion wishes to capitalize on the first assumption is irrelevant in the present analysis. The universality of the assumption across religions is the central point. In religious thought, the physical world is an illusion that cloaks the true essence of existence. How do religions convince people to accept this assumption as an accurate reflection of reality? After all, the metaphysical has been defined such that empirical evidence of its existence is not possible. The answer is that religious thought has a mandatory second assumption for its adherents in the form of faith.

The Second Assumption
Faith is a virtue.

The value of faith is the central issue in the debate over religious thought. If one asserts that faith is a blessing and a wonderful device for spiritual purification, he is religious. If another person proposes that faith is preposterous and only called upon for things one cannot prove empirically or logically, he is a skeptic or atheist. There is no realistic middle ground. Bizarrely, religions tend to frame faith as a moral virtue, which is a tactic that will be revisited and explained in Chapter 12 when morality is discussed. However, faith is really a knowledge-acquisition technique, as can be seen from its definition, in that it pertains to a manner in which one can determine the truth or falsity of an assertion.

Consider the dual assumptions of the existence of the metaphysical and the positive opinion of faith. They operate in tandem to first make a claim (the metaphysical and everything in it exists) and then to provide a means with which to accept it (faith). That is all that religious thought requires, which is not to say that religions do not attempt to muster evidence and logic to support their claims but rather that if they convince their followers to accept faith as a legitimate knowledge-acquisition technique, then they theoretically do not have to bother.

For practical purposes however, most religious believers sense that faith as a knowledge-acquisition technique is not good enough, and the fact that they attempt to muster evidence and logic for their beliefs betrays their intuitive discomfort with the concept. Indeed, the action of accepting some information as reliable on the basis of faith while simultaneously feeling the need to explain other aspects of the belief system logically represents a telling inconsistency.

Since faith entails a dearth of reasonable evidence and logic, it is by definition unscientific and illogical. Therefore, logical arguments cannot be blended together in a system that requires faith from a consistent theoretical standpoint. Practically however, many religious believers employ faith as a safety net onto which key portions of religious thought can fall after the attempted trapeze act of displaying empirical and logical arguments in their favor has failed to reasonably establish their truth.

Why would a religious believer ever mention evidence or logic when he thinks so highly of faith? As will become clear in the next chapter, evidence and logic are worth a great deal to the practical, everyday schema that the brain utilizes to survive and function in reality, and their being arbitrarily abandoned with respect to religious thought creates stress of having to maintain an incoherent duality in the person's worldview.

Religious thought and reason-based thinking employ knowledge-acquisition techniques that are mutually exclusive and show open contempt for each other. To the extent that a person senses the internal conflict of maintaining both together, it is likely that he justifies the clash by conceding that he cannot survive physically without utilizing evidence and logic for practical life but that he cannot survive emotionally without entertaining religious thought.

It is possible that one may suggest that faith is somehow only appropriate as a knowledge-acquisition technique when it comes to the metaphysical realm due to its definitional impenetrability, and the latent assertion is that the contents of the metaphysical realm are exempt from empirical discovery and logical scrutiny, which assumes away the entire debate. Of course, the existence of the metaphysical realm itself is purely speculative in its own right, and if faith in the contents of the metaphysical is going to be stacked on top of faith that the metaphysical even exists, then the probability of error escalates to unacceptable levels. The metaphysical is alleged to be something that exists in objective reality, and the best tools currently available to humanity to determine such questions of fact are science, mathematics, and logic.

*   *   *

Rarely do people engage the assumptions of religious thought, and to the extent that they let them slide past unchallenged to discuss problems with higher-level concepts, they have forfeited the game without realizing it. If one does not challenge the assumption that the metaphysical exists in objective reality, then he is utterly incapable of discrediting anything that religious thought would like to summon from that arena. If one accepts faith as a legitimate knowledge-acquisition technique without assessing the quality of the idea on its merits, then he is likewise hamstrung from bringing analysis to bear on anything that may seem contradictory in religious thought.

This is precisely why the articulation of the terminology and minimum assumptions of religious thought has been so important: to demonstrate that the only way to discredit religious thought is by examining its doorway. Once one has accepted the invitation to enter its world, its two assumptions operate to garner a person's implicit consent to his intellectual disarmament.

The Two Assumptions of Religious Thought
1) The metaphysical exists in objective reality.
2) Faith is a virtue.

Notice how these two assumptions support each other. The first makes a claim that there is an unknown but strangely significant realm of existence in objective reality, and the second declares that the first claim is exempt from both scientific analysis and logical scrutiny. Of course, religious thought dresses up the substance of this intellectual legerdemain behind solemn labels and intricate mythology, but their ultimate effect is to arbitrarily disqualify science, mathematics, and logic from answering questions of fact in objective reality. Everything else that religions have to say is derived from these two assumptions, and one ought to be awestruck of the diabolical genius of religious thought when it comes to the shocking minimalism that it needs to function.

Religious thought's secret recipe for the perceived power that it generates is to 1) make a promise and 2) convince people that asking for evidence of the legitimacy of that promise is unacceptable, either morally or otherwise. Once a religion has convinced its followers to accept these two assumptions, its practitioners then have carte blanche to conjure anything that they like out of the realm of the metaphysical, and its followers will not be bothered to request the basis for any of the alleged knowledge presented to them. If they do, they can expect to be reminded of the terms of their initial contract, most notably, the clause that says that faith will be required for membership.

Courtesy of these extremely advantageous assumptions, religions and their practitioners have become the interpreters of a world beyond human comprehension, the power of which can then be used to make a statement of authority on any topic or occurrence that they see fit. Objectively, it is an unbelievably audacious two-step that provides an infinite amount of possible payoff for the people who claim to hold the invisible keys to the metaphysical gates.

As noted in the previous section, religions do quite a bit more than advocate faith as their only basis for belief, and they always attempt to produce evidence or logic to support their legitimacy. Leaving aside the fatal inconsistency of blending these two knowledge-acquisition techniques in one worldview, Chapters 6 and 7 will engage the practical, reason-based attempts that religions muster in favor of their assertions. After all, evidence or logic that reasonably establishes the truth of religious assertions would make faith a moot point.

Considering the nakedness of religious thought at this juncture, one may wonder exactly how people become convinced to accept its terms. As will be discussed shortly, religions often gain a foothold in a person's intellect by achieving initial delivery via a relationship where pre-existing trust and deference already exist between people. For example, a small child trusts his family instinctually, and religions encourage parents to mix their assumptions and ideology in with the rest of the practical lessons that they deliver to the child. The assumptions of religious thought have no empirical or logical coherence on which to rest relative to a person's practical functioning, and they must be incorporated into a person's identity without his successfully analyzing them, which is a goal that is most successful when a person is young and naturally dependent on others.

Of course, religious thought and religion could not have been conceived to be this brilliantly effective all at once. Surely, all of its mechanisms and constructs evolved to capitalize on natural social gradients that resulted in its mandatory assumptions finding their optimal means of transmission by process of elimination.

This is not to say that the more intricate mythology of any given religion is not constantly in flux because it often is, and those mythologies and moral codes have the latitude to evolve to suit the time and place in which they are delivered. However, the underlying assumptions on which such higher level commentary is based cannot change, and their definitional and investigational evasion speaks to their suspiciousness, not their mystery. As will now be seen in exploring the assumptions of reason-based thinking, the hallmark of systems of thought that are unafraid of the quality of their product is transparency.

3 – The Three Assumptions of Reason-Based Thinking

I am constant as the Northern Star.
— William Shakespeare

The creation of new assumptions for one's life upon departing religious thought is not difficult. In fact, one is content to use these assumptions for everything that he does outside of his religion. For example, how does one know that his computer will start when he hits the power button? Does he have faith that it will? Or does he have a reasonable expectation based on evidence and logic that it will because its hardware has been engineered with scientific principles and research?

If one's computer does not start, would he think that a god has chosen to interfere with its circuitry and cause it to fail, or would he call the helpline of the manufacturer and get troubleshooting advice? Surely, he would choose the latter. It is this practical, reason-based approach that would completely fill one's perspective if not for the arbitrary interference of religious thought in periodically derailing it, and the knowledge-acquisition techniques and overall worldview of reason-based thinking fly directly in the face of their counterparts in religious thought.

The First Assumption
Humanity's only reliable basis for knowledge of objective reality is the senses of the human body.

Clearly, the first assumption of reason-based thinking clashes with the first assumption of religious thought, which is not to say that it implies that the metaphysical does not exist but rather that humanity has no way of reliably determining whether it does due to the nature of its definition and the concomitant disqualification of the body's senses to investigate it. It will ultimately be by operation of the third assumption of reason-based thinking that religious thought's assumption of the existence of the metaphysical in objective reality will be dismissed.

The human brain is the apparatus that creates a person's considerations about objective reality, but it cannot create relevant thoughts or opinions on the subject without data, which must be collected by the body's five senses: touch, smell, taste, sight, and sound. Unfortunately for mankind, the brain's interpretation of the data that it obtains from the senses is occasionally in error, which can produce vagaries of perception. As will be seen in the second assumption of reason-based thinking, humanity has created several methodologies to check the accuracy of the brain's interpretation of the data that it receives.

The knowledge-acquisition techniques of the second assumption of reason-based thinking are science, mathematics, and logic, all of which have their foundation in the senses. This fact is evident in the empirical branches of science from their need to gather sensory data from experimentation, but it is a subtler point in mathematics, logic, and theoretical science, which are disciplines that do not seem to require empirical research in order to advance.

While these fields simplify reality into variables, operators, and expressions that seem disjoint from the body's senses, they still find their source in sensory observations. At their roots, these fields are built on axioms or postulates, which are simple, self-evident truths about objective reality that have been gathered through the senses. The higher levels of these theoretical disciplines similarly absorb such undisputed truths gathered by the human sensory array and incorporate them into their systems. The apparent difference between empirical science and the theoretical disciplines with respect to the human body's senses arises from the latter's translation of sensory data into a symbolic language, which has advantages with respect to piercing the overwhelming complexity of objective reality by using controlled, well-defined terms.

In any case, the knowledge-acquisition techniques of reason-based thinking as memorialized in the second assumption act as sensory-refinement tools, composed of humanity's most confirmed and trusted observations about objective reality. In other words, no matter how complex the tools of reason-based thinking may appear, they all observe the first assumption provided here. Indeed, how could it be otherwise? Even the wholly internal manipulation of abstract variables could not progress according to operations that simply come out of the blue as they would spiral into unrecognizable irrelevance. There must be sound reasoning behind any theoretical action in these disciplines, and the judgment of soundness can always be traced back to basic sensory perception that created the bedrock of the fields in the first place.

Leaving aside the knowledge-acquisition techniques, exactly what other basis does humanity have on which to reliably ground knowledge of objective reality other than the senses of the human body? Imagine that all humans had been born without any sensory capacity whatsoever. Surely, the brain would still function in its internal world, but how could it possibly assess its external world? Logic and theoretical disciplines would be of no use because one would lack the knowledge of the basic axioms to spark the creation of those fields. The brain would have no means of determining that the external world even existed. Indeed, this is precisely the situation with respect to the first assumption's implications for the existence of the metaphysical realm.

The Second Assumption
Science, mathematics, and logic are currently the most reliable methods to explain and predict objective reality.

Science, mathematics, and logic are the knowledge-acquisition techniques of reason-based thinking, and they represent methodologies that both depend on human sensory data while simultaneously guiding the interpretation of said data with prior, stable observations, the accuracy of which is beyond reasonable question. In other words, the term "discipline" is well-used with respect to these fields; they are disciplining the brain's interpretation of new data by bringing parallel connections in past, well-understood data to bear.

"Science" can be a gummy word as there is sadly no shortage of pseudoscientific ventures that resemble true scientific investigation in form but not in substance. Indeed, many so-called sciences are deliberately designed to capitalize on that resemblance in order to give their assertions undue credibility. However, exploring the substantive nature of scientific inquiry will help to separate impostors from legitimate investigators.

At its core, science is a philosophy about acquiring and refining knowledge about objective reality, and the engine that drives its practical experimentation is a technique called the scientific method. The scientific method is nothing more than a refined trial-and-error approach to investigation: one makes observations about the world, develops a question about what the cause of those effects is, creates a hypothesis to answer that question, develops a controlled experiment to test the accuracy of that hypothesis, and then observes the results.

The trial-and-error methodology of the scientific method mimics how the human brain learns naturally. For example, consider a child who is about to have his proverbial moment of touching a hot stove. The child sees a hot stove, becomes overwhelmed by curiosity, and then touches it. He was gathering information about the world by trial-and-error, using the body's senses as his data-collection instruments. The child sensed something about the stove he wanted to learn (whether it would burn him if he touched it), he formed an experiment to test it (touching it), and he got his results (it burned his hand). Thereafter, he has learned that when he sees the stove again under similar conditions, he will burn himself if he touches it. With substantial refinement, this is the investigative method employed by science to render explanations of complex phenomena in objective reality.

While the process may seem routine, the scientific method requires creative ingenuity on the part of the experimenter as there is no perfect hypothesis, test of said hypothesis, or roadmap to generate either of the two. Indeed, some scientists have become legendary in their respective fields simply for devising a test of surprising simplicity while isolating variables in the observed system such that the interpretation of the results and the correctness of the hypothesis could not be reasonably challenged.

This is the exception to the rule, however. The far more likely occurrence is that the broader community of scientists in a field will have to collaborate, share methodologies that each has devised for different tests concerning a given phenomenon, and hone in on the likely explanation for such results while weeding out confounding variables or altogether faulty experiments. In other words, they have to get their hands dirty with both theoretical conceptualization as well as practical experimentation possibly for years on end, depending on the complexity of the question.

Importantly, the collaboration of a scientific community to assess results and create a scientific consensus constitutes the core of what makes its results reliable. To analogize, think of the stock market. Investing all of one's money in a single stock is extremely risky from a mathematical standpoint. The stock may be part of an industry that is subject to supply shocks, the company may be hiding losses on its books illegally, or the company may be considering winding up in the near future. In other words, a single firm is subject to unique risk.

If one instead spreads his money across many businesses in disparate industries that share little overlap in terms of their exposure, he minimizes the unique risk of each company and approaches the minimum risk possible for his portfolio, i.e., market risk. This is diversification. It lowers the expected return on one's investment, but it also lowers the variance in that expected return, i.e., it makes the realization of that level of return more certain.

Diversification is precisely the strategy that scientific communities utilize when they conduct peer review. Each scientific discipline acknowledges that any one researcher's subjective view on an experiment is riddled with unique risk based on his potential for errors and misperception. By refusing to accept results as confirmed until the rest of the scientific community has inspected the methodology of the experiment and the formulation of the hypothesis, science's implementation of peer review makes the policy decision that unique risk is unacceptable without the introduction of rivalrous researchers to bring additional perspective. In other words, science diversifies its portfolio of perspectives on a proposed result across as many different people, cultures, and backgrounds as possible in order to approach market risk, i.e., the minimum level of human subjectivity.

As with its use in the stock market with respect to expected return, diversification in scientific communities slows down the creation of new knowledge, but it also minimizes errors that arise courtesy of any given individual's biases or vagaries of perception. Underneath the fabric of science is the premise that as the number of people trained in the state of the art and participating in the analysis of a problem reaches its maximum, the likelihood of the group's acceptance of results and interpretations that are actually incorrect approaches its minimum.

Even though it takes precautions to minimize errors, science is willing to admit when it has been wrong if compelling evidence surfaces to contradict what had once been an established explanation. There are no presumptions of perfect knowledge in science, and it does not have the power to generate pure certainty about objective reality, as will be discussed in the next chapter. After all, science cannot capture objectivity; it can only approach it by minimizing subjectivity, which is why the second assumption of reason-based thinking touts science and the other knowledge-acquisition techniques as currently the best available methods, i.e., superior relative to other available options but not in an absolute sense.

Before considering the third and final assumption of reason-based thinking, there are three smaller issues to consider. First, some fields fraudulently pass themselves off as scientific. A lack of reasonable precision in language, claims purporting to establish knowledge about objective reality that are neither testable nor falsifiable, and generally stagnant, non-advancing knowledge are all hallmarks of impostor sciences. Is it possible that they have some element of truth to them? Anything is possible. Are they providing people with any reasonable manner with which to investigate the accuracy and reliability of their assertions? No. In this way, they are strikingly similar to any given religion, and it is no coincidence that many pseudosciences borrow elements of religious thought, especially its mythology.

Second, an experiment's having been conducted in a legitimate scientific discipline that demands proper and rigorous use of the scientific method does not mean that the researcher's interpretation of the results of the experiment represents a scientific consensus. Sometimes, religious believers will locate an article or experiment that purports to be proof positive of a Creationist viewpoint and jump straight to the headline without reading the methodology, hypothesis, or the reaction of the scientific community. Peer review and scientific consensus are not quaint niceties for science; they are crucial aspects of the quality control process that it uses to deliver reliable information. To the extent that an experiment does not achieve such recognition, its results do not acquire a veneer of reliability simply by virtue of being a scientific attempt.

Third, the comments with respect to science and scientific inquiry roughly apply to mathematics, and logic is the underpinning to both. Mathematics has the luxury of being able to operate in an artificial world of abstract concepts that are deliberately well-defined. Mathematical applications to science are often useful in quantifying and memorializing patterns in nature with formulas or by discovering anomalies that are true mathematically but do not fit science's current understanding of objective reality. In this manner, mathematics is an integral partner to science that has the power to focus its investigation into areas that a researcher's intuition might never have considered.

Mathematics is an attempt to model the patterns of causality in nature with numbers, variables, and operators, all of which exist in their own pure theoretical world. When mathematics is paired with scientific inquiry however, they synergize into an impressive tandem. Sometimes, mathematical theory will imply a course of action for scientific investigation, and other times, scientific results will crack an impasse in mathematical theory. The union of these two fields creates an effective partnering of theoretical and practical disciplines, resulting in the grinding down of seemingly impenetrable mysteries into an understandable form, all while checking the other's work at each step.

It seems truly absurd to juxtapose the knowledge-acquisition technique of faith with those of reason-based thinking, most notably, on the issue of the reliability of the knowledge that each generates. By its definition, faith makes no attempt to provide any reasonable means of investigating its assertions, which casts the entirety of religious thought into dubious territory, and due to their definitional exclusivity, the knowledge-acquisition techniques of reason-based thinking utterly reject their counterpart in religious thought.

The Third Assumption
A hypothesis is presumed false until proven true under rigorous scientific experimentation, capable of independent verification and reproduction.

While the third assumption is actually a statement of a scientific and logical concept that is already a part of reason-based thinking due to the inclusion of those disciplines in the knowledge-acquisition techniques of the second assumption, it has unique significance in the debate over the existence of gods, and giving the logic of the rule special attention will crystallize some important problems with religious thought.

The third assumption describes the manner in which reason-based thinking establishes the burden of proof that creates the reliability of its knowledge-acquisition techniques. Considering an example of the informal operation of this assumption will help one to recognize its presence in the course of his ordinary, practical thinking. Suppose a person were to tell his friend that he owned a mansion that hovered two inches off the ground. In that case, he would naturally presume that that was not true until he was shown such a spectacle. In other words, people naturally presume that remarkable claims are false until reasonable evidence appears to establish their truth.

Without reasonable evidence, the third assumption of reason-based thinking operates as a filter, sifting out and discarding assertions that lack an acceptable level of support and therefore reliability. The brain will base higher thoughts, opinions, and motivations on assertions that it has determined to hold sufficiently reliable truth, and it is in its survival interest for those thoughts and opinions to be accurate reflections of objective reality.

Imagine it as a screening process for a new job. New candidates are interviewed, quizzed, and then are accepted as employees. After the completion of the interview process, no employer would need to engage in that level of scrutiny of its workers again. They have been cleared for access, and once they have, the success of the business will depend on the screening process having made positive selections.

On the question of the existence of a god, the brain routinely fails to activate its ordinary presumption of disbelief as embodied in the third assumption, and it avoids it for at least two reasons. First, it is a social taboo to challenge the assertions of religions in many places in the world, and the appearance of being dubious with respect to religious thought carries a social price that a person may not wish to pay. Second and more ominously, the thought of activating the third assumption may not occur to a person at all. The reason that the brain may bypass it is because religions tend to deliver the two assumptions of religious thought to a person via a pre-existing relationship with someone he already deeply trusts or on whom he depends, often in a parent-child setting.

In this manner, the objective bizarreness of religious thought artfully avoids detection by a person's third assumption by becoming camouflaged with the other practical lessons a parent teaches a child. Indeed, religions always cloak themselves as fountains of moral rectitude, and their assumptions and mythology are often delivered to children based on that pretense. Even after a person matures to the point where he is equipped to utilize his third assumption to assess general information, the assumptions of religious thought will have already breached his perimeter defense before it had been built, and the person himself will have neither the inclination nor the ability to reexamine every single lesson he was taught before that defense was in place.

Note that religious believers have no problem activating the third assumption of reason-based thinking when it comes to fielding assertions from religions other than the one in which they were raised, which makes sense. The intellectual bypass that religious thought installs in people before their brains have matured to the point of understanding how to use reason-based thinking is specifically primed for the religion that was taught. The brain recognizes the stories, the characters, and the general framework of that religion, but concepts from other religions that are not so recognized will trigger the person's reason-based thinking, specifically its third assumption, to presume that such assertions are false until proven true.

In other words, the brain has not been taught to accept religious thought in general but rather a specific religion's implementation of it. When a person hears assertions from other religions that do not activate his intellectual bypass, the brain does not recognize the concepts, and their objective bizarreness is detected and not spared the disbelief employed by the third assumption of its reason-based thinking. It is only when a person's religion of choice is referenced to his liking that the third assumption bypass is activated, and his reason-based thinking becomes incoherently muddled with religious thought.

Utilizing the concept of a scientific hypothesis, the third assumption of reason-based thinking applies to questions of fact with respect to objective reality. If someone were to argue that his subjective sensations of love or fear could not be tested under the assumption, he would be correct. More precisely, the question of whether he is in fact feeling emotions is a question of objective fact that could be determined from analyzing the parts of his brain that are active, but the issue of how those sensations feel to him is not conducive to scientific inquiry. Their terms are too vague, and they do not represent facts about external, objective reality but rather values about one's internal, subjective world. However, the question of the existence of the places and beings in religious thought is not a subjective one; it is a question of fact with respect to objective reality.

The third assumption of reason-based thinking flouts both assumptions of religious thought. The metaphysical is a location that claims to be a part of objective reality but that has defined itself around the knowledge-acquisition techniques that reason-based thinking employs to refine information. On that basis, the third assumption of reason-based thinking operates to disqualify it as unproven. Obviously, the third assumption's opinion of faith as a knowledge-acquisition technique is patent, given that it refuses to accept any information delivered without reasonable evidentiary support.

Leaving aside the poorly-defined nature of the word "god" with respect to its inclusion in a scientific hypothesis, consider the following assertion: "There is a god in existence in objective reality that has created man and everything in the universe." The third assumption of reason-based thinking operates to presume the falsity of that claim in the absence of further evidence. In other words, it demands reasonable evidence so as to say, "Prove it," while faith, the knowledge-acquisition technique of religious thought, says, "Trust me."

The Three Assumptions of Reason-Based Thinking

1) Humanity's only reliable basis for knowledge of objective reality is the senses of the human body.

2) Science, mathematics, and logic are currently the most reliable methods to explain and predict objective reality.

3) A hypothesis is presumed false until proven true under rigorous scientific experimentation, capable of independent verification and reproduction.

The good news is that the three assumptions of reason-based thinking are the only ones needed to discredit religious thought, and the better news is that a person relies on all of them on one level of consciousness or another throughout his life. If one had never been exposed to the two assumptions of religious thought, he would likely have never systematically digressed from reason-based thinking in his lifetime.

At several points in discussing these assumptions, the motif of vagueness in concepts and language arose, and it will continue to appear, most notably, in Chapter 8 in The Meta Argument. The machinery of scientific inquiry requires reasonable definition into the nature of the objects for which it searches. By aiming to investigate and map patterns in objective reality, the ground that scientific knowledge has already covered must be clearly demarcated.

To foreshadow later arguments in Part One, realize the incongruence of religious thought when it is juxtaposed with reason-based thinking. Religious thought posits the existence of places and beings in objective reality and then disqualifies the tools that humanity has devised and refined expressly to generate reliable knowledge about what is real in that locale. Practically, religions teach their followers to feel with their emotions that there is in fact a god, and what could be a more unreliable manner of establishing a question of fact with respect to objective reality than to encourage one's subjective feelings to lead the way?

Thus, the relentless clashes between science and religion ought now to be understandable. With the sets of assumptions on which they operate rejecting each other so completely, their feuds as institutions are unavoidable.

To clarify the situation, the debate between theism and atheism is the debate between religious thought and reason-based thinking, which is itself the debate between how best to reliably understand what actually exists in objective reality and what is imaginary. That is all that is being discussed in Part One of this book: making a reliable determination of what is real. With respect to the existence of gods, theism is the conclusion of those who employ religious thought, and atheism is the conclusion under the current evidence of those who choose reason-based thinking.

4 – The Asymptote of Certainty

Ignorance more frequently begets confidence than does knowledge.
— Charles Darwin

Almost universally, people desire to have certainty with respect to their knowledge of objective reality. Certainty generates feelings of comfort and predictability and removes anxiety that humans naturally feel towards the unknown. Indeed, religious thought earns much loyalty by offering utter certainty in its explanations, and considering the failure of its knowledge-acquisition technique to entertain nuance, it is actually bound to make its assertions with such force.

However, the knowledge-acquisition techniques of reason-based thinking cannot distill knowledge of objective reality to the potency of complete certainty. As seen in discussing the assumptions of reason-based thinking, humans technically lack the necessary objective frame of reference with which to achieve true certainty with respect to their knowledge of objective reality, though that level of certainty can be convincingly approximated.

Below is a simple chart, which will be a helpful visual aid in compartmentalizing the necessary terminology for the next discussion.

1. Gnostic Theism	2. Gnostic Atheism
• Says there is a god	• Says there is no god
• Claims certainty	• Claims certainty
3. Agnostic Theism	4. Agnostic Atheism
• Says there is a god	• Says there is no god
• Does not claim certainty	• Does not claim certainty

There are two axes to the chart: theism-atheism and gnostic-agnostic, the combinations of which create four possible positions. The axis of theism-atheism relates to a position on the existence of a god, and the axis of gnostic-agnostic pertains to the level of certainty claimed with respect to the conclusion on the theism-atheism position.

The Internally Inconsistent Positions

By virtue of the knowledge-acquisition techniques embedded in their respective assumptions, religious thought and reason-based thinking have necessary implications on the level of certainty that they can deliver in their conclusions about objective reality. Positions 2 and 3 in the above chart, gnostic atheism and agnostic theism, represent pairings of conclusions and levels of certainty that are internally inconsistent, and aside from their discussion now, they will be ignored in the remainder of this book based on their incoherence.

Gnostic Atheism

Position 2 is that of gnostic atheism, which is rare to find in reality. As atheism is the logical conclusion under the current evidence for those who employ reason-based thinking, the knowledge-acquisition techniques that have led to its conclusion on the question of the existence of a god are science, mathematics, and logic. As powerful as those tools are in rendering truths and patterns of causality from objective reality, they cannot produce complete certainty.

As discussed in the previous chapter, the root of all human investigation in reason-based thinking is the sensory array of the human body, which lacks an objective frame of reference to guarantee that it could not possibly inaccurately perceive reality. Despite their immense utility and predictive power, the knowledge-acquisition techniques of reason-based thinking can never refine the interpretation of sensory data to the point of pure certainty, which is clear from the open willingness of scientific fields to revise their knowledge at any point if convincing reason appears to think that past conclusions were in error. The knowledge-acquisition techniques of reason-based thinking can only anticipate patterns in nature by lashing well-accepted and reliable knowledge of past, similar events to the present in order to make reliable predictions of the future. In doing so, they produce extremely high levels of certainty in their conclusions and predictions, just not pure certainty.

Therefore, the position of gnostic atheism represents a confused and self-contradictory mismatch between knowledge-acquisition techniques and the resulting level of certainty in their conclusions. Practically, one can "know" many things about objective reality based on scientific inquiry, but theoretically, acquiring a gnostic attitude with respect to its results is incorrect. In this theoretical manner, gnostic atheism is an internally inconsistent position.

Teasing out the niceties of human knowledge may seem an arduous chore with minimal payoff at this juncture, but when the discussion moves to agnostic atheism, the details will be significant in order to understand exactly what that position says about the places and beings in religious thought.

Agnostic Theism

Position 3, agnostic theism, also has a mismatch between its knowledge-acquisition technique and level of certainty. First, recall the clash that occurs for gnostic atheism: the use of knowledge-acquisition techniques that utilize scientific and logical inquiry to arrive at conclusions of absolute certainty, even though no part of science, mathematics, or logic offers an absolute capability epistemologically. With respect to the knowledge-acquisition technique of faith as employed by religious thought, it naturally creates certainty, though the reliability of its conclusions with respect to objective reality is highly suspect. There are no standards of analysis involved with faith that reasonably allows one to analyze anything. Either one accepts the truth of an assertion without evidence or logic to reasonably establish it, or he does not. To the extent that one is uncertain in his decision, he lacks sufficient faith.

Religious thought does not offer any tools with which to penetrate its mythology, and even if it did, they would be strange and foreign ones to the human brain by the nature of the concepts that occupy the realm of the metaphysical. These concepts cannot be known to the human senses by definition, and if the first assumption of reason-based thinking is understood and accepted, then a person is simply precluded from reliably knowing anything at all about the concepts of religious thought, i.e., there can be no method that produces reliable knowledge if the human sensory array is disqualified from participation.

Therefore, the lack of standards of analysis in faith encourages one to engender a simplistic attitude of all-or-nothing thinking, in which anything less than absolute certainty appears to be complete uncertainty. On that basis, agnostic theism is similarly rare in reality because it occupies a territory where the level of certainty that it holds in its conclusion implicitly contradicts the knowledge-acquisition technique that was utilized in reaching that conclusion. Faith does not come in grades; one either has it, or he does not.

*   *   *

Due to the internal inconsistency of the positions that they maintain, those who espouse gnostic atheism and agnostic theism are on unstable ground. Without question, some people who attempt to hold these positions will linger in the theoretical contradiction of their views, but the respective knowledge-acquisition techniques of religious thought and reason-based thinking tend to act as a centrifuge. If a person believes that the limits of the human senses can only honestly merit an agnostic attitude with respect to any conclusion concerning objective reality, he tends to drift away from the implicit certainty demanded in religious thought.   In other words, he tends towards agnostic atheism. If he instead feels as though the only things worth knowing are those that one can claim to know with utter certainty, the inability of the knowledge-acquisition technique of religious thought to deliver such a level of confidence will not be appealing, and such a person will likely gravitate towards gnostic theism.

The Internally Consistent Positions

Positions 1 and 4 have internal consistency with respect to their knowledge-acquisition techniques and associated levels of certainty and constitute the main camps in the debate on the existence of a god.   Based on the methodologies of science, mathematics,   and   logic,   agnostic   atheism   correctly acknowledges that complete certainty in its conclusion is neither honest nor necessary.   Gnostic theism likewise maintains the logical position on certainty in a system that utilizes faith as its knowledge-acquisition technique.   Leaving aside any assessment of the sensibility of their respective assumptions, agnostic atheism and gnostic theism are internally consistent, which is to say that their positions on certainty follow from their respective knowledge-acquisition techniques as detailed in their assumptions.

Agnostic Atheism

Position 4, agnostic atheism, is a position whose conclusion about objective reality matches its certainty level with respect to the tools utilized to generate that conclusion. As previously discussed, the knowledge-acquisition techniques of reason-based thinking provide a high level of reliability and predictive ability, but they cannot yield certainty. Their results can approach certainty, but they do not come with absolute guarantees. As an example to demonstrate why pure certainty is not forthcoming, it is possible that the laws of the universe could all suddenly break down at any moment. That such an event is exceedingly unlikely and never seems to happen does not mean that it definitely cannot happen. Similarly, it is theoretically possible that one could be trampled to death by a stampede of unicorns. Practically, no one would consider taking steps to anticipate that contingency.

Failing to be theoretically certain is not to say that agnostic atheism is a position that is guessing wildly, which is a common misunderstanding by religious believers who seize on agnostic atheism's honesty in admitting the limitations of its knowledge-acquisition techniques to imply that it has no basis for its conclusions due to its failure to achieve certainty. What a religious believer who makes such an attempt does not understand is the epistemological nature of science, mathematics, and logic. Responsibly refusing to claim absolute certainty is a long walk from conceding that one knows nothing at all, and the same lack of theoretical certainty that agnostic atheism has with respect to the existence of gods is present on any piece of knowledge that scientific disciplines have to offer. In other words, there is nothing special or divergent about the conclusion of these knowledge-acquisition techniques with respect to the existence of gods; agnosticism is theoretically the level of certainty offered in all of their conclusions. In sum, Position 4's conclusion is atheism, its theoretical certainty level is agnostic, and both its conclusion and certainty level follow from reason-based thinking under the current evidence.

The position advocated in this book is that of agnostic atheism, and understanding the nuance between theory and practice in the position is important. The brain only has so many available resources, and if one were to wander about his day always cognizant that he could not truly "know" anything about objective reality, he would be unable to function in this totally theoretical state. Faced with a menu of infinite possibilities in each moment, the brain's practical decision-making would be paralyzed by theoretical noise.

Theoretically, agnostic atheism acknowledges that it cannot know that gods do not exist to a certainty. Practically however, all of the miniscule possibilities that exist in theory, e.g., one's head spontaneously exploding, his next step sending him rocketing into outer space, or suddenly only being able to speak fluent Mandarin, are too unlikely to waste precious cognitive resources attempting to anticipate, even though nothing guarantees that they cannot occur.

Gnostic Theism

Position 1, gnostic theism, likewise enjoys internal consistency with the level of certainty of its conclusion being in harmony with its knowledge-acquisition technique of faith. The topic of faith will be the basis for the entirety of the next chapter, but for now, it suffices to say that faith acts to provide religious believers with a level of certainty that they cannot responsibly claim to have. If one is prepared to utilize faith as a knowledge-acquisition technique for a given assertion, then he will have intentionally scuttled any other tools of reasoning with which to tease out nuances with respect to the reliability of his conclusion by definition.

None of this is to say that faith is the only knowledge-acquisition technique that religious thought or gnostic theism will employ in order to develop the interactions of its higher-level mythology because they regularly graft logical implications onto the motives and actions of the beings that occupy the metaphysical realm. Nevertheless, religious thought and gnostic theism cannot survive without faith, the initial breach of reason-based thinking that generates the metaphysical realm and its cast of characters in the first place, which is why so much energy has been spent building up the tools of the debate. If there is a definite error with religious thought, it lies in its terms and assumptions, not about what it further asserts after those elements have been accepted.

At the minimum, gnostic theism is internally consistent. The knowledge-acquisition technique of religious thought delivers the message to religious believers that certainty is the only manner in which to think about the existence of a god. To the extent that religious believers do not accept certainty, they are likely to default to the three assumptions of reason-based thinking, which means that they may wriggle out of the grasp of religious thought by virtue of questioning the value of faith. After all, people cannot escape their practical need for reason-based thinking in order to live, and if those standards begin to bleed into the religious domain, religious thought cannot survive.

Indeed, many religious believers do not seem to understand that they are operating with a separate set of assumptions with respect to religious thought, which is an unsettling fusion of faith with the certainty that it produces. The assumptions that religious believers have accepted, knowingly or otherwise, encourage their certainty, their certainty reciprocally camouflages their assumptions, and the feedback effect creates a rigid mindset where one tends to see his religion as beyond doubt.

*   *   *

By virtue of their internal consistency, agnostic atheism and gnostic theism are the natural poles for the two ends of the debate on the existence of a god. Agnostic atheism concludes under the current evidence that there is no god and admits that it theoretically can never be certain of its conclusion, and gnostic theism asserts with certainty that there is in fact a god. These are the two teams on the playing field in the debate over the existence of gods and the overall quality of religious thought.   Individuals may incorrectly maintain self-contradictory positions, e.g. gnostic atheism and agnostic theism, but the presumption will be for the remainder of the book that agnostic atheism and gnostic theism are the only camps worth considering.

There is a telling tradeoff at work between the positions of agnostic atheism and gnostic theism on the questions of reliability and certainty in their respective sets of knowledge of objective reality.   Based on the perspective implied by their respective knowledge-acquisition techniques, agnostic atheism prefers knowledge that has assurances of being reliable without achieving certainty, and gnostic theism favors knowledge that is billed as certain without any means with which to judge its reliability.   The stark contrast of that comparison speaks for itself.

Do Atheists Never Have Certainty?

To answer this question and explain the title of the chapter, a quick digression into basic mathematics is in order to understand the concept of an asymptote. To get a visual image of what an asymptote is, consider the graph below.

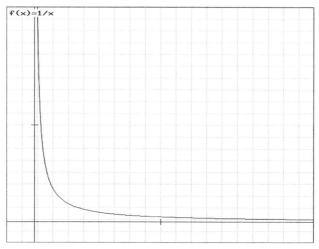

This is the graphical representation of the function y=1/x for positive values of x. The x-axis is the horizontal grid line, and the y-axis is the vertical grid line. The graph of the function itself represents all of the possible solutions to the function y=1/x, i.e., all of the points on the grid, such that the pairing (x,y) satisfies the equation y=1/x. On the solution curve for y=1/x, notice how as the value of x approaches zero, the corresponding value for y gets infinitely large, and as the value of x gets infinitely large, the corresponding value for y approaches zero. Mathematically, the solution curve is described as "approaching" these limits because it has asymptotes in both the x- and y-axis, i.e., the distance between the solution curve and these axes approaches zero but never actually reaches it as x or y gets infinitely large.

For the same graph, imagine the x-axis as "absolute certainty of falsehood", the y-axis as "absolute certainty of truth", and the solution curve as the possible levels of human certainty on statements pertaining to objective reality. With respect to judging a statement to be either true of false using the knowledge-acquisition techniques of reason-based thinking, one's available set of certainty mimics the solution curve above. One can get so close to certainty in a determination that he is practically certain but absolute certainty cannot be obtained. Certainty with respect to objective reality is an ideal for which the knowledge-acquisition techniques of reason-based thinking strive, but it is technically an asymptote.

As an example, the planet earth is spherical, which is not a statement regarding objective reality that is up for reasonable dispute. Theoretically, people have no guarantees that their eyes and other data-collection senses have not systematically failed to observe the earth's true nature. Practically however, man has observed the earth from space, sent satellites in orbit around it, plotted flight paths on its surface taking into account its curvature, and has such a staggering amount of evidence that it is indeed spherical that the theoretical possibility of that conclusion being in error is infinitesimal. With respect to the solution curve regarding objective reality on this issue, humanity has moved so far along it that it is as close as it can possibly be to the asymptote of certainty.

As for whether atheists ever have certainty, realize that the only thing that is thwarting certainty for reason-based thinking is that it is being used to make determinations about objective reality without an objective vantage point from which to view it. The knowledge-acquisition techniques of reason-based thinking have succeeded only in minimizing and purifying subjectivity by pitting many different versions of it against each other, not in creating objectivity.

However, humanity has created an internal world of abstract concepts that can have absolutely certain comments made about them, if sufficiently well-defined. In geometry, the definition of a square is a rectangle with all four sides of equal length. In this world of pure thought that does not rely on referencing objective reality, one can say with absolute certainty, "If I think of a rectangle with all four sides of equal length, then it is a square." It is only when one wants to transplant those ideas onto external objective reality that absolute certainty is forfeited. To the extent that people create an internal world of definitions and concepts, then they are creating objective rules for that world itself, which means that absolutely certain comments can be made about them.

On this nuance, Socrates once said, "I know one thing: that I know nothing." While a seemingly paradoxical piece of humble wisdom, it makes elegant sense in the context of the present discussion. In light of the asymptotic nature of certainty with respect to objective reality, it is likely that the spirit of this quote could be faithfully translated to say, "I am absolutely certain of one thing: that I am absolutely certain of nothing." Surely, he sensed that man lacked a basis with which to measure the definitive accuracy of his knowledge of objective reality but simultaneously understood that he could speak with absolute certainty on the state of his own knowledge, which existed in his internal, abstract realm of ideas.

*   *   *

Humans cannot know objective reality to a certainty, which does not mean that they know nothing. The knowledge-acquisition techniques of reason-based thinking have yielded boons for humanity in the form of cars, bridges, computers, and medicine, all without needing to couch their conclusions in the mirage of absolute certainty. Absolute certainty is a man-made ideal, i.e., it exists only in the realm of abstract thought. As a sneak preview of the later arguments delivered in Part One, gods with their perfection and absolute certainty are likely nothing more than residents of the same domain.

5 – The Knowledge-Acquisition Technique of Faith

The way to see by faith is to shut the eye of reason.
— Benjamin Franklin

Now that a thorough lay of the land has been charted for the terminology, assumptions, and certainty of each side of the debate, locating and attacking the weakest point in religious thought can occur, which will result in the collapse of its entire system, as will be demonstrated in Chapter 8 with The Fundamental Argument. Without question, the Achilles Heel of religious thought is its knowledge-acquisition technique of faith.

In religious thought, faith is something to celebrate and cultivate; it is an honor to be able to have. Faith comes in tandem with an emotion of bringing one closer to a god and often produces feelings of trust in his benevolence and plan. Reason-based thinking sees faith in a completely different light. Faith is the signaling of a location in an argument where a person has arbitrarily chosen to abandon science, mathematics, and logic and represents one's intellectual inability or emotional unwillingness to carry an analysis through to its logical conclusion. When faith is necessary to complete an argument with respect to establishing facts concerning objective reality, then the argument has provided its own refutation.

The Arbitrariness of Faith

By definition, faith is the acceptance of assertions as true without reasonable evidentiary or logical support. To decline well-reasoned and rigorous conclusions of science, mathematics, and logic solely because they do not suit one's taste is tantamount to rejecting the disciplines in their entirety. The knowledge-acquisition techniques of reason-based thinking require consistent application, and if something is going to be exempted from their inspection, there needs to be a sound, logical explanation as to why they are the wrong tools for the job. To permit otherwise is to introduce an inexplicable, arbitrary element to rigorous systems of thought that have been created and refined to avoid exactly that.

When a person asserts faith as the basis for any portion of his reasoning, what he is saying is that he is unwilling to press an issue for a logical answer. Once a person has taken the existence of a god on faith, why not take that god's alleged instructions on faith? Once he has taken god's instructions on faith, why not take the existence of the devil on faith too? Once he has taken the existence of the devil on faith, why not see some people as agents of the devil?

In other words, the landslide cannot logically end once it begins. The introduction of faith into a person's reasoning acts as a self-replicating virus that tears through a person's reasoning because he cannot stop it from infiltrating any topic. By accepting it as a legitimate knowledge-acquisition technique in the first place, he has forfeited the only techniques that could control it.

In all likelihood, one's high opinion of faith is the result of the assumptions of religious thought having gained access to his reasoning before he was capable of assessing their merit, and their awful prize is arbitrary reasoning, which opens the door to well-known cognitive errors. As an example, some religious believers delight in the belief that their god protects his flock from danger. When something eventually kills them however, then he was calling them home. Without standards of analysis to control the brain from incorrectly tailoring reality to confirm its biases and expectations, gods appear and vanish in events as a person sees fit.

A subtle implication of faith is that it suggests one's deference to an authority figure, which does not necessarily mean an individual. By accepting faith and pawning off his intellectual arsenal so cheaply, a person implicitly agrees to accept complete mental defenselessness with respect to anything that his religion tells him. Of course, religions selectively utilize the knowledge-acquisition techniques of reason-based thinking for credibility, but if a person wants to logically press an issue that he does not understand in his religion, faith is always waiting in the wings if he does not relent, ready to remind him that he had agreed to lay down his arms long ago.

In most cases, faith is actually a codeword for one's emotions, and the appeal of religious thought to activate them is a request for a person to allow his feelings to determine what exists in objective reality, which is clearly preposterous. However, what other tools does one have other than his emotions to make a judgment when he has sequestered his intellect? Emotions are an important part of any person's life, but they have their purpose. Reliably determining questions of fact about objective reality is not one of them.

Faith's Struggle for Relevance in the Modern World

In the times and places in human history where people lacked scientific inquiry or analysis, faith must have been a natural last resort. Without an orderly means to disintegrate the overwhelming complexity of causal chains in nature, faith is an understandable surrender, and insofar as the adoption of faith helped people to emotionally cope with so little predictability in their surroundings, it was probably once worth it. Without the knowledge-acquisition techniques of reason-based thinking to analyze and understand nature, man was left to simply shrug his shoulders, cope with significant uncertainty as best he could, and leave the daunting questions of existence to a religious authority figure. In the modern age however, crushing cognitive dissonance awaits those who accept this stale invitation.

The most painful ironies for religious believers arise from their interactions with scientific instruments that now saturate the modern world. The striking discordance of faith in the modern world perhaps hits its apex when some believers challenge the scientific theory of evolution over the internet with messages transmitted via fiber optic cables, satellites, and computers. By employing scientific tools to spread their religious message, they unwittingly send an encoded transmission with every keystroke that the means by which the message was delivered renders the message itself void.

Sometimes, religious believers try to incorporate science into their worldviews and say science is a gift from their god. If that is true, it is a strange gift, considering that the implementation of the knowledge-acquisition techniques of reason-based thinking yields the conclusion that gods do not exist under the current evidence. When scientific results displease the religious, they are quick to point out that science cannot conclusively prove the determination that has upset them. Considering the review of the asymptote of certainty, this is an unremarkable observation and a fallacious one to boot if it is meant to imply that only conclusive certainty is worth achieving.

More than anything, religious believers desire to reconcile faith with their practical mindset that requires evidence and logic, but unfortunately, the knowledge-acquisition techniques are mutually exclusive by definition. If one has faith in a statement, he has neither sufficient evidence nor logic to reasonably establish its truth, and if he has such evidence or logic, he cannot possibly have faith. In the times in history when religions lacked competition from scientific inquiry, the inconsistency was less dramatic, mainly because the vast majority of people lacked the analytical tools and training necessary to feel any cognitive discomfort. Today, science, mathematics, and logic have repeatedly demonstrated their predictive ability and practical value with respect to accurately modeling objective reality, and religious believers cannot help but to incorrectly blend their two sets of assumptions.

As an illustration, consider the dreadful scenario of a loved one being unconscious in the hospital. The entire reason that he was taken to the hospital in the first place was to make use of modern medicine and to have trained professionals attempt to identify and correct problems in the integrity of his body. In such a scenario, religious believers might pray or place religious talismans in the person's room while he receives medical treatment, but if prayer or religious items were going to save him, why did they even bother taking him to the hospital? If the patient recovers, are they going to give the doctors any credit for employing scientific techniques effectively, or will the kudos be delivered to their god? None of what the religious do in this scenario makes any objective sense because they are blending two incompatible sets of assumptions. Modern medicine is operating on assumptions that find the existence of a god highly unlikely, and religions are operating on assumptions that find modern medicine to be unnecessary. To employ both is to understand neither.

Such is the dilemma of faith in the modern age. Faith was born and extolled in a time when man had not yet created, or at least proliferated, rigorous systems of analyzing objective reality. In that environment, faith was mandatory for almost everything except the most basic chains of causality. Today, faith gasps for air under the piles of evidentiary and logical support that the knowledge-acquisition techniques of reason-based thinking have mustered.

In other words, faith is obsolete. It represents humanity's first attempt at acquiring knowledge about and explaining objective reality, and the knowledge-acquisition techniques of reason-based thinking are man's most recent and superior efforts. To think that any amount of faith with respect to questions of objective reality is reconcilable with reason-based thinking is a significant error. Their mutual exclusivity arises by definition. Faith arises only in locations where reasonable evidence and logic are absent, and in that respect, it is literally unreasonable.

Don't Atheists Have Faith?

In light of the time that has been invested articulating terminology and assumptions, the suggestion that atheists have faith may seem preposterous, but it is a tenacious misunderstanding. Atheists often hear the comment, "It takes just as much faith to disbelieve in gods as it does to believe in them." Before getting into the substance of the question, consider the subtle suicide of the comment for the religious believers who speak it. The religious are supposed to consider faith a privilege. Why would they want to allege that a non-believer has any part of it? If faith is a pristine pool of virtue, why use it with the connotation of a slur or weakness? Unwittingly, they sabotage religious thought with the question itself, but due to their maintaining diametrically opposed sets of assumptions, the contradiction is a bucket of water in the ocean.

With respect to the substance of the question, the allegation of faith in atheism implies that one has faith that a god does not exist because the knowledge-acquisition techniques of reason-based thinking cannot conclusively disprove it. However, the third assumption of reason-based thinking operates to establish the correct burden of proof with respect to assertions concerning objective reality, and the presumption of falsehood for those that do not satisfy it is not an act of faith; it is the explicit rejection of taking assertions on the basis of faith. Would one suggest that it takes faith to disbelieve in the existence of unicorns or werewolves? There is no evidence that either exists or logically must exist, and so they are disregarded as products of man's imagination.

Possibly, the question of faith in atheism pertains to the assumptions of reason-based thinking by suggesting that one needs faith to believe that they accurately reflect nature. Are the three assumptions of reason-based thinking without evidentiary or logical support? No. Indeed, they go to great lengths to contain nothing else. The first and second assumptions root themselves in both empirical evidence and logical rules while the third is purely logical.

What is happening when it comes to the insinuation that atheism needs faith is that many religious believers themselves do not have a grasp of what faith is. As most have never bothered to define the word themselves, it morphs into different shapes and causes subtle confounding. When religious believers accuse atheists of needing faith, they likely mean to say, "Trust or certainty that one could not possibly be wrong", which is not what faith means. To play along however, atheists have "faith" in the non-existence of gods to the exact extent that they have "faith" in the non-existence of dragons and vampires.

Splitting the Difference - Pascal's Wager

Blaise Pascal was a brilliant French physicist and mathematician who is widely credited with creating a probabilistic thought experiment now known as Pascal's Wager. The Wager asserts that god, an unknown and presumably unknowable entity, either exists or does not and that human reason is by definition an insufficient tool to determine the issue. Assigning an equal probability to god's existence and non-existence, i.e., 50/50, the Wager then moves on to discuss the payoff structures around the decision of whether to worship god or not. Essentially, the Wager argues that if one worships god he will either realize an infinite gain (going to heaven if god exists) or a finite loss (death with no god in existence to reward his belief). If one chooses not to worship god however, he stands to realize either a finite gain (death with no god in existence to punish his disbelief) or an infinite loss (going to hell if god exists). Given the available payoffs and associated probabilities, the reasoning concludes that one should choose to believe in and worship god. So, Pascal's Wager is not a proof of the existence of a god; it is a game-theoretical strategy of how one should choose to behave, assuming that one cannot ever know whether a god actually exists.

Many people have likely intuited similar reasoning to Pascal's Wager when considering whether to believe in gods or participate in a religion, regardless of whether they have ever heard its formal presentation. One does not need to be an expert in probability theory to understand that a miscalculation with eternal ramifications is infinitely more costly than an error with finite ones, and many people tend to err on the side of demonstrating risk-averseness with infinite payoffs on the line, i.e., they err on the side of presuming that a god exists.

For all of its easy, intuitive appeal, the Wager suffers from major errors. First, the Wager significantly overstates the probability of a person realizing his desired, infinite reward and avoiding his feared, infinite punishment. The Wager reasons that god either exists or does not, and since man cannot bring his reason to bear to settle the question, the issue becomes a 50/50 coin flip. From the perspective of one who may wish to employ the strategy of the Wager however, that probability does not accurately capture his dilemma due to its presumption that there is only one god available in which to believe.

Actually, humanity has known thousands of gods over the course of its history. For illustrative purposes and erring on the extremely conservative side, assume that there have been one hundred gods in human history that have been believed to be capable of delivering eternal judgment. If a person wants to realize infinite gain, a god must not only exist, but he must also pick the right one. Without getting bogged down in the fine points of probability theory, one multiplies the probability of each event taking place on its own when attempting to determine the probability of both events taking place in conjunction. So, consider the following approximation:

Probability that a god exists =	1/2	(50%)
Multiplied by	x	
Probability that the correct god has been chosen =	1/100	(1%)
Equals		
Probability of infinite reward of Pascal's Wager =	1/200	(0.5%)

In this light, there is only a small probability of successfully executing the Wager's strategy and capturing the most desirable payoff, a far cry from the tempting 50% chance suggested by the Wager. The chance of reaching the conjunctive outcome of both there being a god in existence and that god being the same one that the individual has chosen to worship is not even remotely close to 50%. Therefore, the Wager oversells its strategy of realizing infinite reward and avoiding infinite punishment due to the number of available gods from which to choose in human history.

Second, a key assumption that goes into Pascal's Wager is that human reason is of no use when examining the question of the existence of a god because of the inconceivable nature of gods. Leaving aside the integrity of that assumption for now, what about the soul? The soul is the alleged vehicle that must exist in order for these infinite payoffs in death to be legitimate. Man's reasoning ability is not similarly disqualified from examining the existence of the soul in the same way that the Wager assumes it is unable to examine the existence of gods.

As will be argued in Chapter 8 in The Fundamental Argument, there is neither sufficient evidence nor logical necessity to establish the existence of the soul. However, the excuse for not applying scientific and logical examination to gods does not apply equally to the soul. Therefore, the Wager's payoff structure is void from the outset. Even if one were to concede that the assumptions of the Wager succeed in smuggling a god through the barrier of reason, they forget to take the concept of the soul with it. Without the soul's existence being able to satisfy reason, the existence of a god is moot when it comes to the Wager's infinite payoffs. Whether a god exists and is capable of delivering infinite punishment or reward is a pointless question if nothing infinite of one's consciousness remains after death in order to receive such treatment.

Lastly and most importantly, the Wager's assumption that gods are beings that are exempt from ordinary analysis and logic by definition is an argument that contains the logical fallacy of special pleading, also known as stacking the deck. In general, the error can be described as claiming an exemption from ordinary analysis without establishing a logical basis for that exemption. On the subject of gods, simply defining them as beings that no one could ever understand in order to carve out an exemption from analytical treatment represents the definition of special pleading.

The two arguments given earlier against the soundness of the logic contained in Pascal's Wager were discussed because they are additional considerations that emphasize the Wager's clumsiness, but the last argument is all that is needed from a logical perspective to eliminate Pascal's Wager from serious consideration. The assumption that reason cannot be brought to bear on the question of the existence of a god is ludicrous from a logical perspective because no meaningful basis for that exemption has been provided. There is no empirical proof, logical necessity, or even thoroughness of definition of what a god is in order to give an acceptable reason to exempt the concept from the ordinarily applicable analytical tools other than his being defined around them. This is the pinnacle of stacking the deck, and it is a logical error.

Anyway, the three criticisms of the Wager discussed here have been based on attacking both its assumptions and terminology. That the attacks were aimed at those locations of the argument should not come as a surprise. Errors in logic subsequent to the initial framing of an argument are easily discovered, and arguments that contain errors in those locations are too routinely discredited to withstand the test of time. In other words, such arguments have their errors located in the area that people tend to inspect closest for logical validity and soundness. Like religious thought in general, Pascal's Wager has lingered in human history because its fallacies are buried where casual observers do not focus, namely, in the argument's terminology and assumptions.

I think it to be quite a shame that Blaise Pascal's name is attached to a logical attempt as flimsy as the Wager. His intellectual legacy in mathematics and physics is substantial, and quite frankly, he deserves better. As someone who took a major in mathematics as an undergraduate, I have supreme respect for those who have had the ability to create mathematical theory. It is difficult enough to learn to mimic what such minds did, but to be able to generate new mathematics requires stupendous intellect and creativity. The groundbreaking genius of Blaise Pascal is painfully absent from the Wager, but as I have taken a good amount of time to criticize it, I wished to take a moment to make clear that the man who created the thought experiment was much better than this. The fact that one can find his name sprinkled throughout any probability or physics textbook is testament to his intellectual legacy, and it would be a sad irony of history if the vast majority of people knew his name only from his least flattering work.

*   *   *

Why is faith ever a good thing? Of what use is the certainty that it produces if it is simultaneously bereft of reliability? If one never asks those questions and thoughtlessly accepts faith as a knowledge-acquisition technique, then he will be unable to discredit the conclusions that religious thought reaches. As for faith, it is intellectual fool's gold and is likely the net result of a person feeling overwhelmed by the concepts of religious thought and being unable to restrain his emotions from trumping his intellect. Subtly, religions admit as much themselves by camouflaging faith as a moral virtue instead of what it really is, namely, a knowledge-acquisition technique.

Despite the theoretical inconsistency of the attempt when combined with ideas that require faith to be believed, religions muster evidentiary and logical bases for their systems of belief, and before getting to the articulation of the final arguments to discredit religious thought, the practical, reason-based attempts by religions to support their assertions will be examined. After all, religions will not need faith if they actually have reasonable evidence and logic to support what they assert.

6 – Logical Arguments and Empirical Evidence for the Existence of a God

As a rule, men worry more about
what they can't see than about what they can.
– Julius Caesar

The evidentiary and logical portfolio offered by religions will be considered an argument in the alternative for the existence of a god, i.e., an independent attempt to gain acceptance for their assertions if faith proves unconvincing, as it has.   Considering the respective opinions of believers and skeptics on the value of faith and their concomitant stances on the value of evidence and logic, the empirical evidence for the existence of a god and the logical legitimacy of religious thought is underwhelming to say the least.   Either empirically or logically, religions nevertheless attempt to offer a reasonable basis to believe that gods do in fact exist. Clearly, they prefer to offer their followers more than faith as the support beam for their entire structure, and when they do, they all follow the same patterns of argumentation.

Logical Arguments for the Existence of a God

Religions pose many logical arguments in favor of the existence of a god. Some are coherent, most are not, and the rest are truly bizarre. However, the coherent ones boil down to three patterns, all of which are very well-known. The proper refutation of these arguments will demonstrate reason-based thinking in action as well as several corollaries that result from it, most notably, requiring reasonable definition in terms used to establish claims with respect to objective reality. Note that these logical arguments are not religion-specific. They only argue for the logical necessity of a god in existence without deigning to establish the legitimacy of any given religion.

The Cosmological Argument – An argument to escape an infinite regress of causation

Argument: Causality is a logical law that runs through the entire universe. For any given occurrence, there is a preceding cause or set of causes that has resulted in that effect. Intuitively, the law of causality ought to apply to the universe itself. If the universe is the effect, what is its cause? More to the point, infinite regresses of causation are considered logical fallacies and impossibilities. So, what was the first cause that triggered the set of effects that includes both the universe and human life? It must have been god, a being that caused his own existence or who did not need a cause in order to come into existence. Given the unprecedented power that must have been required in order to create the vast energy in the universe, god must be omnipotent, and as he is either his own cause or without need of a cause for his existence, he is also immortal.

Refutation: The Cosmological Argument does not make a serious effort to establish the existence of a god with the associated three characteristics in the definition created in Chapter 1. Its focus is on causality and the unprecedented nature of that causality with respect to the universe's origin. For expedience purposes and for clarity of terminology, the simplifying concession will be made that the attributes of a god will be established if the argument's reasoning is otherwise successful in establishing the logical necessity of the cause of the universe as a conscious being.

First, the entire thrust of The Cosmological Argument rests on the logical need to avoid an infinite regress of causation, and in its solution to the problem presented by the law of causality vis-à-vis the universe, the argument simply breaks the law of causality without justification. The Cosmological Argument creates a definitional dodge of an infinite regress by summoning an entity that itself breaks the law of causality, positing a being that is either its own cause or that does not require a cause at all. In other words, the argument provides a solution that breaks the logical rule that was the cause of the whole problem in the first place.

If all that was needed to fill the logical hole regarding the cause of the universe was an arbitrary moment of self-causation, it could be argued that the universe caused itself. Such an explanation would be of equivalent logical force, more parsimonious, and therefore superior, i.e., if self-causation is on the table, it is logically preferable to cut out the middleman. What is remarkable about The Cosmological Argument is the unassuming manner in which it has its cake and eats it too. For an argument that contains such a blatant error, it somehow generates significant intuitive appeal.

Second, The Cosmological Argument implies that the cause of the universe has a consciousness without demonstrating the logical necessity of that result. The argument's use of the loaded term "god" has the sneaky implication that the argument is generating more power than it is. Creating an argument for the causation of the universe that is couched in the terminology of religious thought, The Cosmological Argument primes the listener with the unwarranted assumption that if the argument successfully establishes the self-causing or uncaused nature of its first cause, then it will have established that that first cause is also a sentient being.

The Cosmological Argument wants to argue that a unique, self-causing or uncaused force is logically necessary to the universe, and even if it were to be conceded that it so succeeded, it does not establish the logical necessity of that force having a consciousness. Without that element, its argument is a moot point, and if one wanted to worship based on nothing more than what The Cosmological Argument logically deigns to prove, he would be left doing something akin to worshiping gravity.

As The Cosmological Argument cannot produce logical necessity for the consciousness of the first cause based on nothing more than its solution to a problem of causality, it has a partner argument, The Teleological Argument, which attempts to deliver that logical necessity independently. Even though The Cosmological Argument is unsuccessful on its merits, The Teleological Argument will be assessed for redundancy purposes since it can be asserted independently and is prone to frequent and casual abuse.

The Teleological Argument – An argument for purposeful design of the universe

Argument: The Teleological Argument contends that the seeming harmony and complexity of the universe necessarily implies the existence of a conscious creator or designer, especially when it comes to the interaction of humanity with its environment on the earth. The argument suggests that the universe and man's place in it could not have occurred due to random chance or non-purposeful action, and as such purposeful action requires a conscious intelligence, the existence of a god is logically necessary.

Refutation: In order to assess The Teleological Argument, the force of its argument must be considered through two independent lenses: from the standpoint of the universe in isolation and from the standpoint of the universe vis-à-vis humanity. The latter of these two considerations is how it is more commonly employed.

First, The Teleological Argument implies that the universe reflects genius and complex design even without reference to humanity's place in it. Of course, one can only shrug his shoulders to that assertion and ask, "Compared to what?" It is not as though humanity has knowledge of another universe as a reference for what an "undesigned" universe would look like. The universe as it is currently understood is a one-of-a-kind entity without a known peer with which to make comparisons on its orderliness. To the extent that The Teleological Argument asserts that the complexity of the universe demonstrates the logical necessity of conscious motive or purpose in designing it, it is meaningless because there is no comparable frame of reference.

However, The Teleological Argument is used more often to imply that the earth and the universe are perfect designs relative to man. In this case, the assertion of orderly design in the universe at least has a legitimate frame of reference and perspective. In this form, The Teleological Argument is the underpinning of Creationism and its more sleekly named but otherwise identical twin, intelligent design. The appeal of the argument is that it is a lay framing of the perceived natural orderliness of the universe from man's perspective, and it takes no effort whatsoever to assert. The argument looks at nature from the casual perspective of the naked human eye, from which it is easy to assume a feeling of dominance over and purpose in nature. After all, man is an apex predator on the earth and outclasses all other animals on the planet in terms of ingenuity and complexity of thought. In other words, the table does seem to be set for humanity on this planet. Man does seem special in this place.

But the planet once seemed flat too. The sun once seemed to orbit the earth. The problem with one's entire argument being based on how things casually appear without rigorous standards of analysis behind that observation is that such non-rigorous observations can be fraught with vagaries of perception. Indeed, this was the subtle master stroke that scientific inquiry brought to the table: decreasing the chances of a vagary of perception by increasing the objectivity of study. Complete objectivity with respect to objective reality is impossible as discussed in Chapter 4, but the minimization of subjectivity sufficiently models the desired ideal.

The point is that the most reliable tools with which to make determinations about questions of fact in objective reality are the knowledge-acquisition techniques of reason-based thinking. By failing to employ rigorous techniques and standards, those who assert The Teleological Argument are saying little more than, "I sense order in the world, therefore there is a god." In other words, they are offering a claim regarding objective reality that should be subject to verification based on empirical discovery or logical necessity, and their support for that assertion is their subjective gut feeling that they sense that this is so.

Considering the unadulterated subjectivity of the argument, the presence of confirmation biases is doubtless. For example, a person espousing The Teleological Argument may point out that the human eye alone is so intricate and efficient in processing data that it would not have occurred but for the existence and omnipotence of a god. Of course, they will simply ignore the known flaws in the eye's design, e.g., the blind spot that exists in the eyes of all vertebrates. The existence of that flaw alone is an argument for the lack of purposeful and perfect design of the human eye, but since it does not fit their preconceived notion, it is discarded. Such is confirmation bias.

The above discussion is sufficient to dispense of the Teleological Argument as nothing more than a gut feeling masquerading as a logical proof, but since it is a favorite tool of many religious believers, consider the manner in which their vagary of perception is likely operating. In all likelihood, they are confusing correlation with causation. Yes, the earth's environment and man's needs absolutely align, but that does not logically compel the conclusion that the former was created to house the latter. If that were the case, one would think that shelter would not be one of man's basic needs for survival or that such a large percentage of the planet would be uninhabitable for man in general. The human body may seem quite vibrant and hardy, but from the universe's perspective, it needs rare and delicate conditions in order to survive.

What is more likely: that the earth was made to support people or that people evolved from other life on the planet to suit the opportunities that the earth was offering? Science says the latter and has tremendous amounts of evidence for what it asserts while religions say the former and offer naked assertions camouflaged as logical attempts. When used to argue for the orderliness of the world relative to human beings, The Teleological Argument is a remarkably self-centered view of the universe that asserts that everything exists just for humanity while never approaching logical necessity for its position.

The God of the Gaps Argument – An argument against science's current knowledge

Argument: As science, mathematics, and logic have not yet answered all questions of causality and origin in objective reality, the gaps in their combined knowledge demonstrate the necessity of a god as a logical explanation for the universe's mechanics. Proponents of The God of the Gaps Argument make their point by asking questions about nature or human existence until the interviewee reaches a point where science's knowledge about the world cannot continue to answer, at which point the interviewer claims that at that exact gap in knowledge a god is the cause of the phenomenon in question. For the purposes of practical debate, it does not matter what the state of the art is in a given field of science; a person asserting The God of the Gaps Argument will invoke it whenever his opponent's personal familiarity with a scientific field has been exhausted.

Refutation: First, note that The Cosmological Argument capitalizes on a gap in scientific knowledge specifically regarding the cause of the universe in order to plug in the logical necessity of gods while The God of the Gaps Argument capitalizes on any gap in scientific knowledge to attempt the same trick. Due to the similarities between The Cosmological Argument and The God of the Gaps Argument, the refutation provided for the former applies similarly here, namely, that special pleading an entity that defies the law of causality does nothing to prove the logical necessity of that entity in explaining an unknown chain of causality.

Both arguments also represent fallacious arguments from ignorance, i.e., arguments that exist due to lack of conclusive evidence to the contrary rather than arguments that affirmatively prove their assertions. The fallacy of the argument from ignorance has special significance in the logical argumentation of reason-based thinking, and it recurs so frequently in the debate between theists and atheists that its logical refutation has been memorialized in the third assumption of reason-based thinking. As has been discussed, the third assumption of reason-based thinking is redundant due to the knowledge-acquisition techniques in the second assumption, but the proper placement of the burden of proof is of such significance that the idea deserves special consideration.

The God of the Gaps Argument is another interesting example of the errors that the brain makes while it struggles to maintain two sets of assumptions that completely conflict. While building up The God of the Gaps Argument, religious believers implicitly concede that science's explanations for natural phenomena are valid because they do not challenge them. Instead, they want to push their opponent into a place where science does not yet make claims of knowledge and only there do they insert gods. Unwittingly, they imply that only unexplained causal chains in physical nature have room for the participation of a god.

If fully adhering to the two assumptions of religious thought, they would not bother making an argument that implies that a god's realm recedes to the exact extent that science's expands. If fully adhering to the three assumptions of reason-based thinking on the other hand, they would accept the gaps in scientific knowledge as temporary and honest gaps in understanding that require more work and investigation. Instead, they inconsistently blend their two sets of assumptions. Due to a fundamental misconception that it is possible to square science into a coexisting worldview with religious thought, inconsistent and incongruent logical attempts like The God of the Gaps Argument and its limitless number of incarnations occur all too often.

*   *   *

The three above arguments address nearly the entirety of the intelligible logical patterns of argumentation in favor of the existence of a god. As with Pascal's Wager, people often encounter the above arguments in their own introspection long before they ever hear of their formal formulation because all three have simple, intuitive appeal, combined with errors that are subtle and difficult to see when one has been raised in religious thought. However, they are all easy to spot when one becomes familiar with their common hallmark: gods are always framed as a default and never affirmatively proven. The reason why they are framed this way will be reinforced upon covering the current state of the empirical evidence for the existence of a god in the next section, but a logical reason why his existence is never affirmatively proven is that the word "god" just does not possess a sufficiently reasonable level of precision in order to be proven. In other words, no one reasonably knows for what he is searching.

Personally, I have had countless exchanges with religious believers that have gone accordingly:

Believer: God created/designed the universe.

Me: What evidence is there to support that?

Believer: What else could have done it?

Aside from being an example of an argument from ignorance, such an answer provides an interesting glimpse into the place that gods hold in the thinking of many religious believers: they are using the word "god" as a personified euphemism for the phrase "I don't know". In order for a person to become an atheist, he must identify and accept that which science does not currently know about nature and existence without feeling the need to plug in gap-filler ideas that lack both sufficient definition and predictive ability. Such ideas only serve to provide the semblance of knowledge and squash the appetite of humanity to investigate the world and its place in it.

Empirical Evidence for the Existence of a God

As noted, the above logical arguments for the existence of a god are non-specific to any religion. Unfortunately, the empirical evidence for the existence of a god is very religion-specific. The reason for this specificity is that the vast majority of the alleged evidence is referred to in scripture, which is the main source for a religion's edicts and alleged legitimacy. Nevertheless, the discussion does not need to delve into the specific assertions of every religion because they all share similar quality in their evidentiary portfolios. Instead, a canvassing of the common threads of the evidence offered by the vast majority of religions along with an assessment of the reliability of that evidence will suffice.

At this point, it would be appropriate to review the definitions of direct and circumstantial evidence, as provided in Chapter 1. For clarity, the chart below provides a simple organizational framework in which any religion's main sources of evidence will be classified.

Direct Evidence; Past	Circumstantial Evidence; Past
• Divine Revelation	• Miracles
	• Scripture
Direct Evidence; Present	Circumstantial Evidence; Present
• Personal Experiences	• Anything, depending on personal taste

Direct Evidence of the Existence of a God (Past and Present)

All of the direct evidence offered by religions for the existence of a god takes the shape of eyewitness testimony. Before delving into what religions claim, realize that they cannot realistically have any other form of direct evidence on the matter because the nature of gods is cloaked in the realm of the metaphysical, resists understanding by humanity, and lacks reasonable definition as a result. A video recording of a god would be direct evidence of his existence, but how would one know that he was seeing a god on camera footage? In fact, how would one reliably know under any set of circumstances that he was capturing direct evidence of a god? Without reasonable definition, there is no way to know how one has found for what he is searching. Eyewitness testimony winds up being a natural default with respect to direct evidence of gods because to have otherwise would be tantamount to providing a definition of what a god actually is.

On the question of the direct evidence that religions do proffer, their assertions arise from divine revelation via a prophet, which has usually resulted in the writing of scripture or source text for a religion. For evidentiary purposes, "divine revelation" is a fancier way of saying "eyewitness testimony", and there are several reasons why it is dubious in this context.

First, there is a conflict of interest problem for those who claim to have received a divine revelation, i.e., there is the presence of motive for a person to intentionally lie about the experience. Gods are recognized as sources of tremendous power, and if one were to convince others that he had been so favored as to speak with such an authority, he would receive deference and honor due to the association. Second, there is a high likelihood of confirmation bias, i.e., an unintentional error in cognition with respect to what had actually happened. In the context of religious thought and its knowledge-acquisition technique of faith, confirmation bias abounds as there is no shortage of vague concepts and poorly-defined ideas for a willing brain to interpret in a stilted fashion. Lastly, there is the omnipresent problem of how one could have reliable knowledge that what he had experienced was a god. Squirrely, nebulous definitions are often tactical advantages for religious thought in the theoretical setting, but they represent its doom when it comes to generating convincing, practical evidence.

With the advent of scientific inquiry, the appearance of prophets whose experiences and revelations have led to the creation of entire religions has suspiciously declined. Nevertheless, it is not uncommon for religious believers in the present day to claim to have spoken with their god of choice or to have otherwise "experienced" him, and humanity has no direct evidence of the current existence of a god other than such personal commentary. Though less comprehensive and impressive than the alleged divine revelation that once yielded foundational scripture, these claims of personal experiences with gods still represent eyewitness testimony, subject to all of the same critiques of credibility and authenticity already discussed.

From the perspective of the knowledge-acquisition technique of religious thought, trusting eyewitness evidence of encounters with a god is not a problem. However, reason-based thinking begs to differ. When a being is hypothesized to exist in objective reality, the knowledge-acquisition techniques of reason-based thinking are the best tools for the job in order to control against vagaries of perception, i.e., experiential evidence gathered without any discernible methodology or control ought to be discarded as unreliable. In religious thought, the knowledge-acquisition technique of faith tends to operate so as to encourage one's conclusions to select evidence that matches. In reason-based thinking however, the reliability of one's evidence operates to determine his conclusion.

On the question of the past or present eyewitness testimony of the existence of a god, the conflict of interest, high likelihood of confirmation bias, and failure to utilize the knowledge-acquisition techniques best-suited to render reliable information about objective reality disqualify the evidence as both damaged and suspect. Of course, there is also the baseline failure in the concept of god itself that makes claims of having experienced one beg the question of how a person could reliably know such a thing without knowing anything about what a god is. Taken as a whole, the relevance of the direct evidence of any given religion's portfolio is apparent, but failures in credibility make the evidence unsalvageable.

Past Circumstantial Evidence of the Existence of a God

There are two sources of past circumstantial evidence that are indispensable for religions: scripture and miracles. Miracles are circumstantial evidence of the existence of a god because witnessing seemingly impossible occurrences in nature requires the additional inference that an unseen god was the cause in order to establish his existence. Classifying scripture from an evidentiary standpoint is more complicated because not all of it is considered to be the exact transcription of eyewitness testimony from a prophet who had received divine information. To the extent that scripture holds itself out as the exact transcription of a divine revelation, then it constitutes direct evidence of the existence of a god, subject to all of the same concerns about integrity raised in the previous section with additional concerns about translation errors or alteration as it moved through the years.

To the extent that scripture is not alleged to represent a written eyewitness testimony of divine revelation, it constitutes circumstantial evidence of the existence of a god, and many religions claim that their scripture presages historical events in order to encourage the additional inference that such impossible knowledge could only have been delivered by the omniscient whispers of a god. In a new trend designed to maintain the relevance of religious thought in the modern era, religions sometimes pass off passages of scripture as auguring accepted scientific knowledge before science itself had acquired it. Regardless of context, these insinuations all wind up in the same place, namely, the connection of scripture with foreseeing the future.

On the interpretation of scripture as having prophesied future events, one's general reaction ought to be, "Who cares?" Even if it were true, how does such a thing establish the current existence of a god? The relevant question in this debate is not whether some omniscient being once existed but rather whether a god with all of the relevant, defined attributes exists today. In other words, it is not worth the effort to chase down the historical chronology of when a prophecy was written relative to if and when the prophesied event happened or to dissect the language of an alleged prophecy to determine if it is written so vaguely as to be satisfied by a wide variety of occurrences. Even if the circumstantial evidence put forth in this manner was conceded in its entirety, its relevance with respect to the ultimate question at hand in the debate is minimal.

On the question of scripture presaging knowledge later discovered by scientific inquiry, the problem is that the language cited comes nowhere near the level of precision needed to create scientific or mathematical knowledge. Scripture tends to wax poetic, and to suggest that there is any science in any of it is either delusional or dissembling. Also, religions conveniently forget about any or all of the clearly incorrect information contained in their scripture later disproven by scientific inquiry while making this argument, which continues to demonstrate a pattern of selecting evidence that confirms their conclusions while ignoring or dismissing evidence to the contrary. Nevertheless, the same problem arises here for religions as it did with respect to allegedly fulfilled prophecies, namely, that the relevance of the evidence is quite low on the question of whether a god is in existence today.

If scripture contained foresight in either science or future events in general, why have those passages done nothing to advance scientific knowledge or avoid such events? Is it more likely that scripture predicts the future by displaying the knowledge of an omniscient being or that human events take place and are then read into the vague and malleable commentary of scripture? If one were to concede all of the prophecies of these books as fulfilled, where would it get these religions? They would still have no evidence for the existence of a god in the present day or any manner of determining how to muster it without defining what he is first.

Along with the appearance of prophets, miracles have likewise witnessed a precipitous decline in frequency after the advent of modern science. Generally, a miracle is the occurrence of the impossible, often with respect to the apparent breaking of the laws of nature. Miracles occur rather frequently in scripture and are used to imply the presence or active interference of a god in the normal mechanics of the physical world. In the modern age, the religious particularly enjoy claiming the occurrence of miracles in the medical arena. Strangely, such miracles always occur in internal, unseen circumstances and never for an amputee or a burn victim so as to assuage their suffering and simultaneously demonstrate the presence of otherworldliness. It would be a remarkable miracle indeed if a man would have an amputated limb grow back overnight, but they do not and never have.

In fact, it has only been scientific progress to offer relief to such people through the development of prosthetic limbs and therapies in how to manipulate them. To call science's contributions in this regard "miracles" is to do incredible disservice to the amount of human effort and ingenuity that has been exerted in creating solutions to these problems. Indeed, the entire arena of modern medicine would have never been created if the blessings of a god were forthcoming to soothe the suffering of humanity. Strangely, miracles also never seem to occur that run against someone's fortunes, i.e., those who see miracles always tend to see them as pockets of physical impossibility that produce boons but never sorrow. Of course, the entire topic of miracles would be put to rest if someone would simply preserve the occurrence of one on recording equipment in order for it to be later examined for its credibility.

Miracles should not be hard to find if they exist, yet they are at best soft gossip among the ranks of religious believers. The awkwardness regarding miracles is that they never seem to occur when well-known causal chains are in consideration. How many times have people witnessed the phenomenon of dropping something and seeing it pulled to the earth by operation of gravity? Why does that law never break for a miracle? What about the phenomenon that the human body cannot process oxygen in water, i.e., that it cannot breathe underwater? The many people who have perished as a result of these natural laws speak to the demand for such miracles to take place, yet the supply never seems to accommodate any of it.

No person has skydived with a parachute that has failed to open, only to miraculously have his velocity reduce until he landed gently on the ground unharmed. No person who has fallen through a sheet of ice and been unable to surface for air has survived that event any longer than his lungs could permit due to a miraculous suspension of the body's need for oxygen. And, no, the fact that a skydiver plummets into the earth and survives the impact does not constitute a miracle solely because the impact failed to kill him. If trading death for horrific bodily injury represents the miracles of which gods are capable, then their omnipotence demonstrates peculiar restraint.

Scripture and miracles are the crown jewels of the religions of the world, and they advertise them heavily on that basis. Scripture is surrounded with a taboo of solemn respect, and miracles are contemplated with wondrous excitement. Sadly, neither deserves the billing. If scripture were so valuable for its prophecies, one would think that it would proactively utilize its knowledge rather than claim sublime victory after the fact. As for miracles, they are a fitting device for gods in that they operate to save people in unknown ways, always when scientific knowledge or human witnesses are unavailable to view the magical intrusion of a metaphysical hand into the causal chains of the physical world. It is all very convenient, and as far as the credibility of the evidence goes, nothing about scripture or miracles creates a sense of legitimate curiosity that either may indeed be the handiwork of a god. Indeed, their flimsy evasiveness tends to suggest the opposite.

Present Circumstantial Evidence of the Existence of a God

As mentioned in the above table, present circumstantial evidence of the existence of a god could be anything. Why did it snow in Kiev yesterday? Why do magnets of opposite polarity attract? Why does nature exist at all? Since the concept of a god is amenable to only the barest of definitions with respect to his capabilities and personality, there is nothing to restrain a person from seeing circumstantial evidence of his existence everywhere. For example, it is not unusual for a person to hike in the outdoors, come to a clearing where he can see a vast expanse of nature, and feel thunderstruck by the magnificence of it. The dwarfing feeling of awe one can have for natural beauty is then imputed to the primed concept of a god in the person's brain, and circumstantial evidence for the existence of a god is created. There is no way to isolate or categorize all of the possible forms of this evidence because it is literally infinite. All that can be done is to discuss why so many things and events, indeed all things and events, can be considered to be circumstantial evidence on the question of whether a god exists today.

Although the lack of definition in the word "god" cuts both ways in the evidentiary portfolio of religions, it pays dividends in this instance by creating a bottomless pit of confirmation bias for their followers. Gods are a perfect black box into which one can throw everything he does not logically or scientifically understand about the world because their lack of definition means that anything goes. Why does science never conduct an experiment to search for the existence of a god? Even if gods were not arbitrarily defined around the core assumptions of reason-based thinking, for what would science be searching? How would it know if it found it? This is the reason that many people have been unable to pry themselves out of religious thought: they have entered a state where they believe in something that they do not understand.

As to the authenticity of present circumstantial evidence on the existence of a god, one need not enter this hall of mirrors in search of an exit because there is no meaningful evidence being captured to establish any of the three, necessary qualities of gods. If one perceives beauty in the world with gasps of marvel and attributes that moment to a god, he is really asserting that a god created all things and that his magnificence is evident from the elegance of his creation. All that is happening with this category of evidence is that the people who claim it have felt an inclination to sublimate their own emotions or place in the world by activating their favorite catch-all concept of the unknown. Indeed, it is emotion-based evidence purporting to establish factual aspects of objective reality, and the cognitive errors likely to stem from that pairing have already been discussed at length.

Present circumstantial evidence of the existence of a god amounts to precisely nothing because it is asserted without reasonable definition of what is being credited or how that entity is affecting the world. In other words, the evidence of this category constitutes one big set of arguments from ignorance, the logical error specifically addressed by the third assumption of reason-based thinking. As stated at the outset of the discussion, all of the evidence discussed in this section is completely contradictory to religious thought's core knowledge-acquisition technique of faith, but the frequency with which religions will claim independent evidentiary support merits its own review. Indeed, a complete rout of all that religions claim for their legitimacy is called for considering the tenacity with which their concepts grip their constituents.

The Overall State of the Evidence for the Existence of a God

With respect to the assessment of any evidence offered in support of the existence of a god, it is important to keep in mind the precise question at hand: does a god currently exist? The definition of "god" implies that if a god has ever existed, then he exists now as he is immortal, but religions never bother to prove such a thing by necessity. Instead, they subtly pack that all-important element into their terminology in an attempt to smuggle it past casual investigation.

Even if they were true, what difference could any of the miracles and divine revelations mentioned in scripture from generations long since dead possibly make? Even if they were reliable and authentic, they do not get the religious any closer to proving that a special being currently exists today, only that one existed back then. No evidence or reasoning is ever provided that reasonably establishes the presence of such a being today. From an intuitive standpoint, the distant past is a most unusual place to begin an investigation for an omnipotent being allegedly in current existence, and the leap in logic required to slingshot the implications of such dubious evidence from antiquity into the present is precisely why faith is indispensable for religions. That the most interesting and desirable evidence of the existence of a god arises as one goes further back in time is telling, especially when coupled with the astonishing dearth of evidence with respect to his existence today.

There is no need to enter the dusty realm of specific scriptural history when searching for a god, and the fact that the religious feel compelled to do so is an unwitting manifestation of the weakness of their position. People rummage through history books to discover the thoughts and actions of Booker T. Washington, Julius Caesar, and Mahatma Gandhi, but that is because no one suggests that any of those people are still alive. Gods are not relevant in people's lives because they are alleged to have once existed; they are relevant because religious believers operate under the faith-based assumption that they exist now. Following the same pattern to learn about them that one would take to learn about Genghis Khan does not bode well for the case that they still exist today, if they ever did.

So, the evidentiary portfolio of all religions with respect to reasonably establishing the existence of gods is a stupendous failure, exacerbated by the fact that attempting to offer any evidence at all in tandem with the knowledge-acquisition technique of faith betrays their frantic desperation to garner legitimacy at any cost. Faith is what counts in religious thought, not evidence or logic. To muster evidentiary attempts while simultaneously maintaining faith as a legitimate knowledge-acquisition technique is an attempt to stitch together the biggest butterfly net possible, so that when it is whirled through the air, it will maximize its catch through its targets' utter confusion about where the net begins and ends.

The fact that atheism even exists speaks to the audaciously poor quality of the evidentiary portfolios of the world's religions. After all, reason-based thinking desires evidence and logic, and if there were a reasonably specific definition for a god and concomitant evidence of his current existence, atheism would be a lonesome conclusion indeed. Atheism is not the static, unchanging conclusion of reason-based thinking with respect to the existence of gods; it is the conclusion that it reaches under the current evidence.   Like all scientific conclusions, the emergence of convincing evidence at a later point that demonstrates that a past conclusion was error will result in a change in position. However, one does not count on reversing a well-reasoned assessment of objective reality based on the knowledge-acquisition techniques of reason-based thinking, especially considering the practical stonewall that the terms of religious thought have erected around themselves.

7 – Logical Contradictions Around Gods and Final Considerations

Conversation is a game of circles.
– Ralph Waldo Emerson

Aside from the lack of evidentiary and logical support for religious assertions, contradictions abound with respect to gods, based on the minimal definition that has been created for them. Of course, unsupported assertions of knowledge with respect to objective reality are presumed false by the third assumption of reason-based thinking, and one does not have to actively chop down the structure of religions in light of their evidentiary and logical emptiness. Nevertheless, their logical incoherence merits review for redundancy purposes. After canvassing some of the logical absurdities of religious thought, the final section will tie up loose ends as to what gods really are. Many people have spent and continue to spend their entire lives in service to their religions, and clarifying the matters in question to their simplest elements is an important last step.

Logical Contradictions Around the Existence of Gods

The following collection of contradictions in religious thought represents what religions might be inclined to label "mysteries of faith". Regardless, they do not represent an exhaustive list. Entire books could be written on nothing more than the plentiful errors and oddities of religious thought. Why do bad things happen to good or innocent people? Why does humanity's free will seem to operate as the fine print in a contract for religious membership, absolving god from any responsibility for the pain and suffering in the world? If the devil punishes sinners for all of eternity, does that not make him good? Seemingly, there is no end to these contradictions, and only a brief coverage will be performed here. As will be seen, most of these contradictions arise from the discordant screech of laying the theoretical, heroic figures of religious thought on top of the practical suffering that humanity endures.

The Problem of the Existence of the Devil/Demons/Evil

Since religions deal in absolutes, they create two clean poles of human morality, good and evil, and the structure of religious thought personifies these extremes. Gods are the source of all good, and devils or demons are the source of all evil. Leaving aside the cogency of framing the staggering range of all possible human behavior as either "good" or "evil" in an objective sense, a problem arises for the theoretical beings of religious thought vis-à-vis the practical state of human civilization. Since gods are both omnipotent and benevolent by definition, they presumably want the best for their creations. So, why would they permit the existence of entities that deal in evil? Why would a god who wields omnipotence permit such evil or suffering to exist at all?

The existence of evil in the world has proven to be the ultimate double-edged sword for religions. On one hand, the existence of misery and sinister behavior in the world is what makes their alluring promise of salvation relevant. On the other, the minimal, indispensable characteristics of a god are undercut by the fact that people must turn to help from the very being that created their anguish in the first place. At the intersection of these two concepts lies a serious clash. If gods are benevolent and omnipotent, then why would one ever need to be saved? From where could danger possibly come with the existence of a being with that level of power and tenderness?

Many arguments to solve the problem have been offered, some of which include:

1. Earthly existence is just a test or proving ground to see who will be deemed worthy of heaven, and a god will in fact destroy evil at the end of this world.
2. Man must be purified by pain and suffering before he can enter heaven.
3. Man misperceives what evil really is, i.e., god knows what is best for us, and he actually is acting in a benevolent fashion.

Arguments 1 and 2 are non-starters. Argument 1 suggests that a god, whose omnipotence gives him the power to do anything, intentionally and knowingly created humanity defective and set up the world as a test to see which of his creations would prove worthy. In other words, Argument 1 is the standard appeal to the human-blaming concept of free will in order to explain the existence of evil. Of course, a god would not actually acquire any information about people from such a test due to his omniscience, and the choices that they made would always have been anticipated. Also, Argument 1 betrays god's trait of benevolence in that he would be intentionally making people's lives harder to bear, seemingly for sport since he is in full control of how to create them.

Argument 2 does no better because it also implies that a god, capable of anything, deliberately chose to make people in such a way that they would actually need purification by pain and suffering, no matter how they exercised their free will. Either way, a clash between the omnipotent and benevolent characteristics of gods ensues such that both cannot be said to be true simultaneously. If gods could have avoided creating evil and suffering but did not, their benevolence makes for a bad joke, and if they could not have avoided creating evil and suffering, their omnipotence is destroyed.

Argument 3 is the most sensible answer to the problem for religions, yet they do not often employ it. Ostensibly, their reluctance to endorse it arises from the fact that it undermines arguments that the devil and hell actually exist, which stands to sacrifice a sizable incentive to participate in religion. It is also likely that Argument 3 cannot be seriously maintained in a moral system that deals in absolutes. For a god to be the ultimate source of actions or results that man finds universally obscene, the pristine pools of heaven and the murky pits of hell begin to mix, and the cure may be worse than the disease as far as religions are concerned.

Anyway, Argument 3 is the best selection for religions because it stays true to the core religious assumption of faith, i.e., it dismisses human knowledge as trifling and irrelevant. By asserting that people cannot comprehend anything about the true nature of the world or what is actually happening, faith delivers the message that they should not bother to try. Of course, the use of faith in this manner would pitch the person into a position of complete and abject powerlessness, but it is at least logically aligned with the spirit of the two assumptions of religious thought.

As an example of the problem faced by religious thought on this issue, consider an infant who dies of malnutrition. He has had no time in the world to form moral thoughts of any kind, and he never had the capacity to be intentionally cruel towards another person. He is blameless. In short, he has had no chance. He was born into a circumstance outside of his control, his life was short and tormented, and then he was gone. To a casual observer, his suffering offends any reasonable notion of justice and would go far to discredit the existence of a god overseeing such a state of affairs. Of course, a devil is a convenient scapegoat, but blaming him only begs the question of why a god would permit him to exist in the first place. If there is a god in the world, permitting such wanton agony to take place seems either a decisively vicious exercise of his omnipotence or a bizarre interpretation of his benevolence.

There is no avoiding the problem for religions, however, and it represents the most uncomfortable contradiction in their mythologies.

The Problem of the Meaning of Life

From the standpoint of religions, all physical things are fleeting, which is a viewpoint that is given singular emphasis because of the assumption of religious thought that the metaphysical exists in objective reality. The metaphysical realm is where all of the action takes place if one is religious, mainly because it is the location of all things immortal and permanent. What one can see and sense is only a hint, a glimpse of the amazing promises of splendor in the metaphysical. On the other hand, the consequences of an ill-considered life are also dealt with there. One can either live in bliss or misery for all eternity, and the manner in which one conducts himself in the physical realm of existence will determine his destiny. Thus, religions give people an ultimate meaning of life that guarantees bliss and joy no matter how horrible or banal their present existence may be so long as their instructions are followed about how a god expects people to behave. So, why would a god not just make people deliriously happy and immortal in the first place? Of what use is this world to a god?

If a god made man and knows everything about him, then what information could he possibly gain from putting people through such a test? It is at this juncture that the religious enjoy deploying their throwaway term "free will", which is meant to imply that a god has deliberately relinquished control of what people do, but thanks to the casual flexibility in meaning that the term enjoys, they also use it to imply that a god does not know what a person is going to do. If that is true, then he is not a god by definition as his lack of omniscience implies less than omnipotence. If he is not omniscient, he is not omnipotent, and if he is not omnipotent, why bother to pray to and worship him?

Regardless, the framing of the world as a divine experiment or proving ground leaves a massive logical hole in the system of religious thought when two of the core attributes of a god are considered simultaneously. Is this all some sort of demented game to him? Then he is not benevolent. Does he really not know what people are going to do with their lives and thus requires this world to determine who deserves heaven and hell? Then he is neither omniscient nor omnipotent. The contradiction here represents a painful irony because so many religious believers claim that their religion gives them a deep sense of meaning and purpose, without which they would be unable to engage their lives. If one looks with any effort on what that meaning is built however, it leads one down a contradictory path where the preciousness of its promise loses its luster.

The Problem of Divine Justice in the Afterlife

Any incarnation of religious thought contains concepts that distribute justice to people such as heaven, hell, reincarnation, obliteration, or limbo because religions understand and cater to the innate social desire of humans to have moral deeds rewarded and immoral ones punished. Indeed, for what reason would one want to worship a god if he was completely arbitrary in what he was doing? Considering that religions establish a justice system that often carries on into eternity, the stakes are high when it comes to choosing and worshiping a god, as the payoff structure of Pascal's Wager demonstrated in Chapter 5. There are two problems with this portion of religious thought. If a god made man and his eternal justice awaits his creations to weigh the depths of their morality, why are people responsible for the flaws that a god put into their personalities and character? Secondly, what exactly is just about meeting the finite crimes of man with infinite penalties in the afterlife?

Again, religions cavalierly inject free will at this point as though to say, "Look, god made you, but whatever you did from there was your decision." Leaving aside the earlier discussion of free will and its implications for a god's omniscience and omnipotence, gods cannot have it both ways. Religions cannot assert with logical consistency that a god is responsible for the creation of man and everything else in existence and then suggest that he is somehow without responsibility for any of man's sinister actions because of the nebulous concept of free will. Cause and effect ripples through all of nature and life, and there is no greater cause than a god, a being allegedly responsible for the creation of both man and the universe. To claim that a god has no responsibility for the trajectory of a person's life while simultaneously arguing that he created all things is yet another example of how the ideas of religious thought betray each other if they are followed to their logical implications.

In light of the subtle and advantageous contortions of free will in religion, it is obviously a conceptual turnstile designed to preserve the desirable attributes of gods in the midst of the undesirable reality of human suffering. If one must allow for some arbitrary element of free will, so be it. The inclusion of that concept cannot save a god from the blame of knowing exactly what a person was going to do during his entire life anyway, lest he cease to be a god. A related concern is the question of whether a god can be logically blamed for the wrongs people do. If he is to retain all of his main attributes, then the answer is clearly yes, and since a god cannot deny total responsibility for the nature and actions of any given person, what sort of justice is it to reward or condemn that person for his nature or actions for all of eternity? If a god exists, a person is what he made him to be. There is not enough free will in the world to attenuate that connection sufficiently so as to warrant the sort of infinite justice that religions claim. One can give religions all of the slack in the world with respect to free will to let gods off the hook for the suffering of man; it still does not save them from the logical discomfort that they created man to be capable of atrocity and aggression in the first place.

On the second question, what is just about condemning or rewarding people for the behavior that they exhibit during their finite lives when the terms of those sentences are eternal? Where is the proportionality of crime and punishment in such a system? Only a warped sense of justice would laud the merits of such sentencing guidelines, and they are made especially distasteful when colored by the above discussion in regard to the responsibility of gods for the behavior of people. In other words, the eternal justice system of religious thought is a legitimate nightmare, fraught with abuse unbecoming of a deity. The solace to be found in its concepts is that its horror is directly linked to its preposterousness.

The Problem of Differentiating Between Religions

Technically, the last problem is not a logical issue surrounding the existence of gods as much as a game-theoretical conundrum surrounding the religions of the world. As a conclusion, atheism is often roundly rejected by religious believers, which is a consistent decision since they have accepted the assumptions of religious thought as accurate reflections of objective reality. However, they still must choose from the available religions in order to achieve their goal. In other words, their rejection of the application of reason-based thinking to the question of the existence of a god in objective reality leaves atheism to wither on the vine, but when it comes to comparing religions to each other, there is no such clash in assumptions and no sensible metric with which to differentiate between them. If there is a god and worshiping him matters, how does one pick the correct religion?

Considering the two assumptions of religious thought, there is no way to make an intelligent differentiation as there are no standards of analysis in the knowledge-acquisition technique of faith other than deference to an authority figure or scripture, which begs the question at issue. If one is going to take an assessment of what any given religion advocates with reason-based thinking, then one will wind up rejecting them all due to their common, non-negotiable cores that contain the assumptions of religious thought.

Alarmingly, most religious believers do not acknowledge their blind spot in this regard. Through their eyes, they are members of the one true faith as created by the one true god, which is a remarkable fortuity for them considering it is often earned simply by being raised in families that taught them the same religion. With the three assumptions of reason-based thinking, the answer to the question of how one picks the correct religion is that the question itself is flawed because it presumes the legitimacy of religious thought. One cannot rationally pick the correct religion. One can only choose between religious thought and reason-based thinking, and if he chooses the former, he can only play a guessing game from there.

Consider another perspective on this point. It is safe to assume in the present day that Zeus, Apollo, and Poseidon are not taken seriously as real beings. So, what reliable information has been determined about them to remove them from humanity's discussion of the afterlife? Have they been disproven? The answer is that nothing about these gods has been discredited; their mythology has simply fallen out of favor due to social and cultural changes. Religious believers cannot rationally explain how they are mocking Zeus but praising their gods nor can they have any rational basis for asserting that any given phenomenon that is credited to a god is actually due to theirs as described and worshiped in their religion. What they have is emotional reasoning masquerading as intellectual analysis, and while emotional appeals work quite naturally for expressing that one loves another, they are meaningless when it comes to establishing whether that someone even exists in the first place.

*   *   *

Hopefully, it is now apparent why so much time was invested in setting the table in the debate. Religions are able to create a façade of internal coherence because their terms do not have any reasonable meaning, but their errors are hiding in plain sight. The trick that religions employ to feign legitimacy is to generate terms purporting to establish places and beings in objective reality that are sufficiently defined as to be alluring but evasive enough to counter reasonable investigation. Even the absolute minimum roster of concepts and definitions of religious thought cannot tolerate its own company from a logical perspective, which is remarkable considering how much more complex they can get.

The Practical Irrelevance of a God in Nature

Modern scientific inquiry has delivered humanity an unprecedented amount of comfort and predictability with respect to its environment. Casual reflection on some of the products of the scientific method that many people take for granted reveals the remarkable achievements of reason-based thinking as a methodology. Engineers have dug transit tunnels under huge bodies of water, erected skyscrapers capable of withstanding hurricane force winds, and designed spacecrafts that have allowed man to escape the gravity of the earth itself. Medical researchers have produced antibiotics to tame ailments that had once annihilated past generations while creating immunizations to eradicate others entirely. Surgeons have developed techniques to correct failures in the body's many systems, even to the point of transplanting crucial organs. All of these fields are sourced in reason-based thinking, and the impact of their progress ripples through civilization to increase both the quality and quantity of people's lives. Indeed, a man that lived only a hundred years ago would be at an utter loss to comprehend how the world could have become so unrecognizable in such a short period of time.

Modern scientific inquiry has existed for roughly three hundred years, yet humanity has accomplished more in that time in terms of manipulating and stabilizing nature to suit its needs than in the entirety of previous human existence. Its methods are not a magic trick; they have captured and crystallized nature by adhering to a logical assumption of causality in the physical world. In fact, the knowledge-acquisition techniques of reason-based thinking go well beyond spotting one-time causality and look to map patterns in nature. They have become so successful in the endeavor that they have created the above-mentioned marvels of technology, often by collaboration of multiple disciplines.

So, does a god interfere in the world when bridges collapse or when electronic devices fail? There is no reason to think so. Indeed, the failure of gods to interfere in the world when people are replicating well-known scientific results is telling. Consider that billions of people walk and drive on the earth every day without one of them rocketing off into space due to the cessation of gravity. That phenomenon is itself an unwitting experiment that silently testifies to the seeming inexorability of physical causality. A religious believer desirous of carving out locations in the physical world for the necessity of a god cannot explain why that law is never broken. If the physical world obeys a law of causality that interacts exclusively with its own elements, then the existence of a god in objective reality is unnecessary to explain the existence or the operation of nature.

Of course, the knowledge-acquisition techniques of reason-based thinking are currently unable to explain and predict every aspect of the physical world, but they have accumulated tremendous information that enjoys significant reliability. Gods are an all-or-nothing concept by virtue of their definitional omnipotence, and as a result, one ought to logically see them everywhere or nowhere. Considering the predictability that scientific inquiry has visited upon nature's systems, the emphasis is on nowhere.

As a last example of the irrelevance of gods, consider the mathematical field of actuarial science. Roughly speaking, actuaries are accountants with a significant, additional layer of complexity. Accountants take into account the future value of money with the concept of interest, and actuaries take another step to predict future decrements in people's lives, e.g., death. On the question of predicting death specifically, actuaries do their jobs by assessing trends of mortality in certain industries and geographical locations, i.e., they are utilizing probabilistic tools and historical trends to make future determinations about large groups. Actuarial predictions will be unable to determine which specific people will die in a given group, but they will be able to speak with a high level of accuracy on how many people will die in a given time frame. Indeed, entire industries are built on the backs of actuarial science and the predictive glimpses into the future that it provides.

On the present question however, the mathematical techniques of actuaries demonstrate just how predictable nature can be even with respect to human mortality, which is often conjectured by the religious to be the domain of gods. If gods routinely call humans home for eternal judgment, why does their beckoning never seem to regularly deviate from the group predictions of actuaries? From the standpoint of nature and its law of causality, there is nothing special or unique about human death. It is as predictable as any other cause and effect in nature if sufficient information is provided, and the fact that that information is currently lacking to explain a natural phenomenon of any order does not create a justifiable reason to introduce an arbitrary concept such as a god.

Perhaps the ultimate schizophrenic manifestation of the irrelevance of a god in nature is a religion contracting with engineers and architects to construct a house of worship. The structure's integrity will be based on engineering principles, which are based on reason-based thinking, which utilizes knowledge-acquisition techniques that conclude under the current evidence that gods do not exist. So, what the religion will have paid for when the building is complete is the creation of a monument to honor a being that the monument itself strongly implies does not exist. Could there possibly be an irony more exquisitely complete than that?

The Mandatory Causation Between Gods and Men

Before turning to the next chapter in which the comprehensive arguments against religious thought will be considered, it will be fruitful to zoom out and get perspective on the debate in a macro sense. The entire question at issue in this debate revolves around two things: gods and men. Between gods and men, there is no dispute that one created the other; the only question is the direction of that causation. Are men the physical creations of a god or gods, the power of which exceeds what humans can understand? Or are gods the bizarre product of humanity's imagination, conceived to explain magically that which people could not rationally? The answer to one of these questions is no, and the answer to the other is yes. Determining how to accurately pair the appropriate answer to each question represents the entirety of the dispute. Framed in this manner, it seems such a simple game, and in an emotional vacuum, it truly is. Sadly, emotions come to bear on the question improperly, and the simplicity of what is at issue becomes blurred.

If gods and men represent a cause and effect in some direction, it is telling that only one of the two has reliable evidence of actually existing. The assertions of religious thought that a god created both man and the universe, is currently in existence, and cares about the moral decisions of humanity have no foundation in either empirical evidence or logical necessity. So, the only reasonable direction of causation is that man is actually the creator of gods. In other words, gods are an example of the creative power of the human brain horrifically backfiring on itself by conjuring an idea that terrifies the emotions and that the intellect has difficulty subduing due to its vagueness.

The conclusion that gods, the soul, and the metaphysical in general only occupy the domain of the human imagination and not objective reality makes the most sense. Of course, the failure of religions to achieve successful verdicts from the knowledge-acquisition techniques of reason-based thinking is precisely why they must exalt faith as a legitimate knowledge-acquisition technique in order to establish the actual existence of its key places and beings. Nevertheless, there is one place that gods, the soul, and the metaphysical exist with certainty: in the imagination of humanity. That religions cannot produce reasonable evidence or logic to demonstrate their existence outside of those confines means that their ideologies as accurate representations of objective reality are defunct.

Final Considerations

Consider the performance art of magic. Magicians specialize in deceiving the senses, often in elegantly simple ways. Witnessing a magician's illusion produces awe, wonder, and a sense that the impossible has happened. How could a man levitate? How could a woman be sawed in half only to later emerge whole? How could a man transport himself across a theater within the blink of an eye? The answer is that none of these things are actually happening but rather a well-disguised, logical cause is producing the effect. Sleight of hand, misdirection, and rigged equipment conspire to deceive the audience into believing that the natural laws of the universe have been broken and magnificently so.

Magicians are experts at finding gaps in human perception, and they understand how to manipulate the abundant cognitive errors of the brain for the entertainment of their audience. Yet there is always a logical explanation for the illusions that they create, the laws of the universe are never fractured as they appear to be, and magicians do not have special powers. So, becoming an atheist is not a totally dissimilar feeling from being told how a magic trick is performed in that what once seemed so unbelievable and awesome becomes clear and linear. The brain begins to understand that it was not nature that impossibly bent but rather that it was the brain itself that had misperceived what was at hand. This realization produces a feeling of convergence, which will be discussed in Chapter 9. Convergence is the emotional byproduct of the intellectual understanding that one's religious storyline has collapsed into his practical, predictable version of objective reality upon the realization that the brain had made cognitive and perceptual errors in propping up the former.

What is god? God is an idea, encapsulated by a word. If that were the end of it, the word "atheism" would never have been uttered. However, religions bill themselves as channels to their gods thus asserting their existence in objective reality, and reason-based thinking does not buy it. The triumphant effectiveness of the knowledge-acquisition techniques of reason-based thinking lies in a policy decision they make with respect to objective reality: the prioritization of reliable knowledge. Without question, humanity would love to know every bit about objective reality and human existence with pure certainty, but it is not possible. The option that most closely mimics that ideal is the capturing of highly reliable knowledge, and to the extent that offered explanations about objective reality do not demonstrate reasonable reliability, they are dismissed until they earn some. Based on this philosophy, atheism is not the conclusion that gods do not exist in objective reality; it is the conclusion that believing that they do under the current evidence is ludicrous.

8 – Three Arguments to Discredit Religious Thought

Am I not destroying my enemies when I make friends of them?
– Abraham Lincoln

For the entirety of the first part of this book, the table has been set in order to reach the point where the necessary assumptions and perspectives have been assembled to compile refutations of religious thought. Chasing down all of the necessary turns and detours that religious thought requires to be believed has been important because only then could its essential nature be cornered, which it works hard to avoid having done to it. As will be seen, religious thought struggles mightily to avoid this treatment for good reason. Its practitioners sense that if people succeed in pinning it down, then what comes next will be dissection of its properties, and if its properties are subject to close scrutiny, then the entire affair will be revealed for what it is: a shell game.

In the interests of redundancy, there will be three refutations of religious thought presented, which will each stand on its own merits. You likely already have a sneaking intuition about the framework of these arguments, but resist the temptation to skim the details. We have come a long way, and the final step deserves the same focus as all of the intermediate ones to achieve a thorough treatment of the topic. At long last, we have reached the heart of the matter.

The Fundamental Argument

I. Faith is not an acceptable knowledge-acquisition technique because it does not produce claims of knowledge with respect to objective reality that can be assessed for their reliability.

The definition of faith is the acceptance of the truth of an assertion in the absence of both empirical evidence and sound logic that reasonably establishes it. From an epistemological standpoint, faith is a knowledge-acquisition technique that entails deference to an authority, either internal or external. However, this begs the question of how exactly one is to know whether such an authority is legitimate. In the world, there is no shortage of people and institutions that hold themselves out to be authorities on a range of subjects, and if one is armed with nothing but faith, he has no methodology with which to judge one authority reliable and another fraudulent. Without regard for evidence or logic, the choice between any of these authorities is arbitrary, and the actual decision will likely rest on emotional considerations.

So, faith is a codeword for arbitrary or emotion-based reasoning, both of which are fraught with errors when used to attempt to explain questions of fact in objective reality. Devoid of standards of analysis that demonstrate reasonable reliability in their determinations, faith gives no reason whatsoever to instill confidence in what it concludes. The methodologies of science, mathematics, and logic are currently the best tools that humanity has devised to reliably assess claims of knowledge with respect to objective reality, and faith falls entirely short of trumping their use.

Truly bizarre reasoning lies under the surface of all arguments that rely on faith. Suppose that a person believes that the earth's moon will combust tomorrow. No matter what authority he produces to justify his faith in the assertion, a natural question arises regarding why he is putting stock in the source of that information. His answer to that question will fail to have reasonable meaning due to the nature of faith. His reasoning is as follows: the earth's moon will explode tomorrow because the authority who delivered that information has said so, and he has chosen the correct authority because it has produced insufficient evidence and logic to support the declaration. The arbitrariness of his reasoning is evident, and if faith ever yields correct information about questions of fact in objective reality, it overcomes the odds that it stacks against itself by flouting reasonable evidence and logic. If faith is a necessary part of one's claim of knowledge with respect to objective reality, then he does not have an argument at all; he has an unlikely guess.

II. The metaphysical is presumed not to exist in objective reality because its existence has not been reasonably established by either empirical evidence or logical necessity.

Leaving behind the discarded knowledge-acquisition technique of faith in the investigation of questions of fact in objective reality, the knowledge-acquisition techniques of reason-based thinking are the clearly superior options. A hallmark of the scientific method, courtesy of logical reasoning, is that a hypothesis is presumed false until proven true by reasonable experimentation capable of independent verification and reproduction. Indeed, logicians would recognize this as an applied version of forbidding arguments from ignorance, which are logical errors that unreasonably reverse the burden of proof from the person proposing to have unique knowledge onto the skeptic to disprove it. On the present question, the existence of the metaphysical is an assertion of fact with respect to objective reality that requires reasonable evidence of its actual existence or arguments demonstrating its logical necessity. If the proponents of its existence fail to produce such argumentation, then the existence of the metaphysical in objective reality will be presumed false as it will be unproven and without basis for reasonable belief.

On the question of empirical evidence for the existence of the metaphysical, there cannot be any by definition. If such empirical evidence existed, it would have to be physical in order for man to be able to sense it as evidence, and it would thereby cease being metaphysical. So, collecting empirical evidence of the metaphysical is impossible by the nature of man's senses relative to what the metaphysical claims to be. Therefore, the proponents of the actual existence of the metaphysical in objective reality must prove their assertion by showing that that realm is logically necessary to avoid it being discounted as an unproven and imaginary concept.

As for why the metaphysical realm must logically exist, the bizarreness of the arguments in favor of the assertion has no limit, and the staggering number of them is testament to the attractiveness of theoretical meandering to religious thought. In any case, the existence of the metaphysical realm adds a layer of complexity to existence, the inclusion of which makes no substantive addition to the explanation of the physical world's existence or operation. To argue that an aspect of the physical world is unknown because it is sourced in the metaphysical realm does not add meaningful information with respect to how the physical world operates, let alone prove the indispensability of the metaphysical. More to the point, nothing about the metaphysical realm can be known to man as it defies human senses and investigation, and as such, how would man ever reliably know that it was essential to the universe even it were true? The metaphysical is intentionally defined around human intellect, and the case for its logical necessity suffers the consequences of alienating itself in that fashion.

All things being equal, logic favors parsimony in explanations, and the metaphysical realm adds much complexity to the model of the world with no explanatory payoff. As such, its logical necessity is dubious at best, only rescued from complete bankruptcy by the ability of its proponents to relentlessly gin up abstractions and link them to the metaphysical by sheer force of will rather than soundness of logic.   Utilizing the knowledge-acquisition techniques of reason-based thinking, there is neither reasonable empirical evidence nor logical necessity for the existence of the metaphysical in objective reality, and therefore, the hypothesis that the metaphysical exists in objective reality is unproven and presumed false.   Based on the current state of information, the only place that the metaphysical reliably exists is in the imagination of humanity.

III. Gods are presumed not to exist in objective reality because their existence has not been reasonably established by either empirical evidence or logical necessity.

With the dismissal of faith as a legitimate knowledge-acquisition technique, the tools of investigation became the knowledge-acquisition techniques of reason-based thinking. With the collapse of the metaphysical realm, investigation for gods is now limited to the physical universe.   As with the existence of the metaphysical, the proponents of the hypothesis that gods exist in objective reality bear the burden of mustering sufficiently reasonable support for that claim, either empirically or logically. Failing to carry the burden of proof will result in the dismissal of the hypothesis as unproven and the continuation of the presumption that it represents a false statement.

On the issue of empirical evidence for gods, anyone looking for a god would have a difficult time accomplishing the task since the lack of a rigorous definition does not provide a meaningful way of knowing if and when one finds one. The same problem would have occurred in attempting to utilize scientific inquiry to locate the metaphysical but for the fact that the definition of the metaphysical acted to disqualify the scientific method as a fruitful means of investigation from the outset.

In any case, gods are not wholly without definition, and if one is to look for a god via empirical investigation, searching for a consciousness that has the ability to break the laws of nature under reasonable experimental conditions seems an acceptable starting point. The compromise of this rubric ignores key definitional aspects of a god, but if religions cannot develop evidence to satisfy a minimal bar, then they will also fail any test covering other characteristics. Since there is no consciousness in nature to which one can point that has the power to break causality in nature, there is insufficient empirical evidence to demonstrate the actual existence of a god.

Many religions point to past stories and alleged historical events to claim that a consciousness once existed that satisfied the earlier, compromised qualifications for the existence of a god. However, these comments are of minimal relevance when what is at issue is whether a god exists today, and on that question, there is no evidence of a consciousness presently in objective reality that has demonstrated the ability to break the laws of nature. With respect to past legends of people or gods that routinely performed the impossible, they need not be challenged unless those entities can be proven to exist today, which is an effort that fails decisively when the metaphysical realm has been eliminated from consideration. Therefore, there is no empirical evidence that a god exists in objective reality.

On the issue of the logical necessity of a god, the law of causality in the physical universe is the central assumption of concern. While scientific inquiry does not yet know what caused the universe, there is no logical necessity to establish that the cause had either a consciousness or, if it did, that it still exists today. Beyond the unknown first cause, chains of causality in nature have been isolated and understood to an extent that they do not seem to ever be broken, either by random chance or by deliberate action from a conscious being. To the extent that chains of causality in nature are not yet explained, there is likewise no affirmative reason to insert a god in those locations in order to explain the continued operation of the universe. To do so does not provide an explanation of the phenomenon, and it also acts to betray the concept of a god by implying that he chooses to avoid tampering with causal chains that humanity has currently mapped without providing reasoning for that restraint. Logically, there is no need for a god to exist in the natural world in order to explain either its causation or functioning.

In addition, the same arguments provided in the above paragraphs for gods, apply equally to the soul, heaven, hell, demons, and angels. All of these places and beings entirely lack both empirical evidence and logical necessity in the physical world, and without the metaphysical realm as an available option, the hypothesis that any of these concepts exist in objective reality is presumed false due to a failure to carry the burden of proof. Without faith to grant these concepts exemptions from scientific and logical scrutiny, their failure to achieve a reasonable standard of reliable existence is apparent.

IV. Agnostic atheism is the most logical position on the question of the existence of gods under the current evidence because the knowledge-acquisition techniques of reason-based thinking cannot produce absolute certainty yet the hypothesis that gods exist in objective reality must be presumed false.

With the discrediting of faith as a reliable knowledge-acquisition technique and the resulting collapse of the metaphysical realm of existence as both empirically unproven and logically unnecessary, the associated mythology of religious thought loses its escape hatch from reliable methods of assessing objective reality and fails as a result. Therefore, atheism is the most logical position to maintain on the existence of gods. Considering that man's knowledge of objective reality has no objective reference point, he can never achieve complete certainty about questions of fact with respect to objective reality, no matter how refined his perception may be by the scientific method and logical rules. Technically, some level of theoretical uncertainty in atheism must exist due to the knowledge-acquisition techniques utilized in arriving at that result. Nevertheless, the dearth of evidence for the existence of gods and the lack of their logical necessity means that the uncertainty in the ultimate conclusion of atheism is minimized to an extent that makes the conclusion practically certain.

Summary of The Fundamental Argument

The Fundamental Argument attacks the core of religious thought, disintegrating it from the ground up. Without faith, the metaphysical realm is upended as a concept that accurately reflects objective reality, and from there, the remainder of the mythology freefalls.   The creation of this argument bears witness to why the two assumptions of religious thought that were highlighted back in Chapter 2 are its non-negotiable elements. Without their protection, the remaining concepts in religious thought lose their arbitrary exemptions from the knowledge-acquisition techniques of reason-based thinking, which operate to disavow them as inaccurate, unreliable, and unproven.   The knowledge-acquisition techniques of reason-based thinking are completely incompatible disciplines with religious thought, and if religions cannot legitimately justify why their assertions should escape their analysis of objective reality, then they must collapse.

The Practical Argument

I.   If a god does exist, he would provide clearer guidance regarding acceptable human behavior and would ensure that his own existence was beyond reasonable doubt.

Gods have the characteristics of benevolence and omnipotence by definition, which is to say, that they axiomatically have the power to do anything and that those actions will be in the best interests of mankind. Over the course of history, much anguish and torment have been endured by man due to religious disputes alone, which have sprung from both internal and external disagreements. Internally, battles have been fought over the correct interpretation of scripture and morality, resulting in the fracturing of religions into sects. Externally, holy wars have been fought between competing religions that have wreaked havoc on the populations unfortunate enough to be in their path. In brief, significant human suffering and confusion could be avoided with the interference of a god to simply validate his current existence as well as articulate the moral code that he desires from people in order to favor them in the afterlife. The failure of a god to so intervene suggests one of three things: he is powerless to do so, he does not wish to do so, or he does not exist in objective reality.

If there is a being in existence that holds itself out to be a god but that is unable to participate in the world in such a manner, then he is not omnipotent. Indeed, he is a far cry from omnipotent. What is being requested by his simply showing up and clarifying both his current existence and his rules for humanity is a feat so trifling and minor that his inability to accomplish it suggests that he is not only not omnipotent but rather powerless. Gods are suggested to be the beings that created the universe itself. A being that simultaneously possesses the unprecedented power of bringing the entire universe into existence while being unable to manifest in that universe represents a ludicrous conceptual clash. If a god could create the universe and everything in it, it would seem to be the slightest bother to show up for humanity and demonstrate not only that he currently exists but that he has precise demands of humanity with respect to its moral decisions. In any case, a being that lacks such power does not merit worship and, in all likelihood, could not logically exist due to the staggering creative ability that he would have to possess in order to create both man and the universe while somehow lacking the petty capability of appearing within that creation.

If there is a being in existence that holds itself out to be a god but that does not wish to clarify the quandaries that revolve around his existence in objective reality and his wishes, then his benevolence is dubious. If this world is as the religious suggest, i.e., a proving ground for those worthy of the eternal prizes of a god, then it is hardly fair to permit the game to be played in the presence of reasonable dispute about the rules. The sheer number of religions and sects that mankind has known with their concomitant moral codes speaks to the dispute that rages over what it is that a god wants from people if he does indeed exist. There is great injustice in leaving such gambles to men when their eternal fates hang in the balance, and his decision to not clarify both that he currently exists and what behavior will result in the successful acquisition of his favor represents a contradiction in his benevolence. Secret or obfuscated laws are offensive to the human sense of fairness, and that breach is made all the more severe by promising an eternity of suffering for being incorrect. In short, a being that is capable of delivering this level of clarity to humanity but who declines the invitation is not benevolent and is a being unworthy of worship because of it. Even if one were to conclude that such a being was worthy of worship by sheer virtue of his unlimited power, one would be unable to do anything more than arbitrarily guess what moral behavior was favorable, which would be a strategy with a minute probability of success.

Therefore, a god's refusal or inability to prove his current existence to humanity as well as provide clear instructions of how to win his favor renders him a being unworthy of one's attention. Indeed, both outcomes render such a being unlikely to exist in objective reality due to the resulting incoherence of his theoretical traits given his practical inaction. Considering the disqualification of two explanations of the silence of a god on the issue of clarifying questions that humanity has about him, what remains is the conclusion that he does not exist in objective reality. If a god did exist with the traits of both omnipotence and benevolence, surely he would delight in exposing those religions and sects that misappropriate his name and influence. Indeed, religions themselves are preposterous from the standpoint that they consist of men allegedly speaking on behalf of gods, which would surely be unacceptable to a deity under any circumstances. So, the practical inaction of gods with respect to clarifying their existence and rules for their creations suggests that no god in fact exists in objective reality.

II. If a god does exist, one's worship and belief would be unnecessary because he would prioritize one's capacity for moral behavior towards his fellow man.

Gods have two characteristics of omnipotence and benevolence that make them relevant to humanity from the standpoint of bothering to worship them. One would hardly be interested in worshiping a being that he thought was unable to protect him from danger or that did not care enough to do so. However, a being that possessed unlimited power would be unlikely to care if his creations worshiped him. After all, the power of an entity that is capable of a feat as staggering as creating a universe would hardly be appreciated by humans, entities that possess only the tiniest sliver of such potential. Therefore, a god would be indifferent to the praise of humans as they would be unable to understand what they were worshiping, and even if they did, he would gain nothing from such praise. A god would have no use for homage, least of all from entities of his own design. If he is truly benevolent and cares about the moral decisions of man, he would value the manner in which people treated each other and not him.

Consider the rank injustice that would result if the opposite were true, namely, that gods only care about one's behavior towards his fellow man insofar as it does not interfere with worshiping them. If that were the case, the most sinister of people could abuse and torment mankind with impunity so long as he showed the proper respect for a god or, more saliently, did so in the name of defending or honoring the correct god. When one prioritizes what he feels a god would favor over the best interests of his fellow man, he is at liberty to wreak havoc in the lives of others who have done him no harm, save lying in the path of pleasing his god. The suggestion that a god who requires nothing in order to improve his own existence or survive would desire such a result contradicts his character trait of benevolence. A god who is benevolent could well consider any time spent worshiping him as time wasted that could have been spent assisting his other creations that actually needed help. Gods cannot prioritize their own feeble honors bestowed on them by beings whose offerings serve them no purpose over one's fair and decent treatment of his fellow man if they are to logically maintain the character trait of benevolence.

Based on their core character trait of benevolence, gods would analyze human merit by placing the substance of their behavior over their form, i.e., by inspecting their capacity for decency to those who could do them no favors in return. Gods do not require omniscience in order to sense the potential for self-dealing in humans worshiping them. After all, promises of great and permanent reward linger in their minds, and humanity's worship of gods is tainted by that self-interest. In other words, the conduct of worshiping a god is formalistic, unnecessary, and sycophantic. If a god truly assessed human conduct for its pure merit, he would search for the moments in a person's life to examine how he treated people whom he believed could do nothing to return the favor. To do so would be to inspect the substance of a person's character and his capacity for decency and respect without the confounding element of self-gain to muddle the picture.

Who is more deserving of the rewards of a god? Is it the man who displays utter indifference to the poor in his community but who prays in public to curry the favor of a god and potentially increase his reputation by appearing to be humble in the eyes of others? Or is it the man who does not believe in the existence of a god but anonymously donates his time or money to help feed and educate people that are blamelessly without their own means to do so? If the answer is the former, then one is condemned by such a being no matter what he chooses. If he is decent to others instead of gods, he will be sent to hell for prioritizing the needs of people over the gluttonous desire of gods, and if he does not, he will find hell of his own accord by leading a cold existence, stripped of significant connection to humanity. Regardless, such a cruel choice cannot exist if a god is truly to maintain his characteristics of benevolence and avoid the flimsy logical trap of placing form over substance.

III.   The existence of a god is largely moot because the proposition that human consciousness survives the death of the body has not been reasonably established by either empirical evidence or logical necessity.

As the game-theoretical payoff structure of Pascal's Wager implies, the most salient aspects of religious belief and conviction are contingent on the proposition that the consciousness of human beings is without end, i.e., that the soul exists. If this were not the case and the consciousness were extinguished with the death of the body, then the existence of a god borders on moot in that his wrath or favor has only a finite time to come to bear on a person's life. So much of what drives religious conviction arises from the promise that not only is there an afterlife but that one's experiences during it will hinge on his piety during his mortal life. Without the faith-based presumption that there is an afterlife for human beings, the question of whether gods exist in objective reality becomes one of marginal interest.

This portion of The Practical Argument relies on similar reasoning as provided in The Fundamental Argument, but it focuses on something more tangible, i.e., the human body. A god is an idea that no one is willing to ground in anything to which one can relate on a practical level because it is a being that is alleged to be truly unparalleled and unprecedented. On the other hand, the soul is considered the metaphysical analog for a person's personality and overall essence, and the fact that it is starkly absent is suspicious indeed.

In the present state of modern medicine, humanity still has much to learn about how to treat disease and correct systemic malfunctions in the body. However, what never comes up when one visits a cardiologist or an orthopedist is the soul, which is not a coincidence because, anatomically speaking, it does not exist. This is to say that there is absolutely no empirical evidence for the existence of the soul, not just in humans but in any other animal on the planet. Religious believers likely find this point obvious and meritless as the soul is a metaphysical construct, but the same slack that one cuts for the lack of empirical evidence for gods cannot be done for the soul. If the soul does in fact exist, then it is truly who a person is, yet no one can find any trace of it. Waxing poetic about how man's deepest and most sincere emotions represent the soul does nothing to demonstrate that the soul is actually a being that exists in objective reality. If that is all that can be done to demonstrate its existence, then the soul is nothing more than a ship, carrying the most precious of cargoes, that never comes up on radar and never comes into port.

The theoretical necessity of the soul in objective reality is likewise unproven as is the metaphysical realm in general of which it is allegedly a part, but the present argument will only concentrate on the soul's logical necessity in physical nature. Is it not a satisfactory explanation to say that man's subjective emotions and thoughts are both functions of his brain? What reason is there to believe that they have a different source, much less an actual being that has no presence in the physical world? For the religious model of the human experience to be accurate given the dearth of empirical evidence for the soul's existence, the physical brain would have to have some metaphysical-to-physical convertor apparatus that would act as a transformer in order for the soul to be the seat of one's consciousness and emotions.

To further conjecture in this vein is a waste of time, not only because of the fantastical aspect of what is at hand but also because no additional explanatory force to the human condition will be forthcoming while continuing to add significant, inexplicable complexity. The existence of the soul, like all other entities in the mythological structure of religious thought, need not be proven downright impossible to lack logical necessity in objective reality, and absent both that and empirical evidence, their existence can only be presumed to be a phantasm.

If the soul does not exist, the question of whether a god exists has drastically less import as one's consciousness will not survive death. Of course, the same arguments against the existence of the soul apply equally to that of gods, but the soul is special in that it purports to be a part of people, i.e., something that is somehow linked to their physical bodies. That the soul cannot be located anywhere in nature and that its existence is not logically indispensable to an explanatory model of human beings means that there is no current reason to believe that it exists in objective reality. The ramifications of the soul being only a mirage in the desert of human experience include the radical increase in human indifference to gods and their possible power to manipulate and interfere with their lives. In other words, the extreme dubiousness of the soul's existence in objective reality does not mean that gods likewise do not exist but rather that their existence becomes nearly a moot point when the threat of eternity no longer weighs in the calculus.

Summary of The Practical Argument

The Practical Argument is less interested in discrediting the existence of gods than concentrating on undermining the aspects of religious thought that drive people to care whether a god exists in the first place. The first argument implies that a god who cared about humanity's behavior would provide more definitive instruction than what is currently available, the second argues that worshiping a god is a pointless exercise given his alleged characteristics, and the third is that there is likely no afterlife. Taken together, these three arguments contend that worshiping a god is a waste of time and that the question of whether one even exists has no practical import to a person's life. The point of The Practical Argument is that even if a god were to exist, the most logical course of action is to live without actively thinking about him.

The Meta Argument

I. Religious terminology proposes places and beings purported to exist in objective reality but is insufficiently defined as to be testable. Therefore, the existence of such places and beings must be presumed false.

In order to delve deeply into the unwarranted assumptions and plentiful contradictions offered by religious thought, the simplest of arguments against it has been deferred until now, which is that religious thought is an incoherent mess of poorly-defined concepts. Religious thought attempts to swim both ends of the pool: it simultaneously wants to claim supremacy over objective reality while ensconcing from where that power comes in concepts without meaningful definition. This is a subtle trick that permits a disqualifying failure of religious thought to masquerade as majestic mystery. Exactly what are these things and places that religious thought claims exist? What are gods? What is the soul? What is the metaphysical? The minimal definitions created for them in this book have been developed in order to speak about their higher implications and incoherence, but they are flawed at a much more fundamental level. Why do these concepts feel like photo negatives of human knowledge, i.e., deliberately existing in all of the places that man's reliable explanatory powers do not?

The core idea of all of the mythology of religious thought is the metaphysical, which is why it has been discussed as one of its mandatory assumptions. The metaphysical is the escape valve for all that religion cannot prove. It warehouses gods, souls, angels, devils, heaven, hell, and more. If those beings and places do actually exist in objective reality, then it seems that the metaphysical is the only place worth knowing. So, what is it? Defining it as "Nothing that anyone can understand while they are alive" is feeble, yet that is all that religions offer of it. As for gods, how would one know a god if he passed one on the street? Without a definition of what gods actually are, how would one be able to differentiate between a legitimate prophet and a madman or a con man? These minimalistic definitions create fertile ground for the individual to fill in the blanks.

What the concept of a god creates with its current definition is merely the silhouette of a being, a sketch of unimaginable power, hope, and fear. Without more information, the existence of gods in objective reality is not testable because no one knows for what he is looking. Of course, the murkiness of the definition acts to disqualify it from serious consideration because all assertions are presumed false until proven true, and one cannot prove a hypothesis true that one cannot describe with reasonable precision. It is telling that religions posit only one experiment in order to test the accuracy of their constructs of the world, namely, death, and any system of thought that makes one's demise a necessary predicate to gaining affirmative proof of what it asserts is a suspicious brand indeed.

On that point, consider the game-theoretical strategy that religions employ by making death the location of their laboratory. If everything that religious thought says is true, then one would indeed find that information in the afterlife. If religious thought is incorrect however, man's cognition ceases with the death of his body, and he will not be around to bring news of that falsity to others who live after him. Overall, this is a rather enviable position for religions to occupy: one will either obtain proof of the belief system in death, or if the system is untrue, there will not be any requests for refunds. The ability of religions to deploy this strategy is a direct consequence of the laziness of the lexicon of religious thought.

After all, one can fabricate any set of hurdles to obtaining evidence regarding his assertions if one can convince inquiring minds to allow him infinite latitude in determining what will constitute evidence, and a sneaky way to obtain that wiggle room is to refuse to reasonably define one's terms. If a system of thought were a house, the contents of which are of great interest, then the keys to the doors are the system's concepts and terms. If those concepts and terms are poorly-defined, they will be unable to open the locks, and the interior of the house will remain a mystery. Religious thought employs an identical tactic. By filing down the precise grooves of the keys to its locks, it transforms itself into a logical black box with no means of entry, and safely insulated from penetration and inspection, its reasoning becomes unacceptably opaque.

Ultimately, it is important to know what words mean, especially when they purport to establish questions of fact in objective reality. When certain ideas and their related terminology are held out to have the significance that those of religious thought do, clarity is truly mandatory. Subjective emotions like love or awe escape precise definition because they are internal and are expressions of value instead of fact. This is not the nature of the metaphysical, god, or the soul, however. These concepts are proposed to exist in objective reality, and as such, their failure to be reasonably defined makes them unacceptably insulated from testing for their accuracy. As one cannot test the accuracy of these concepts, they must be presumed false as no well-defined and testable hypothesis can be rendered that includes them. That religious terminology evades precise definition does not make what religious thought asserts about objective reality to be mysteriously true; rather, it makes it presumptively false.

Summary of The Meta Argument

At many points in this book, The Meta Argument has been referenced, especially when practical considerations concerning evidence of the existence of a god has been at issue. The Meta Argument is an attack on religious concepts themselves as being so poorly-defined as to be de facto undefined and therefore meaningless. In essence, The Meta Argument is an appeal to intellectual fair play. If one wants to claim knowledge of an entity of staggering significance in the lives of man, then he is expected to bring some reasonable level of precision to the table about what exactly this entity is and how one can know what he believes should he accept the invitation to participate in religion. To allow otherwise is to open a lavish intellectual loophole that incentivizes sinister attempts to speak on behalf of a being of tremendous power and thereby garner the deference given to such an entity by proxy.

Conclusion

We have reviewed three independent refutations of religious thought, all targeting different weaknesses. It should be noted that our construction of three arguments against religious thought is in no way meant to imply that this is an exhaustive list. Other arguments and considerations that concentrate on these and other areas of religious thought are certainly possible. The arguments that we have covered have only been meant to provide variety: The Fundamental Argument attacks religious thought on its assumptions and theoretical terrain, The Practical Argument engages religious thought through a practical lens without bothering to delve into its theoretical nature, and The Meta Argument questions the fabric of religious thought itself by casting suspicion on the slippery nature of its terminology. These arguments and their summaries ought to be read multiple times in order to internalize the pressure points that they squeeze.

At this juncture, realize how much we have accomplished. The vast majority of people in human history have not had the luxury of confronting religious thought in a composed and deliberate manner, which is not to say that its ideas are complex but rather that they are disorienting and prone to emotional confounding. What has saved us from the quagmire of its threats and directives has been the implementation of well-reasoned standards of analysis that ensure levels of reliable knowledge with respect to objective reality and control the imagination from jumping to unwarranted conclusions.

Many discussions of reason-based thinking and atheism have stopped at this point where religious thought has been discredited. However, our journey is only half over. Up until now, we have worked exclusively to extract the faulty circuit of religious thought from our thinking. We are left with a gap in an integral aspect of identity, and we must now build up our new identities systematically, finding new, rational solutions to questions that religious thought once answered.

PART TWO

REBUILDING IDENTITY

9 – The Emotional Lessons of Discrediting Religious Thought

We have it in our power to begin the world over again.
– Thomas Paine

With religious thought out of the picture, the rebuilding phase must begin. As has been discussed, religious thought is nothing more than a set of assumptions about the world. Unfortunately for the present task, they are often long-held, dear assumptions, and with them discredited, one must cope with the toppling of opinions and outlooks that had rooted themselves in his very identity. Many people intuit that religious thought does not add up to their satisfaction, yet they remain trapped in its assumptions because they are at a loss for how to own their emotions without them.

It is this gap in education that keeps far more people in religious thought than who otherwise desire. How to dismantle the intellectual fallacies of religious thought is not exceedingly difficult given the tools of the modern age, but it is one's emotional dependence on it that so often operates to override his intellect's ability to make determinations on its merit. To that end, one must strive to earn emotional discipline, which is a crucial concept that will be reviewed at the end of the chapter. Before that however, the likely emotional ramifications of abandoning religious thought will be covered in order to enable a person to anticipate what he can expect from his departure.

Emotions Focused on the Self

Considering how one's religion incorporates itself into the identity of the individual, most of the internal emotions surrounding the transition to consistent reason-based thinking are tumultuous. Simply because one has figured his way out of religious thought does not mean that his emotions will instantaneously concur with that conclusion. Old habits die hard, and the exit from religious thought requires the flexing of emotional muscles whose growth has been stunted by the promises and ideology of religious thought. In atheism, there is no longer a divine support system to comfort a person when life treats him roughly, and he now lacks the ability to defer his deepest dreams to another life where they will be realized. One's outlook has become more realistic. Before covering the more sobering emotions, the discussion will begin with the exhilarating feeling of convergence.

Convergence

Leaving religious thought produces a surprising feeling of relief when one has achieved an acceptable level of intellectual certainty regarding his conclusions. In religious thought, the self is splintered into the physical body and the soul, one of which possesses immortal access to unknown realms. Indeed, existence itself is bifurcated into the physical and the magical, and one accepts complete intellectual helplessness in trying to understand the latter. A byproduct of participating in religious thought is daydreaming and waiting for the magic to come to operate on the dreamer. In other words, splitting apart one's self and expectations along these lines tends to make a person content to sit and wait, always expecting that somehow and somewhere his goals will find him. Upon rejecting religious thought, all of these mystical places and versions of the self converge, and the brain feels the rush of becoming supremely present and aware. It is an electric feeling of empowerment and clarity that most people do not expect. After all, religions do their job well when it comes to making life without them seem terrifying and empty, but once one calls that bluff decisively, the surge of convergence that races through a person is rather unforgettable.

Convergence has a similar feeling to an epiphany with the difference that epiphanies tend to happen unexpectedly while one is not consciously tackling the subject matter about which he feels that he has obtained a great truth. Indeed, convergence is not about the acquisition of great knowledge; it is about the relief of abandoning cumbersome, defective knowledge. The soul collapses into the brain, the metaphysical collapses into the physical, and gods collapse into the imagination.

Indeed, many mystical things about the world that do not necessarily have anything to do with religion come under one's control. For example, religions have no monopoly on pretending to have incredible, profitable knowledge about the world and the future. That technique is and always will be a favorite claim of con men and hustlers, and with reason-based thinking, the apprehensive curiosity that one might have had for a psychic or tarot card reader dissipates for the same reason that one no longer tolerates the directives of religious ministers.

One begins to connect the dots that the practitioners of pseudoscientific fields all speak about beings purported to exist in objective reality in suspiciously similar ways, i.e., vaguely. The knowledge-acquisition techniques of reason-based thinking demand precision and transparency, and that these other fields and practitioners relish their opaqueness means that they have things to hide or, more to the point, things that cannot stand up to scrutiny. Convergence is the emotional feeling that syncs with such an intellectual realization. It is the feeling that no matter how unbelievable a given phenomenon in objective reality may seem that there is always a logical way to understand and get intellectual control of how it has happened.

It is tempting to think of convergence as the brain's signaling that it has reached the final stop on its journey, but that would be a mistake. Convergence is a rewarding step on the path to a new equilibrium of consistent reason-based thinking, but it is not a graduation ceremony. Religious thought infects one's identity and thinking with many ideas and assumptions, some of which will only surface with introspection, discussion, and practice, and convergence will occur before the brain has chased down all of those old habits and eradicated them.

Nevertheless, convergence demonstrates an individual's significant progress away from religious thought, and one will not have to guess when he feels it. Note that "convergence" is my name for this feeling, and one that makes sense considering my recollection of the sensation. I have bothered to name it at all because I have found it to be a surprisingly universal experience for people who have left religious thought. That it has not been named previously to my knowledge speaks only to the smothering effect of religions and their protective taboo in society. Thanks to the same influence, the remaining emotional effects of exiting religious thought will be trying, though no less rewarding if faced properly.

The Existential Crisis

The existential crisis is a sensation of having lost meaning in one's life without believing in the existence of a god. Without question, this is the issue of supreme importance to those considering departing religious thought. After all, religions teach people that the world and their lives amount to nothing relative to their mythological beings, so religious believers have become accustomed to devaluing their physical experiences. In place of a natural view of the world, religions manufacture meaning for their followers. Even though that meaning is rather squirrely and nonsensical, at least it is a plan, and if desperate enough, people will accept any purpose for their lives, no matter how objectively horrifying or arbitrary. To have that meaning debunked leaves a person with feelings of loss, meaninglessness, and even outright depression.

It is also normal to feel bouts of panic when contemplating the existential crisis. It is an alarming and isolating sensation, and as one goes through this period of turmoil, he should expect it. Also, the collapse of religious thought likely has resulted in a deep appreciation of the time one has in his life, and the prospect of indefinitely wasting more of it can cause stress of its own accord. Regardless, it is important to feel the whirlwind of emotions that result from the existential crisis. Processing all of the disorienting and upsetting emotions is needed exercise for one's emotional coping mechanisms, which have atrophied under religious membership.

Indeed, many religious believers with whom I have spoken have said things like, "I think I am probably an atheist, but I just cannot live without meaning." Through the lens of their religions, what these people sense about exiting religious thought feels like a yawning canyon in identity to their imaginations. It feels vast, uncontrollable, and non-negotiable. It makes one want to turn away from it, and many people do exactly that. For now, the existential crisis will only be discussed in order to explain its inevitable appearance as one leaves religious thought. In Chapter 13, the solution to the problem of the existential crisis will be delivered when a person's place with respect to the self is discussed.

While one is religious, he can easily kick away all of the unpleasantness in his life to his god via prayer or church participation. With the loss of those options, one is left with an underdeveloped sense of how to own and process his emotions. Eventually, one's emotional resources develop, and at the end of this chapter, important techniques and resources to facilitate that development will be reviewed. As a snapshot of the solution reviewed in Chapter 13, the existential crisis is an emotional symptom of an intellectual error, and though one will need to bring emotional resources to bear on the issue, one's intellect need not sit out the struggle. Indeed, safe passage beyond the existential crisis is achieved by both one's intellect and emotions working in tandem.

In my experience, the existential crisis was a problem that drained my time and emotional resources as I worked to extricate myself from religious thought. When I recollect with a friend about the feelings that ran through each of us as we wrestled with our decisions to reject religious thought, we both recall a distinct ebb and flow. Some days, we would feel completely fed up with religion and convinced that it was not only factually incorrect but toxic. On other days, we would feel resignation or depression at our inability to relieve our malaise, unwittingly having blended a reason-based outlook with latent religious viewpoints. In retrospect, we were repeatedly running headlong into the same intellectual impasse and becoming disheartened by our failure to find a way around it. Many people who would not otherwise tolerate religious thought in their lives wind up doing so because they have lost hope that they can bridge this divide, which is a precedent that will end in Part Two of this book.

Disorientation

Many are raised with a religion before they can knowingly consent to participate. Carried through religious institutions while still infants or young children, they receive regular reinforcement that the assumptions of religious thought and messages delivered by the religion are not only accurate but reliable bases for knowledge, and they become convinced that a god exists. When that basic understanding of existence is discredited, it tends to leave a person flabbergasted. To have such an elemental piece of knowledge go by the wayside is beyond disheartening; it seems outright impossible. Past experiences that were once attributed to the power of a god now require new explanations, and others fall apart entirely as mirages. Taken together, these experiences create a feeling of disorientation. Coming to the realization that the beings that one once knew and who he felt had known him back had never even existed, a person feels lost. Unlike the existential crisis, the feeling is not one of being lost in meaninglessness but rather feeling at a loss to explain how one could have been so wrong about something so important.

Disorientation is the result of the staggering accounting of wasted time, emotions, and effort invested in a system of belief now discovered to be defunct. At the early stages of departing religious thought, one is not inclined to place a value judgment on how he feels about all of the time and effort that he cannot recover. The focus is on the self, specifically the failure of one's own intellect to catch what has turned out to be a cataclysmic security breach. The collapse of an integral belief system such as one's religion leads one to take a mental inventory of his internal thoughts and processes, i.e., the brain is now alarmed that its mistake calls for a reassessment of other conclusions. Of course, a person is not capable of doing that level of mental cataloguing and file-pulling consciously, but he becomes aware of the size of the task at hand via the stress and disorientation that the insecurity of his intellect triggers.

The good news is that only the knowledge and assumptions that the brain deduces are rooted in the assumptions of religious thought and its associated mythology are subject to its diagnostic check. Any views that lack an apparent connection to religion will not carry the same taint of suspicion, i.e., the brain does not suddenly go into a manic state of self-doubt and turmoil across the board. Instead, it cordons off the topics and opinions that bear obvious relation to religious thought and operates normally in all other respects. A long-term problem arises from the fact that one may hold opinions many degrees removed from religious thought, which are still dependent on that ideology's correctness but that will not be immediately recognized as related. One can only deal with those issues as they appear, but it is often a shock to realize just how many opinions and decisions one has based on religious thought.

In bracing for the negative aspects of departing religious thought, it is important to count on the positive things in the process as well. On the issue of disorientation, the good news is that one's brain is on the case when it comes to figuring out how it has gone wrong, and the better news is that it proceeds in that task in a deliberate and methodical fashion. Having discarded a set of assumptions that the brain was forced to expend energy maintaining, one will feel a sense of relief and simplicity in the world. Without those assumptions, the brain frees up substantial resources by no longer having to juggle contradictory viewpoints on life, objective reality, and knowledge. In other words, one removes a massive obstacle to the brain's ordinary functioning when he exits religious thought, and with its newly-found consistency in the assumptions it uses to analyze information, it will only improve its decision-making as it learns to handle and process information with rigorous standards of analysis.

Regret

With regret, one fixates in an unconstructive way on the past, and as a result, one's perceived mistake continues to rob time from the present. The time spent in religious thought doubly stings of regret because its intellectual emptiness seems so obvious from the outside but also because one's value of time has increased significantly with his departure. Aside from generalized regret, the emotion can also surface with respect to specific actions that one once took or did not take solely on the basis of the directives of his religion. Obviously, one's perceived level of past investment in his religion will correlate directly with the level of regret experienced upon departure.

Regardless of its form, regret is an emotion one is certain to face as he rids himself of religious thought. Unlike the existential crisis, there is no elegant intellectual solution to regret; one will mainly have to engage it with his emotions in order to conquer it, which is difficult. There is no going back to redo things that one may wish to do differently, and there is nothing that will give any payback for the time invested in one's religion. The only thing that can be done is to learn from those past mistakes to guard against their repetition. After all, the past will never come again quite like it once did, but patterns from it will recur in the present and future. The emotional work that one invests in confronting and examining regret is likely to be arduous as the feeling can cause significant despair, but there are objects of value to be salvaged from it nonetheless.

As one works through the tumultuous longing of regret using the techniques and outlook mentioned later in this chapter, it is important to remember to stop and feel relief sometimes that at least one solved the puzzle when he did. Many people go through their entire lives without ever understanding the nature of religious thought or bothering to meaningfully confront it, and the clarity that one earns by ridding himself of it ought to be used as a diving bell in which to surface for gulps of air while plumbing the depths of regret. The sensation of regret carries important information for a person, but the emotional pain that envelops it will exact costs in how it is extracted.

Emotions Focused on Others

Many of the inwardly-focused emotions that result from the discrediting of religious thought are waves that slam against the hull of a person's sense of self, but the detoxification process also produces outward-focused emotions that lead one to reexamine certain relationships. These interpersonal emotions are the result of the brain's conducting a diagnostic check and searching for the reason why it had erroneously accepted religious thought in the first place. The brain signaled the beginning of its troubleshooting search with the jarring disorientation of having bedrock assumptions and beliefs discredited. Another part of the process involves the brain's investigation into exactly how it had made errors in assessing the quality of information that it had trusted enough to incorporate into its own identity. Assuming that one was raised in a religion, the likely culprits for the brain's failure in this regard are the people in whom it had placed trust to relay accurate information about the world and who the brain had permitted to bypass its usual demand for evidence of assertions on that basis.

Betrayal

The level of betrayal that one will feel upon discarding religious thought will depend on what level of culpability one determines a given person has had in facilitating his religion's indoctrination of him. Some people in one's life may have been blameless in implanting the assumptions of religious thought and vouching for their credibility while others were perhaps instrumental in the process. To the extent that a person has deliberately encouraged a person to accept a religion, some feelings of betrayal towards that person are likely. If one further concludes that that person has deliberately encouraged one's religious conviction without believing it himself or to gain cynical advantage, betrayal can grow into a sense of outrage due to the perceived exploitation. On this basis, it is not uncommon for a departing religious believer to experience a period of anger or resentment towards the ministers of his former religion because their encouragement to join the religion, promotion of religious thought, and personal gain from one's acceptance of both are evident.

Having gained a new appreciation for what it means to be alive now that the assumptions of religious thought have been discredited, one can feel robbed of precious time by those who one determines ought to have reasonably known or perhaps did in fact know that religious thought had built its foundations on fault lines. It is natural to feel contempt towards people who have encouraged one to be religious depending on their perceived intent, but the decision of whether to sever relationships with people on the basis of their prior behavior is nothing to be determined in the heat of the moment. The outrage of betrayal and the strip mine feeling of exploitation by those who once garnered the most delicate of trust create an emotional tempest that will dominate and blur the intellect's ability to think clearly. The time will come to reassess what relationships to conclude based on determinations of one's relative blamelessness or active intent to deceive after the successful recreation of identity and liquidation of the more venomous assets of one's emotional inventory.

If one encounters feelings of legitimate hatred during his assessment of betrayal, it is imperative that they be confronted immediately. After one has reasonably determined that he has been betrayed, hatred can percolate to the surface due to the innate disgust of humans for actions that capitalize on their trust in vicious or ruthless ways. However, hatred is corrosive to the person who holds it, and its presence in a person's emotional portfolio constitutes an emergency that warrants the cessation of all other emotional work until it is corrected.

Distrust

Depending on the amount of betrayal that one senses from those in whom he had once placed routine trust, feelings of excessive distrust of others, especially authority figures, may occur. Unlike the other emotions previously discussed, a minimal, baseline level of distrust for others is sensible and healthy in a person's life to the extent that it is manifested rationally and is based on fair concerns. However, distrust as it is likely to be experienced in this transitional period goes too far and approaches misanthropy. A person in the process of extracting the assumptions of religious thought from his identity will tend to overestimate the number of people who were "in on it" when it comes to what he perceives as his systematic duping, which is a natural overcorrection.

Through the core assumption of faith, religious thought unapologetically fosters artificial trust in its practitioners and worldview. When it is discarded by a person as false, the feelings that result can poison the entire well when it comes to a person's desire to place trust in anyone but those he knows intimately. It is important to remember that religious thought always appears obviously incorrect once one has brought an orderly challenge to it and exited its assumptions. However, religious thought feels very different from the interior, and one can temper going too far with his distrust by realizing that most religious believers are likely authentic and sincerely believe that their behavior is appropriate.

Imagine a pendulum attached to the ceiling of a room. Without interference, it will hang straight down and remain at rest. Further imagine that the pendulum is tied all the way to one side of its arc so that it cannot move. When the rope that holds the pendulum in place is cut, it will hurtle all the way to the other extreme of its arc, oscillate back and forth slowly losing its harmonic motion, and eventually come to rest. One's distrust in this setting follows a similar pattern. By virtue of faith being a core element of religious thought, a person's pendulum of trust is artificially strapped to its highest level of credulity with respect to his religion. When a person abandons religious thought, his trust inverts into nearly total distrust, eventually calming down to the point where the momentum of religious thought's collapse will be gone. At that point, one is free to make determinations of people's trustworthiness based on their personalities, past experiences, and general reputation without the collapse of religious thought still rippling through him.

*   *   *

In general, these are the internal emotions that will result from abandoning religious thought, which is not to say that every person will definitely confront all of them but rather that they represent the highest level of emotional backlash in the self. What any given person actually experiences will be unique to his circumstances, religious commitment, social setting, age, family background, etc. Therefore, the generalized advice above cannot be tailored to predict one's specific experiences. Instead, they aim to brace a person for maximum impact.

If one were to experience all of the negative types of emotions to a high degree, it would be safe to speculate that that individual was highly-invested in his religion, likely convinced others to join, and probably gave the religion itself significant amounts of his time and money. In other words, the level of one's perceived financial and social investment in his religion is directly proportional to the number and strength of negative emotions he will encounter upon his departure. Unsurprising a revelation as that may be, one ought to sympathize with the fervently religious in light of this concept. To the extent that they have any inkling of the incorrectness of religious thought, surely they also sense that the emotional transformation that awaits them if they were to elect to engage it would be an especially brutal one.

External Effects on the Person

Aside from a person's introspective work on his emotional balance, his exit from religious thought may have social ramifications that could produce additional friction, especially in terms of one's immediate family and community. If one decides to stop joining others at their customary house of worship or withdrawals from family prayers, he cannot help but serve notice to others of his internal change, and his family and local community are the ones who are best positioned to both receive that message and exact costs on the person for delivering it. For some, this is a terrifying prospect. The level of anxiety and fear about divulging a decision to no longer engage in religious thought will be directly proportional to how ardent one's family and community is with respect to their religion, especially if those groups have a high level of homogeneity with respect to their affiliation.

If one lives in a small town where everyone belongs to the same house of worship, the prospect of withdrawal from religion is daunting. If one is a member of a family that speaks about a religion often and in glowing terms, then the threat to one's most intimate group membership could be suffocating. If one lives in a large city where there is a wide variety of religious membership or has a family that only pays occasional lip service to religious thought however, the external pressure is far less significant. In Part Three, some special aspects of group interactions will be explored in order to examine how groups operate to exert latent pressure on the individual in order to alter his opinion and behavior in this regard.

Regardless of the situation in which one finds himself with respect to his family and community on the question of his rejection of religious thought, ostracism and lesser levels of social condemnation represent serious problems for the individual, especially if he is a child or young adult. In order to survive, religions need to bind people together into clumps in order to manufacture a setting where the assumptions of religious thought and their concomitant beliefs will receive the reinforcement that they lack in practical life. Without regular reinforcement of the veracity of those beliefs by a minister of the religion as well as the community as a whole, they tend to fall into disuse, and so it is not illogical to expect the rough handling of departing members who choose to remain in the community. After all, their successful and peaceful departure from the religion constitutes an implicit threat to the integrity of the group.

Considered in a vacuum, the stress of such a situation on the individual is problematic, but when considered in conjunction with the aforementioned emotional stress with which a person will have to cope as a result of his own internal process, the situation becomes rather serious. In this situation, social ostracism exacerbates all of a person's internal, emotional hurdles, and intentionally or otherwise, it achieves the goal of increasing their difficulty with ruthless efficiency. By potentially sabotaging a person's familial and community support structures, the pressure on the individual to conform his opinions to that of the group hits its apex. While necessity is the mother of invention, the average person can only be expected to endure so much. In a situation where a person is undergoing internal turmoil of his own and has had his support structures removed, it takes a person of exceptional resolve to be able to generate the will to continue with his decision to exit religious thought, well-considered though it may be.

Considering the stakes and the high probability that a person will not be able to simply leave his family or community, a person has to make judgment calls. What are the costs and benefits of going through the motions of being religious in order to relieve some of the applied group pressure? Does he feel a need to engage the people around him in what he perceives to be a mistake in participating in religious thought? Does he require the acceptance of his family and community in order to be happy? One's answers to these questions will change over time, perhaps drastically, and attempting to answer them while progressing through one's emotional transformation is rash and unnecessarily risky.

There is too much at stake to make a hasty decision without having made an honest assessment of what sort of risk that one accepts by openly flouting religious thought. Regarding the discussion of the emotion of betrayal in the previous section, it was determined to be prudent to avoid ending relationships with people by whom one feels betrayed due to their espousal of religious thought while one is still in a state of emotional turmoil. In this section, that advice is extended to the recommendation that one be circumspect in assessing the likelihood of another's ending his relationship with him on the basis of abandoning their once-shared religion.

No matter what one decides to do with respect to telling people in his family and community with respect to his forfeiture of religious thought, he should recognize that he takes a chance either way. If he chooses to tell people, he risks social ostracism and other penalties from his relevant group associations. If he decides not to tell anyone, he risks his own internal turmoil of participating in activities that he finds absurd if not outright deleterious to a person's life. All that one needs to determine before he makes his decision is where his priorities lie.

To date, I still have not bothered to tell some people in my family that I am an atheist simply because it is not relevant to our relationship, and even if I had, my guess is that they would have thought to themselves, "Who cares?" With others, I have sensed their likely non-religious views and broached the subject in my own time and way. Most of them agreed with me, some were indifferent, and a few did not like it. Simply by bringing up the topic of religion in anything but a solemn and respectful manner, one is flouting a social taboo, which can have unpredictable results. Unfortunately, giving individualized advice with respect to the proper handling of these matters is not possible without first having personal information about one's life, resources, and priorities, and one ought to err on the safe side if significant instability in his life appears imminent.

Emotional Techniques and Resources

Some of the emotions discussed are capable of capturing a person for prolonged periods of time, and reading about them here and anticipating them is one's first line of defense. However, anticipation is only good to compensate for the initial shock to the system, and emotional work will be required to properly engage the process. Since one can no longer use religious thought and its associated mythology as a support structure, he must develop replacement techniques. In general, the recovery period entails necessary development and exercise of coping mechanisms that have atrophied, and they have fallen into disuse because of one's prior belief in a god whose omnipotence and benevolence were taken as axiomatic. Obviously, one would not need to muster the level of coping he would otherwise require for a traumatic event when he believes that his interests and family are being protected by such a being.

Without his religion, a person's emotions have to mature and come under his control, and while sheer force of will can take a person most of the way, one ought not feel that he has to go through it all alone or that he has failed by looking for additional assistance.

Acquiring Emotional Discipline

First and foremost, encountering negative emotions and their potentially increased strength should be seen as an opportunity rather than a crisis. When one feels delight or joy, it is a wonderful experience, but one can hardly be said to have learned anything from it. Emotional pain and discomfort are nothing to fear. Indeed, they often hold significant personal truths within their grasp, and one will never discover them until he can manage to conquer his fear and apprehension of feeling the emotions that accompany them.

After all, what are one's emotions? They are the brain's delivery of subjective sensation in response to stimuli, and the most unpleasant of them often constitute subconscious elements of the brain leaking signals to the conscious portion by expressing fear, embarrassment, panic, etc. In other words, they represent information about the self, and exploring their terrain and why they surface in certain environments is a skill that is sadly absent from modern education. Of course, the social value of education focusing on analysis, technical expertise, and intellectual rigor goes without saying, but the person who has obtained the highest level of achievement is the one who has acquired both intellectual and emotional discipline. Note that the phrase "emotional discipline" ought not to be interpreted as some robotic state where a person restrains himself from feeling anything. Indeed, it is quite the opposite.

As opposed to shutting down, emotional discipline is achieved when one actively engages his most uncomfortable emotions in order to intercept and decode the information that they convey to the conscious portion of the brain. Acquiring emotional discipline is a task in experiencing negative emotions, and the reason for the asymmetry is because one does not generally shy away from positive emotions or exploring why they occur. Indeed, a person will have little problem determining what has made him happy and attempting to recreate that environment as often as possible. However, people do not like to feel emotional pain, and the irony is bittersweet that by avoiding the complete processing of such emotions they doom themselves to making their recurrence more frequent.

After all, one cannot learn to develop emotionally or conquer the things that trouble him if he is failing to discern deep information about the reason why those things hurt him in the first place, and one's negative emotions represent an instance where opportunity knocks constantly, yet few recognize it as opportunity. Just as one knows that physical pain has a definite source in the body and concomitant course of medicinal action to cure, one must learn to reinterpret emotional pain as electrified packets of information floating down the river from his subconscious, which will be invaluable to capture despite the unpleasant sting of their retrieval. The opportunities to learn about and improve the self are all around a person when he leaves religious thought, and they ought to be seized with vigor.

What is regret? It is a wistful emotion that signifies a person's depression over past, perceived failures and contains a latent recipe for action to seize similar opportunities if and when they come again. What is embarrassment? It is a burning emotion that buckles the steel of one's self-esteem and signals the presence of fear and insecurity in one's self-image. These emotions are unpleasant, sometimes unbearably so, and despite its obvious need, obtaining the composure and will to examine them in the moment is an art that few people understand even exists.

Unfortunately, modern society does not provide adequate training for how a person ought to confront and interpret his emotions, which is an omission that almost entirely explains how religions retain any foothold in the world in light of the objective absurdity of their intellectual assertions. With people uneducated on how to handle their emotions, religions command somewhat of a monopoly on emotional support structures, flawed as they may be. The knowledge-acquisition techniques of reason-based thinking are incredibly clever tools, devised and sharpened by some of humanity's most memorable people, but they cannot make a person complete alone. In order for a person to self-actualize, the power of his intellect must be complemented by the proper engagement of his emotions.

Imagine parallel railroad tracks that trail off into the distance. As those distinct lines trail away, they appear to bend towards one another until they connect at the horizon. Such is the nature of these complementary elements of a person's identity. In many ways, they are complete opposites and ferocious rivals, but as one develops them with concerted rigor, he will come to realize that they have the paradoxical quality of meeting at the apex of achievement. In other words, the perspective that one gains from mastering one bears a striking resemblance to the perspective achieved from mastering the other, which is an odd, yet delightful fusion indeed.

The most difficult aspect of achieving emotional discipline is that one must be utterly honest with himself about how and why he feels certain things, which is no easy task. No one likes to admit his personal flaws or lesser nature, but it is precisely the ability to do so that operates to disinfect and quarantine them from manifesting in one's behavior. An additional source of confounding is that no one can really help a person as he performs the task of introspection, which is not to say that nothing can be contributed from external sources but rather that the heart of the matter will always lie within the person himself. If he is unwilling to confront the most painful aspects of his emotional profile, no one else will be able to do it for him.

Again, the goal of one's emotional work is to complete the maturation and unification of the self. The knowledge-acquisition techniques of reason-based thinking provide the best tools for analysis of questions of fact, especially with respect to objective reality, and the information-intercepting technique of emotional discipline provides the best tools for the assessment of questions of value, especially with respect to the self. When these powers mature and fuse together, a person will have gained mastery of both his internal and external worlds, and his potential in that state is dramatic.

Of course, religious thought derails this process and robs the person of opportunities for fruitful introspection by virtue of the emotional support techniques that it offers. Surely, religious rituals like prayer and meetings provide emotional comfort in the short run, even if that reprieve is granted by way of a façade and comes at the high price of intellectual arbitrariness. Regardless, the techniques and implications of religious thought dull and externalize a person's worst emotions, and while they may get a person by for a while, they are not doing him any favors in the long run. Without confronting negative emotions squarely and leaving off pretense, they are destined to recur, and when they exact awful revenge for ignoring them, most people will sadly never realize that they represent another manner in which the body communicates with itself to express pain from which it is begging the conscious portion of the brain for attention and relief.

Living in the Moment

A necessary corollary of the experience of convergence is one's increased value for time, specifically the time he has to live. By burning the imaginary ships of his future escape, one feels compelled to act in the present to experience the world and remedy the ills or injustices that he may perceive. To live in the moment is not an expression of indifference to anything that may occur in the future; rather, it represents the acceptance of the present as the only location in which anyone ever exists. Tomorrow never truly comes, and even the moment that just passed is long gone. Living in the moment signifies the acknowledgement of this chronology.

To the extent that living in the moment gives a person a connotation of carefree and footloose hedonism, that treatment of the expression is rejected in this discussion. Its meaning here implies valuing action over hope, urgency over hesitation, and directness over side-stepping. To live in the moment is to take no instant for granted because one is never distracted from his purposeful action in any one of them with hesitation with respect to the past or the future. It is a technique of nurturing purpose by constantly giving effect to it.

Of course, the concept is an asymptotic ideal that one can never truly reach because people have both strong memories as well as stressful concerns about the future, but its practical lesson is that one's excessive dwelling on the past and future aspects of his life steals from his present. If one follows such a pattern to the extreme, he could easily wake up one day and wonder how his entire life has passed him by, and the answer is that it did so while he was functionally ignoring it.

Living in the moment is an emotional readjustment to compensate for the loss of the implicit guarantee of religious thought that one's consciousness will never terminate. In the religious worldview, one's present moments are diluted into worthlessness by being covered by an avalanche of them. After all, how could one take much interest in any one thing when he has an infinite number of them? Where is the value? What religious thought bills as providing infinitely more actually makes a person value his chances for action in life infinitely less by destroying the value he would have ordinarily placed in his finite time.

By discarding religious thought and living in the moment, the natural value of the present returns to its original, unadulterated concentration, and one celebrates the restoration of his natural equilibrium by filling his moments with purposeful action. One's actions are the manner in which he attempts to give effect to his meanings in life, and simply because necessary implications of those meanings extend into the future does not mean that the person is failing to live in the moment. Living in the moment is an expression of concentrating all of one's action and emotion in the now in order to achieve the goals that one so desires, whatever they may be and whenever he expects to realize them.

Locating a Non-Religious Community

The last topic pertains to acquiring emotional support for those who feel overwhelmed in situations where they have discredited religious thought but remain emotionally tangled in their own feelings or have had their natural support structures undercut by vindictive members of their family or former religion. Departing religious thought is not an easy thing to do because it can be an addictively simplistic way of both thinking and feeling. It is important to realize that the need to reach out to others for guidance and stability during the transitional period is natural, and there is no shame in it. Sadly, most societies in the world do not provide a purposeful counterargument for religious thought as a matter of course, and those who have had to go in search of it understand the travails and isolation of the process.

The good news is that the feeling of isolation is an illusion. Many people have endured the feelings and confusion associated with wondering how religious thought can flourish so widely, all while being objectively nonsensical. More still have felt smothered by families and communities who likely did not understand why they could no longer participate in religious thought. To the extent that one feels that his emotions are fluctuating beyond reasonably safe parameters, one's objective should be to find some of these people and communicate with them.

In the modern age, the internet has become a precious tool for religious skeptics in order to replicate the emotional support and intellectual discussion that one may need while he transitions from religious thought. Simply seeing other people speak about reason-based thinking and atheism can have a calming effect that the same doubts and concerns that have been floating in one's head are not the work of a madman.

If one lives in a small community and feels deep terror at the prospect of his community penalizing him for his lack of faith, the internet is a unique place of safety for such reason-based thinkers where they can learn, develop, and eventually find themselves prepared to no longer need such support. Of course, locating a skeptic group that holds meetings in person serves the same purpose, but if one feels unease about the potential for personal stigma in this regard, he can preserve his anonymity on the internet while still obtaining the information and camaraderie that he seeks. Included in the Acknowledgements section at the end of this book are several people who I have personally witnessed having such effect on others in online settings, and there are plenty more who would do the same if needed.

*   *   *

If the emotional benefits of reason-based thinking and atheism have come as a surprise, it is an understandable one. So much of the dialogue between theists and atheists on the question of the existence of a god acts as a centrifuge separating emotions from intellect, and atheists are very accustomed to having to tease out the emotional connections that religious believers always claim to have with their gods in order to highlight the incongruence of using emotions to establish a question of fact in objective reality. Unfortunately, this customary pattern of argumentation has the effect of making atheists sometimes forget the torrent of emotions that come with exiting religious thought, if they ever had to perform it themselves. It is an emotional and social process as well as an intellectual one.

What is perhaps most unfortunate is that atheism has tremendous emotional arguments on its side, but in the course of debating religious believers, emotional considerations are ignored in favor of dealing decisive logical blows. Nevertheless, the discussion of both the positive and negative emotional impacts of departing religious thought is momentous, and it is my personal hope that atheists will more often take the time to deeply understand and then showcase to inquiring minds the abundant emotional benefits of being intellectually stable and coherent. Logic and reason are precious commodities, but they are not the only ones that people have. To advocate their use to the exclusion of discussing the emotional benefits of atheism is to severely undersell what it has to offer and acts to implicitly cede ground to religious thought that it does not deserve to occupy on its merits.

10 – The Intellectual Detoxification Process

For when you gaze long into the abyss, the abyss gazes also into you.
      – Friedrich Nietzsche

In the previous chapter, the emotional ramifications of one's discarding the assumptions of religious thought were reviewed, and the next topic is not entirely disjoint from the emotional process. However, the intellectual permutations of departing religious thought have the quality of occurring in a linear fashion, which merits independent attention. Unfortunately, religious thought implants some subtle but momentous ideas with respect to what a person values in the world. All too often, a departing religious believer will overlook these thoughts because they are usually not explicitly stated, and when they do, they run the risk of mistakenly finding their reasoning in error and turning back to religious thought. In other words, their emotional panic will overrule their intellectual conclusion.

The assumptions and mythology of religious thought are so central and embedded in the brain's worldview that it cannot give them up all at once. Instead, it conducts a triage of sorts. The brain follows a predictable path out of religious thought, and along its way, it sacrifices that which it can no longer justify while trying to maintain other ideas that it still desires. When it is all over, it will have arrived at its new destination, having succeeded in the complete extraction of the assumptions of religious thought and having achieved a state of consistent equilibrium.

Customized Religion

The starting point of the process is one that is experienced by all religious believers, regardless of whether they have any intention to leave religious thought, and it is the concept of a customized religion.   When a person's religion offends his morality or understanding of logic or science, he will first alter his interpretation of the religion. If the source of the offending material is scripture or other sacred text, then the person will choose to see the passage in question as mistranslated, metaphorical, or intended to apply only to earlier civilizations. All of those excuses are perfect escape valves for the religious mind that has the dual goal of both easing its own cognitive dissonance as well as saving the pristine infallibility of its god.

In the brain of a person who is making a customized religion, any perceived error in scripture or text will be chalked up as human error. Such evasive maneuvering speaks to the complete lack of interest that a person in this stage has in questioning the core assumptions of religious thought and how the brain will move by reflex to shield those assumptions from total system failure, which will be achieved if the god in question is perceived as fallible in any way.

The universal customization of religion to suit the taste of those who practice it is symptomatic of the fact that religions are almost entirely based on scripture, and scripture can be read to mean virtually anything. Filled with metaphor, imprecise terminology, and often conflicting directives, scripture cannot possibly be followed to the letter of the law by anyone because the terms of its legislation are undefined, as was articulated in The Meta Argument in Chapter 8. So, the hollow concepts of religious thought are filled up and given effect by the people who read them and see what they want to see in them, and when a person looks into emotionally significant stimuli that are objectively vague and meaningless, he tends to see himself, though he likely will not recognize it. The human brain projects itself onto vague data because it wants to fill in the gaps of meaning with respect to what it is facing in order to understand it, and to avoid further complexity in an already problematic situation, it selects pieces of a template that it knows best: itself. It is a bizarre and fascinating backfire of the intellect that demonstrates the paranoia that the brain has with respect to utter vagueness and uncertainty in its surrounding environment.

The brain's solution to its data-processing dilemma would not be an issue if it recognized itself in its transplant, and that it almost never does is a chilling failure. In other words, people fail to understand that the cognitive resources of the brain routinely fail in predictable ways and overestimate how perfect the brain can be in how it assesses data. With respect to religious terminology, those failures on an individual basis are reinforced by the coming together of people in groups who all recognize the same codewords being used but fail to understand that they all have different interpretations of what they mean. When they worship and pray, they are each lamenting and imploring funhouse mirrors of themselves to save them. They are worshiping a celestial silhouette of their ideal selves, immune from death and capable of anything. When one sees the actions of the religious in this light, the heavy sadness of their prayers hits home: they are asking themselves for help, and they cannot provide it because they are busy waiting for themselves to answer. It is doubtful that there could be a more gut-wrenching paralysis of action.

In any case, customized religion is the brain's first step on its journey towards intellectual detoxification, and it is a universal one, even for religious believers who never intend to leave. As discussed repeatedly in Part One, religions do not offer any reasonable basis for the correctness of their respective approaches, creating an environment of vagueness in which people naturally gravitate to portions of their religion that suit them best. By virtue of the murkiness of any given religion, its customization by its followers is inevitable and encouraged.

Personal Spirituality

When a religion pushes a person far enough away with offenses to either logic or morality, the next step the brain will take is to sacrifice the concept of participating in a group when it comes to believing in its god of choice. The person is still not considering challenging the core assumptions of religious thought, but he senses that he cannot tolerate its rigidness when taught in groups due to perceived corruption, hypocrisy, etc. The brain's solution to this stress is to exit, which makes sense. If the brain senses clashes that are either too severe or too frequent, e.g., between what it itself deems to be moral and what his religion tells him is moral, the brain does not then leap into the frightening discussion of whether a god actually exists. Instead, it ignores any questions pertaining to gods, especially with respect to their existence and infallibility, and moves to smear the ministers and interpreters of its god's will that have twisted his message and true meaning. The person is on a sinking ship, and the concept of god is loaded with such emotion and meaning that every other item in the hold will be thrown overboard before that one is even considered.

As an aside, remember what is meant by the word "religion" in this book: a system of belief that utilizes religious thought and conducts rituals and meetings in order to commune with or appease a god or gods. Personal spirituality is not technically religion because the person has withdrawn from an organized group of meetings to opt for a more personal treatment, and the significance of this maneuver will become clear when we discuss group phenomena in Part Three.

The solitary nature of personal spirituality makes its likely ethos difficult to describe because it takes countless forms. At one end of the spectrum, those who are personally spiritual may take the entire ethos of their customized religion and continue to pray or conduct rituals; they will only withdraw from the religious community with which they once affiliated. At the other extreme of personal spirituality, a person may retain a hazy sense of a god and some general morality without bothering to pray or perform rituals at all. In other words, "personal spirituality" is not a term that enjoys great clarity; it is more of a miscellaneous catch-all for religious beliefs and practices that have been heavily bastardized to suit one's personal tastes with the characteristic hallmark of one's having abandoned the religious group. In other words, there is a continuum of forms for the personally spiritual, and where the brain chooses to land in this continuum is not always predictable. However, it is safe to speculate that the more socially and intellectually entrenched a person is in his customized religion, the more resemblance his personal spirituality will bear to it.

Regardless, the person who enters a phase of personal spirituality does so because he has taken personal offense to something that his religion has taught, whether logical, scientific, or moral, and the offending comment has created a state of strong cognitive dissonance in him. On one hand, he considers the source of the displeasing information to be immaculate and above reproach, and on the other hand, the information is so starkly incorrect or offensive to the person that he cannot stomach it. At this point, the brain has to remove the irritant one way or the other, and its path of least resistance is not to question god (that offends the still-intact assumptions of religious thought) or to question himself (that causes internal disorder) but instead to shoot the messenger. From there, the person is free to interpret scripture as he sees fit, consciously excising that which offends him and extolling that which he finds pleasing. After all, the vague and metaphorical language of the directives found in scripture is routinely molded into personalized form by whoever reads it.

Customized religion and personal spirituality share substantial similarities. Indeed, they are nearly identical insofar as their theoretical characteristics are concerned. The substantive difference between them is formalized group membership, which may seem of small significance, but to the contrary, religious thought needs regular group reinforcement in order to survive because its worldview and directives will fade into irrelevance in an environment where reason-based thinking reigns. As will be discussed in Chapter 15 when the group psychology employed by religions is reviewed, conformity of opinion that provides necessary reinforcement for religious thought deteriorates when an individual is on his own, devoid of cues from his congregation.

Deism

After the customization of religion and the disintegration of group belief in personal spirituality, the next step the brain takes is towards deism. There are many flavors of deism, but they all tend to revolve around the same general concept: there is a god, but he does not interfere in the world. The appeal of this philosophy is that it solves many conceptual problems that exist when one is uncomfortable with the presence of misery in the world vis-à-vis a god's existence while preserving one's general desire for ultimate meaning. When one perceives atrocity and human anguish, it is difficult to understand why an active, interfering god would permit such things to happen, and as discussed earlier, there is no logically compelling explanation for it. It is also possible that the concept of human morality as framed in objective absolutes would be salvaged to the extent that a person would find it desirable. As far as the brain's triage of religious ideas goes, this is its last attempt. If it cannot accept this minimum roster of religious characters, then there will be nothing left of religious thought to entertain.

Deism is a very short walk from atheism. The god who created the world and then left is nearly identical to the one who does not exist, especially if he has no interest in the moral choices of humans. The brain stops at this juncture because what it is desperately trying to avoid is encountering a profound existential crisis that it senses will occur if the concept of god is jettisoned. When the person enters this stage of detoxification, he fails to realize that he is still erroneously maintaining what will later be referred to as The Ultimate Assumption, which is a subtle corollary to the overall ethos of religious thought.

While in religious thought, the brain was taught and freely accepted the notion that a person's life has infinite, ultimate meaning, integral to his religious identity. Without it, the brain will be forced to ask some very elemental questions about its identity, and it senses and naturally avoids a crisis of that order. Although deism is a natural middle ground, a person will not be content to occupy it for long if he has accepted and embraced reason-based thinking. The Cosmological and Teleological Arguments have the flaws discussed in Chapter 6, and they in no way constitute a convincing foundation to support a belief in a god. Those arguments are the kernel of what compels deism to exist at all, and if they fail as they do, there is virtually nothing left to justify one's belief in the existence of a god in objective reality.

When a person's intellectual detoxification stops on deism, his beliefs are only serving the purpose of protecting his identity; they rarely, if ever, extend outside of the person himself due to the totally passive role that he believes that his god takes in the affairs of the world. Relatively costless though it may be, the deistic philosophy still collapses for the same reason that religious thought did in the first place. The word "god" is no more defined, there is no additional showing that the concept of god is necessary to explain and understand nature and its existence, and there certainly is no empirical evidence of a god's existence.

Doubtlessly, many people who mentally discredit religious thought wind up as deists because it seems to offer a comfortable compromise. On the basis of both intellectual consistency and emotional discipline, I recommend progressing through this strangely appealing stage because a hefty fear is about to be faced in the next step, which represents a momentous opportunity for personal investigation and knowledge, and once it is done, the final equilibrium of atheism awaits.

Nihilism

After one leaves deism, he has unloaded nearly everything of religious thought. In all likelihood, he still retains some subtle assumptions about the nature of his existence, but he has nothing left that he recognizes as religious thought. Because of a lingering intellectual thorn in his side, the stage he enters poses significant problems for those who approach it without understanding where that thorn is located. At the moment one reaches this level, he is standing on the edge of emotional oblivion. Nothing has meaning, least of all one's life, and all seems lost. The world seems a grotesque and unseemly play with actors who do not realize their own pitifully redundant and insignificant roles, and the self feels empty and devoid of any meaning.

Nihilism towards all things in all ways reflects the intellectual stage that coincides with the existential crisis described in the previous chapter. They are two sides of the same coin and produce profound feelings of meaninglessness and loss. Nothing makes a person shudder more completely than to lose meaning in his life, and religious thought has both solved and exacerbated this problem for its adherents. Seeking meaning in one's life is a big reason why people gravitate towards religious thought, but religions simultaneously inflate their proposed solution to existential crises by making people dependent exclusively on them and suggesting that nothing else matters. As will be seen, the emotional dependence will not usually be tested by a normal religious believer, but those who do wish to leave soon realize that the hell with which their religion had been threatening them does in fact exist, courtesy of religions' having tampered with their followers' core assumptions with respect to what a person ought to value in life. It is not the cartoonish hell of red devils running around with pitchforks or the darker gothic hell of elaborate torture devices and agonized screams but rather a hell of silence and emptiness. Sadly, there is only one exit.

While one is in this stage of nihilism, he is deeply troubled by his inability to answer the question: "What is the ultimate meaning of life?" To escape, one must have the realization that his problem lies in the subtle assumption about existence that he makes when he asks the question in the first place, namely, The Ultimate Assumption, which will be addressed in depth in Chapter 13. With reason-based thinking, one has concluded that gods and the soul do not exist, but The Ultimate Assumption has likely slid by undetected. The source of the horrible discomfort that a person feels when he is in the midst of a nihilistic mindset is the unwitting application of a religious concept to a reason-based worldview.

With the discarding of The Ultimate Assumption, the person achieves a state of emotional atheism, which is to say the relaxation and relief associated with his emotions and drives coming into agreement with his intellect. Progressing through nihilism is a huge opportunity for emotional development and maturation, and it should not be squandered. The appreciation for the finiteness of consciousness and the concomitant sense of urgency that washes over a person when he permits the implications of reason-based thinking to completely saturate his worldview signals the complete collapse of religious thought. When faced properly, the fear of meaninglessness dissipates as all fear does, and the power that it has held over a person returns to him. The surge of empowerment marks the conclusion of the detoxification process from religious thought and the beginning of the shift into actively relearning how to live life in harmony with one's emotional and intellectual consistency.

The Final Equilibrium of Atheism

When a person finally discards the entirety of his religion's cast of characters as well as its subtle assumptions regarding his place in the world, he has achieved a state of atheism. His emotions have been given the time they needed to grow up and accept that which his intellect has determined to be an accurate reflection of objective reality. The assumptions of reason-based thinking have been determined to yield the most predictive value and reliability, and now all that a person needs to do is recalibrate his frame of reference for the world.

The ultimate and permanent no longer exist; the relative and temporary are what remain. The hazy and metaphysical have given way to the specific and natural. Life has become more textured, nuanced, and complex. All-or-nothing thinking now seems simplistic, even suspicious. Melodramatic religious thought appears naïve and childish. Nevertheless, a beginning atheist may be at a loss to understand how to live his life from this new perspective, which is an understandable confusion considering his personal change. For now, the concentration will be on how a person strategically operates his life from a temporal perspective, taking it as a given that he has meaning that he wishes to protect or realize.

The ability of humans to create, maintain, and manipulate abstract ideas in their brains is a double-edged sword. On one hand, the ability to generate such abstraction has permitted man to create items and techniques for the betterment of his own life that are wholly without parallel in the rest of the animal kingdom. On the other hand, the human brain has the ability to bewilder itself with its own creativity by incorrectly muddling purely internal creations with the actual nature of objective reality. A timely example of this backfiring is the current topic, religious thought, which contains ideas built in the abstract that people have routinely misperceived as being a part of objective reality.

The good news is that simple lessons are available to an individual courtesy of nature and the rest of the animal kingdom, of which he now has no obstructions to seeing himself as a part. Human beings have significant, additional complexity that other animals do not, but the behavior of other animals contains baseline lessons to teach about harmonious, proactive behavior. For example, deer do not seem to get locked into existential crises. Dogs do not seem to mope about a failure for their lives to turn out the way they had thought. This is because they live in the moment.

While some animals are rather clever and have been discovered to be far more intelligent than man had originally thought, their lessons for man arise from their relative simplicity. For one, other animals do not expect anything of nature in accommodating their existence. If food or water becomes depleted in a given area, they respond to those circumstances and continue to a new location without dwelling on the hardship or taking it personally. Humans are capable of lamenting unfavorable situations in life and tend to drain a lot of energy in the process, thus exacerbating an already problematic situation. Of course, the energy one may waste in this regard might have been invested in determining how to take steps to actually achieve one's desired goal, and to the extent that one does not accomplish this, his inability to control the past from coloring the present has exacted costs in the form of time.

In atheism, time is the ultimate currency because one cannot reasonably conclude that his consciousness will survive the physical death of his body. If there is a touchstone in the final equilibrium of atheism, it is that one must stop waiting for things to happen to him. The natural world does not owe man anything, and if a person is to realize the happiness and dreams that he desires for his life regardless of their form, his likelihood of success is maximized by launching proactive attempts to achieve them himself.

The ability of a person to compensate and adjust his course through life to account for changes in surroundings or circumstance is a hallmark of a high level of achievement in intellectual and emotional strength. In religious thought, a person's nature becomes rigid with expectations and strange, quasi-contractual arrangements with unseen forces that make him feel as though he need not yield to circumstances when others might think it prudent. After all, a religious believer thinks that an omnipotent being favors his existence and cannot help but be understandably filled with feelings of entitlement in certain regards. However, the ideal mindset of an atheist is the opposite of rigidity. The blows of the world will come to a person's life of their own accord, and the inflexible individual is likely to snap from their bombardment. If one's worldview and actions instead have fluidity and adaptive resilience, he will find the storms of life to be no less frequent but rather less likely to inflict damage or extract time by virtue of their occurrence.

Consider the force of nature that is water. In some respects, it is the most powerful substance in the world. Massive boreholes like The Grand Canyon are testaments to the force that it can exert. Yet it has no ability to be meaningfully struck or damaged in its own right, and its adaptive fluidity can be seen by pouring it into receptacles of different shapes and witnessing how it effortlessly molds to its surroundings. This is a natural model for a person's state of mind that an emerging atheist should try to cultivate. Fluidity and adaptability are important resources to mentally generate without the fictions of religious thought. The world will come to deliver blows to a person regardless of his cleverness, and he stands the best chance of sustaining the worst of them by making his mentality fluid to the point such that there is ultimately nothing to strike.

*   *   *

One ought not to feel disheartened if he finds that he lingers in any one of the transitional states detailed above. Indeed, a huge number of people occupy the phase of personal spirituality for a substantial amount of time, probably because it represents a comfortable location, containing both personal independence from religion and continued emotional support from its concepts. Unfortunately, people often do not see the patterns of their own lives recurring in others, and the detoxification stages discussed here have been endured by far too many people, myself included, who have felt that no one else would understand their experiences.

Even with advantageous advance knowledge of these stages, there is an emotional maturation process at work that operates in tandem with these intellectual steps. Indeed, Chapters 9 and 10 constitute a pair that should not be read in isolation; they augment and complement each other. To understand the advisories of each is an excellent start to the rebuilding process of a person's identity and one on which higher concepts and discussions will soon be built.

Applications of Reason-Based Thinking

Before continuing with higher steps of rebuilding one's identity, the attention will first shift to flexing one's newly found intellectual muscles with respect to some ideas and practitioners that many people find bizarre or difficult to understand. The discarding of religious thought has cleared a tenacious obstruction to understanding these puzzles. Now, it is simply a matter of allowing reason-based thinking to operate without being arbitrarily detoured.

The following topics are important house-cleaning for one's reason-based thinking. They have been chosen because they are things that most people casually refer to as "stupid" or "obviously wrong", but few know how to explain exactly why. As an atheist and reason-based thinker, it is important that one be able to systematically understand why he does not believe something. Indeed, many people consider the atheist position "stupid" or "obviously wrong", but that is because they answer to religious thought, the assumptions of which they likely do not understand. Emerging atheists can do better than that, and indeed they must, if they are to avoid repeating the errors encouraged by their former religions and the resulting shock to the system endured when they were exposed. As will be seen, utilizing reason-based thinking thoroughly and consistently will cause the frayed fringes of society to weave back together neatly.

Superstitions

What use is it to carry a rabbit's foot on one's keychain? What is the significance of having a black cat cross one's path? Many cultures and people develop strange superstitions such as these, and while they all seem patently absurd, it is safe to say that most people would prefer to never see a black cat cross in front of them. In other words, there is a tiny bit of a person that gives the superstition a shred of credence, and if he were to see a black cat walk past him, he might think, "Well, I could have done without that." But what is it about superstition that makes it simultaneously unbelievable yet interesting? What are the general characteristics of a superstition?

All superstitions are insurance policies meant to summon good luck or stave off bad luck in the future, or they are omens that portend either good or bad luck to come. They also usually have an arbitrary talisman that creates the superstitious environment, and at the center of every superstition lingers the concept of luck. What is luck? How is one going to know it when he sees it? Is one going to have any reliable standard with which to determine when the talisman that he is carrying is actually creating luck?

Consider the following scenario. Two people, Greg and Claire, both have rabbit's feet in their pockets and are standing in line next to each other at a bank when bank robbers enter. They steal money, and on their way out, one of them fires a bullet into a chandelier, which falls onto Greg, leaving him paralyzed from the neck down for life while Claire is unharmed. Did Claire's rabbit's foot work? Did Greg's fail? They were in essentially the same situation at the same place and moment in time with the same protective device, yet one suffered tremendous harm while the other did not. In other words, all other variables being as equal as possible, all that remains to determine why Greg or Claire was positively or negatively affected is the nebulous concept of luck.

Now, go back and read the two previous paragraphs by trading out the word "luck" for "god/actions by god" and "rabbit's foot" for any given holy device. It is no coincidence that the discussion's logical force is unchanged. The secret as to why lies in considering what the words "god" and "luck" really mean, and utilizing identical reasoning as appeared in The Meta Argument, the fact that no one can deliver a reasonably precise meaning for either means that both concepts are fishy.

In this manner, superstitions avoid being decisively smashed by casual reasoning as they are using terms and concepts that are inherently vague and unscientific and therefore resist being inspected for accuracy. Many people intuit that superstitions are illogical or impractical, but it is difficult to slam the door on them all the way because their errors are buried in their terminology, which is rarely considered on casual reflection.

Surely, a religious believer will feel at liberty to ramble about his god and his benevolent tidings, but he will not be able to prove how he knows that he exists in the first place. He will not be able to reasonably say where his god presently is located. In short, he does not know anything about his god; he simply feels wonderful emotions and is filling in the blanks with a hazy personification. The same is true of luck, minus the personification aspect. These words express identical concepts; they are gap-filler words that people use when they sense personal meaning in an event but are at a loss to explain why. The only difference between choosing one or the other is whether a person wants to load a religious personification into the situation.

How about a chain letter? A chain letter is a superstitious document that recommends that one pass it along to a number of friends and family while remarking on some great rewards that people have not-so-coincidentally received for doing so and some horrible suffering that others have endured for breaking the chain. Does that sound familiar? It should. This characterization is exactly what scripture is. A chain letter has no evidence or logic at all for its promises of happiness or harm to be visited upon those who either continue or break its chain of being passed along and neither does scripture to the extent that it commands people to live by its edicts and spread its word.

Both documents are operating on the same principle for their proliferation: they are counting on a person's fear of the unknown and inability to realize that the knowledge-acquisition techniques of reason-based thinking apply. Exactly what is going to cause all of one's hair to fall out if he does not make 27 copies of a letter and mail it to his friends? Exactly what is going to send a person to some place called hell if he does not indoctrinate his children and family with the laws and customs of scripture? No one can say. All they feel at liberty to remark on is the threat, and from there, they are content to take their chances that one will not possess sufficient discipline to restrain his imagination from running amok.

Conspiracy Theories

What are the characteristics of a conspiracy theory? A conspiracy theory is any idea or explanation of events that is light on evidence of the posited conspiracy, heavy on innuendo, and almost always implies behind-the-scenes collusion by powerful people. The hallmark of a conspiracy theory is the heavy reliance on insinuation and implication, however. Preferred evidence comes in the form of guilt by association or weak and highly suggestive circumstantial evidence. Of course, not all conspiracy theories are made equal. Some are far more believable than others because they have more quantity of circumstantial evidence or better quality of it, and others seem to intentionally test the bounds of human credulity. In other words, one has to analyze evidence based on its sources and overall reliability before he can be bothered to put any stock in what it purports to establish.

Sadly, there are people whose minds are gripped in paranoia and who select storylines around events that confirm their fear, which is the work of a brain that is permitting its emotions to bully its intellectual capacity. Everyone knows at least one person who gets worked up about conspiracy theories, and they often broach the subject with, "You really didn't know about this?" or "This is going to blow your mind." In other words, they tend to develop a know-it-all personality, which is understandable considering the depth of knowledge and information that they have convinced themselves that they have obtained.

With reason-based thinking in place, a clean and uniform approach can be brought to bear for any given conspiracy theory, which is that one's level of credulity ought to increase in direct proportion to the quality and reliability of the evidence one is providing to support it, and emotional appeals will not do. In fact, emotions are of no use whatsoever when making determinations of question of fact with respect to objective reality, and another's appealing to them is suspicious.

As with superstitions, religious thought follows a similar pattern. Indeed, religious thought represents the ultimate conspiracy theory. Without a reasonably convincing foundation in evidence or logic, the people who champion both religious thought and conspiracy theories in general are doing so from an unhelpful emotional perspective, and the conclusions that are drawn are held with certainty. Indeed, how could they not be? One has made a decision to accept less than reasonable evidentiary and logical support for what he believes, and in the process, he has abandoned the same tools that would have allowed him to have added texture to his level of knowledge. Without them, he is basically operating on the basis of faith.

As with religious thought, the operation of conspiracy theories bears all of the hallmarks of a brain at a loss to ground itself in reliable information, and it causes incredible discomfort and stress in a person's life. By making one's belief contingent upon reasonable evidence and logic, one has an anchor to ground his intellect from being tossed about in the winds of his emotions, and there is no emotion more capable of producing that turmoil than fear.   Sharing the hallmark paranoia of conspiracy theorists, religious believers are endlessly paranoid about even whispering that they do not believe in a god because they have been taught that he is everywhere and hears everything.   They can be paranoid about missing church or prayer for the same reason. They are all playing a game that they cannot win because their emotions have stacked the decks against them from the beginning.

Fortune Telling, Psychic Readings, and other Pseudosciences

The core of fortune telling, psychic readings, and other pseudosciences is their claim to have special ability to predict future events.   Practitioners of these fields use various techniques and objects to summon information like tarot cards, crystal balls, reading palms, or entering a trance.   While collecting data from these sources, they begin to correctly detail aspects of a customer's life that have already happened and then proceed to deliver news of what will happen to him in the future. A skilled practitioner can make this experience feel alarmingly accurate and sobering.

So, what is happening here? How could these people have such powers? Of course, the answer is that they do not, but understanding how they create their effects is subtler than debunking physical magic. Magic tricks appear to break laws of nature, and one can always physically investigate and deduce that they have a logical explanation.   Psychics and the like perform similar tricks, but they do so with verbal information instead of physical impossibility. As such, their magic is safely hidden in their brains, so all that can be examined is what they say.

When it comes to predictions of pseudosciences, the trick is once again that nothing said is specific enough as to be testable or falsifiable. What sounds more like the prediction of a psychic: that one will have money troubles in the near future or that one will lose six hundred and eighty-three dollars in the stock market this coming Tuesday at 3:42 PM? By making hazy comments that tend towards universal applicability, the practitioner lets the customer fill in the blanks as he sees fit. Money, love interests, and deceased family members are all ripe territory for psychic predictions because nearly everyone has an interest in hearing predictions about each one.

They will also study a person's reactions and responses to probing questions to guide the direction of what they predict. This general technique is known as cold reading and will be discussed in Chapter 14 when the con of hot reading is also considered. Cold reading is a subtle technique that can feel quite powerful if one only sees it done to him and has no other opportunity to see the practitioner's patterns. Regardless, it is a method of getting a customer to unwittingly yield personal information, which in turn renders later predictions more impressive. If one were to sit expressionless in front of a psychic without responding to questions, their predictions would feel less impressive.

Like magicians, ministers and practitioners of other pseudosciences aim to appear to be able to break the laws of nature without ever actually doing so. Magicians practice sleight of hand; practitioners of pseudosciences practice sleight of mind. Both are attempting to strike the right balance of vagueness that seems like specificity. After all, anyone who goes to a psychic (or a house of worship) wants to believe that the practitioner can do what the sign in front of his business says he can do. On average, all the practitioner has to do is be perceptive and let the customer's primed desire to believe that he knows his future do the rest. Is the customer wearing a wedding ring? In what general age group is he? What type of clothes does he wear? Everyone wishes to think they are completely unique, but people follow patterns. Successful practitioners of pseudosciences will be able to spot those patterns and use them to divine good guesses about the person's life.

Consider the striking similarities between religions and the *modus operandi* of these pseudosciences. Scripture gives vague predictions about what the future holds for its adherents, often delivered in the context of a person's greatest hopes and worst fears, and some ministers even attempt versions of cold or hot reading in their congregations. There is a common vein to all of this, namely, that great knowledge is claimed, and nothing specific is ever said. Surely, that pattern has created a tired repetition, but it should also feel relaxing in demonstrating that the linguistic tricks of charlatans have now been rendered obvious and one-note. Despite their befuddling scenery and chicanery, they are all nothing more than unethical merchants, selling different flavors of the same brain candy.

Non-Religious Metaphysical Entities

Ghosts, spirits, and tormented souls have captured man's imagination for centuries. Whether it is an abandoned mental hospital, a lonesome house, or an old subway track, ghosts and apparitions supposedly haunt any place that has the proper history for it. Haunted structures always seem to be older and with a dark history in some respect. People who claim to have interacted with ghosts often have heard faint sounds, felt temperature changes, or have had a general, creepy uneasiness about where they were. These events almost always take place in the dark of night, and the person who senses the presence of ghosts often has knowledge of the unique history of the structure in which he senses them.

Psychics sometimes get involved in these situations as well in order to determine the presence of spirits, and séances are another rarer venue in which the supernatural is invoked with the aid of a psychic or medium who claims to have intimate knowledge of this strange realm. In common parlance, this is the realm of the supernatural, home to untold numbers of horrible, invincible creatures with a strange interest in humanity. While many of these creatures tend to have ties to religious mythology, many of them occupy a realm of general fear since religions do not often bother to reference them directly.

Of course, a significant amount of time has already been spent in Part One to demonstrate that there is no reason to suspect that the metaphysical realm actually exists in objective reality, and so there must be another explanation for these phenomena.   For one, it is telling that almost all ghost encounters happen at night. Much as the previous phenomena in this section occupied the dark places in a person's brain, ghosts and spirits occupy the dark places in his sight. When a person enters an old, creaky house or a structure that otherwise appears to carry age, he is primed for encounters with ghosts, i.e., he expects to see such things based on the folklore surrounding ghosts.

If spirits do exist, they are oddly constrained from appearing in new buildings or in the daylight. The fact that psychics and mediums engage this area as well shows how other practitioners of pseudosciences have come to parasitically capitalize on the already-parasitic conceptual priming that religions have instilled. Ghosts are either souls that cannot enter heaven or are demons trapped in the physical realm. Both of those concepts are lifted directly from religious mythology, and that other spurious fields utilize religious concepts so effectively creates undesirable company for religions. With reason-based thinking, one can only deduce that what is felt in dark corners of dank cellars is one's own fear, being given shape by the fictional ideas that have been implanted into his brain culturally and projected onto the poorly-defined darkness.

Summary

The common lesson in all of these areas is that having specificity in thought and language is the way to conquer one's fear of things that are alleged to exist in objective reality. If a fear is irrational and unsubstantiated, the best chance one has to discover that is to organize his thoughts rigorously without letting panic factor into the assessment. If a fear is legitimate and likely however, bringing precision in ideas to bear on addressing the problem is similarly one's best chance of thwarting the danger.

In other words, one's precision will permit a person to generate the most linear course of action to extricating himself from the situation. The understanding that one's most intractable fears lurk in his imagination and that the rest of these seemingly external dangers are actually projections from within him is a major source of the feeling of convergence. This handful of lessons alone ought to be valuable enough to create a great feeling of ease that some of the more unsettling aspects of folklore and mythology belong in the same category as gods, namely, fairy tales that have gotten out of control. If one wants to control his fear, he need only think precisely, and he will be taking his best available strategy to conquering it.

11 – A Person's Place with Respect to the Universe

When I became convinced that the universe is natural, that all the ghosts and gods are myths, there entered into my brain, into my soul, into every drop of blood the sense, the feeling, the joy of freedom. The walls of my prison crumbled and fell.

— Robert Green Ingersoll

After the extraction of religious thought, Chapters 9 and 10 delivered methods and perspectives for one to achieve much needed emotional and intellectual catharsis. As Part Two is intended to mimic a systematic rebuilding process, issues of substantial emotional import were discussed at the outset because prolonged participation in religious thought is an emotional addiction first and foremost, and the stabilization of the self cannot be anything other than the first order of business as a result. One's emotions have the power to effortlessly overpower the intellect, and unless tools were first delivered to stabilize the self, any intellectual structures hastily erected would have toppled in the emotional aftershocks.

Now, the integral intellectual rebuilding can begin, and the first block to be placed on one's new, level foundation of identity will be the determination of a person's place in the universe. The scope of the block to be placed on top of it will be narrower and focus on a person's place in society. The scope of the last will be narrower still and will focus on a person's place with respect to the self.

Beginning with a person's place in the universe, the discussion will delve into the state of the art in multiple scientific disciplines, and a new storyline for the existence of the universe, man, and all things will emerge that starkly differs from the origin stories told by religions. As comprehensive scientific discussions go beyond the scope of this book and the expertise of its author, this chapter will only survey the currently accepted understandings of several important events in the history of the universe that bear relevance to a person's identity. The explanations that follow span a variety of disciplines, including chemistry, biology, physics, and astronomy, and if one's interest in these areas exceeds the brief discussion provided, consulting scientific texts or scholarly journals for additional technical clarification is appropriate.

The Origin of the Universe - The Big Bang

Presently, astronomers and physicists agree that the universe began as a miniscule, super-heavy singularity that detonated and sent all of the matter inside of it racing apart. The explosion is what is referred to as The Big Bang, and the use of the term "singularity" is just a sleeker way of saying "something unprecedented in man's current knowledge". According to the convergence of several methods that are based on the extrapolation of certain aspects of the current universe backwards in time, The Big Bang took place well over thirteen and a half billion years ago, though no one yet knows how it was caused or how it generated so much energy and matter. Indeed, science only claims to have reasonable knowledge of what occurred an instant or so after The Big Bang, and so, the singularity itself remains a mystery. After The Big Bang however, the laws of the universe operated on the newly released energy, and matter began to unevenly clump together due to the effects of gravity, which ultimately resulted in the formation of stars and planets, including humanity's own solar system, sun, and earth.

Religions assert that a god caused the universe by causing the singularity that resulted in The Big Bang. Obviously, this is an expression of The Cosmological Argument, already put to rest, packaged in scientific terminology. If religions defined the word "god" as simply some unknown force, there would only be a dispute of semantics between them and science, each calling the same thing by different names, i.e., "god" versus "singularity". Of course, religions do not define the term with such minimalism. They proceed to personify the force, give it a personality, claim it still exists today, assert it has a special interest in humanity, suggest it speaks with certain people, and declare that it cares about man's moral decisions. As far as science is concerned, there is no empirical evidence or logical necessity for any of these conclusions, and from the perspective of reason-based thinking, the singularity is only an unknown point of causation.

Questions regarding The Big Bang and the limits of the universe are dizzying because their scale utterly dwarfs the human brain. In its brief history, humanity has only recently gained the ability to meaningfully stretch its senses beyond earth, and so much of the progress in human knowledge with respect to The Big Bang has occurred in the last fifty years. Unsurprisingly, the spike in knowledge with respect to the origin of the universe coincides with the development of instruments with increased power and sensitivity, especially computer technology. The processing speed of computers has permitted observations and calculations that were previously impossible, either because the speed with which an observation would take place would be too quick for the human eye to precisely measure or because the amount of data one would need to analyze in an experiment would be too vast to compile in a realistic amount of time by hand.

In other words, The Big Bang theory will continue to be refined and shaped over the coming years. Presently, it sits on the cutting edge of scientific knowledge with one big question mark lurking in the center of it that bends the imagination to explain due to both its distance in time and defiance of observation. Many ideas have been proposed to attempt to model the available data into a framework that explains not only the singularity but what existed before and outside of it. It is possible that there is a limit on what science can understand in this regard if it cannot devise a way to somehow extend man's senses beyond the universe itself, a thought that is itself seemingly incomprehensible. Nevertheless, humanity's recent trend of drastically accelerating the processing speed of computers and sensitivity of scientific instruments can only strengthen the chances that perhaps these questions that seem so impossible now will indeed have accepted explanations in the future. After all, no one could have imagined that scientists would have determined as much as they have about the question as it stands right now.

The Origin of Life - Abiogenesis

Taking the earth's formation and existence as a given, a fundamental mismatch arises between the past and the present, namely, how all of the thriving life presently in existence on earth could arise from a past that saw the earth as a freshly compacted ball of elements. So, how did life begin on earth? The answer to this question and the scientific term for the phenomenon of how organic life could arise from inorganic material is abiogenesis. Realize that abiogenesis has nothing to do with The Big Bang theory. The models are distinct, independent, and grounded in different scientific disciplines. Abiogenesis takes the existence of the earth and the universe as a given in order to then explain how life could have begun from there.

At this point, there is not a single scientific theory that is favored to exclusively explain how life on earth began, mainly because multiple avenues are known as feasible manners in which organic matter could arise from inorganic material. One such setting is the so-called primordial soup, which describes an early earth, unrecognizable to man, in which the chemical composition of the atmosphere and water combined with the electrical charge of a lightning strike could produce amino acids, a building block of life. Recently, the discovery of complex organic molecules in meteorites and cosmic dust has revealed that such material is not as rare in the universe as had once been thought. Between its possible creation from several terrestrial chemical reactions and its potential delivery by extraterrestrial objects, explaining how organic molecules could have arisen in inorganic settings is surprisingly not troubling.

Organic molecules are only half of the story, however, and the manner in which they could organize to form a cell capable of reproduction is less settled, though not without many cogent explanations. Cells present in today's life contain complex structures like strong external membranes, genetic material, and proteins. Surely, the earliest cells looked nothing like them, and the most likely order of operations for primitive chemical combinations to shape into a cell is difficult to establish, mainly because there does not appear to be an inexorable path that had to take place. Obviously, examining today's life provides a roadmap of what a basic cell would need, but the distance in time, the foreign conditions of the earth's early chemical composition, and the sheer availability of options for how it could have happened makes honing in on one explanation for the process that did in fact occur a difficult task.

Again, this is the importance of the knowledge-acquisition techniques of reason-based thinking. To the casual eye, one can observe living things exclusively being born from other living things, and the notion that it could have ever happened otherwise seems impossible. Similarly, time seems uniform, and one could hardly imagine a manner in which time is actually altered. However, increases in gravity actually have the effect of slowing time down, and one would never have guessed such a thing from casual observation because the surface of the earth produces a rather uniform gravitational influence on time to those who are standing on it. Indeed, satellites in orbit around the earth must have their internal clocks very slightly adjusted to compensate for the lesser effect that the earth's gravity has on them.

In other words, things are not always as they seem, and common sense when it comes to understanding objective reality is not an asset. What common sense amounts to in this arena is a set of static, preconceived notions that have been determined by casual observation, which have not been refined by rigorous methodologies, expressly created to fend off vagaries of perception. When such common sense is brought to the table in terms of using the knowledge-acquisition techniques of reason-based thinking to understand objective reality, its activation amounts to having already jumped to conclusions that will resolutely resist being contradicted by evidence. Common sense may have its uses elsewhere in interactions with people, but in establishing questions of fact pertaining to objective reality, it leads to very poor creativity with respect to understanding and explaining evidence that contradicts its conclusions.

On that point, the word "life" is a major hindrance to understanding abiogenesis because it is a word and concept that comes loaded with the common sense of past civilizations. As people have historically known it, life was seen as intrinsically distinct from inanimate nature, and from a casual standpoint, there is easy, commonsensical appeal to the dichotomy implied by the word. With the knowledge-acquisition techniques of reason-based thinking zooming in on the smallest components of nature, people have learned that there is nothing unique about living things when it comes to what composes their bodies, i.e., the difference between "life" and inanimate objects is an issue of form and not substance at the chemical level. People and living things are indeed special, just not across the board, and the vagaries of perception of past, unrefined observation have subtly entered the lexicon, inadvertently chaining the imagination to their assumptions. All of this is to say that if one is having trouble understanding abiogenesis or how it could create "life", taking a step back to assess one's linguistic arsenal and the concepts that they imply is a wise manner in which to shake off past common sense in favor of accommodating what current, superior evidence has to say.

Unfortunately, most people never hear about abiogenesis in the course of their ordinary schooling, likely due to the lack of a decisive scientific theory to teach. Plus, abiogenesis is a more subtle building block to the storyline of humanity's existence. From the perspective of religious thought, the focus of the origin of life skips directly to humanity, and there is no parallel religious concept that bothers to compete with abiogenesis. Indeed, the discrete, instantaneous creation story of religions has been splintered into the first step of abiogenesis and the second step of evolution, together representing a continuous, integrated narrative.

The Origin of Man - Evolution

At this point, the universe and elementary life have both come into existence. So, how did man get here? The answer is the scientific theory of evolution, which is an extremely well-supported explanation for the diversity of life, including the origin of man. Based on comparing fossil record, DNA sequences, and anatomical structures, biologists presently assert that the complex, diverse life existing on the planet today in fact evolved from simple, primitive cells, which existed about three and a half to four billion years ago. Clearly, these first entities were the simplest of life, but their having developed the ability of cellular reproduction would ultimately result in the remarkable diversity of life present on the planet today. As with the independence of The Big Bang theory and abiogenesis, whether these first cells were formed by abiogenesis is moot to understand evolution. Evolution does not deign to explain the existence of life; it is an explanation of how life that already existed could have developed so much diversity.

To picture how evolution operates, consider a certain type of bacteria that causes disease in humans. If humanity discovers an antibiotic that has success in killing it, a new environmental factor has now been introduced that will affect the bacteria population. Due to random genetic mutations, some of these bacteria may fortuitously have a resistance to the antibiotic, but the ones that do not will die faster on average and have less opportunity to create offspring that will inherit their genetic material, specifically their inability to resist the antibiotic. With respect to the next generation of bacteria, the genetic characteristics of its members are more likely to be similar to those bacteria that originally had the mutation to survive the antibiotic as those specimens would have had an advantage in successfully creating offspring.

As more generations pass and the antibiotic continues to reduce the lifespan of those bacteria that cannot survive in its presence, what may have started as a rare characteristic in the population will become a common trait. This example of evolution is in the setting of bacteria gaining drug resistance to an antibiotic. The antibiotic has acted as a selection mechanism for a certain trait in the bacteria, and the population has evolved in response to that change in environment.

The above example of evolution is sometimes unhelpfully known as microevolution, i.e., a change in the frequency of heritable traits within a species due to environmental changes, and so-called macroevolution is the long-term evolution of populations that results in the formation of entirely new species. There are no substantive, intrinsic differences in these processes other than time, and the artificial dichotomy that they create represents another example of preconceived notions creating errors on par with the prior discussion with respect to the word "life". Put differently, macroevolution is the term used by those who cannot refute the process of a bacteria population gaining resistance to an antibiotic or humans creating different breeds of dog but who cannot comprehend long-term changes in "type", e.g., a water-bound species evolving into a land animal. The choppy discreteness of such thinking is a relic, and its appeal arises from the casual vagaries of perception of the past coloring the well-examined and controlled evidence of today. In other words, evolution is evolution, and if certain flavors or implications of it seem bizarre, that is because incredible amounts of time and loss of species have operated as to obscure the process from common sense.

Through this lens, humanity's existence and relationship to the rest of life on earth has an elegant storyline. Evolving from the most basic form of life over a huge amount of time, humanity is merely another link in the chain. Man is a part of the animal kingdom, not above it. There is nothing inherently special about people, relative to other animals when it comes to what composes their cells and bodies. In fact, the only thing that makes man truly unique stems from the remarkable brainpower that he commands, relative to other species. Man's isolation on the planet is revealed as a self-imposed term in solitary confinement, and nature itself develops additional texture. Without the soul and the escape valve of the metaphysical, people only have their bodies, habitat, and a vested interest in maintaining the integrity of both. Dominion over nature becomes stewardship, and man's ability to manipulate and alter his environment has a note of personal responsibility.

The scientific theory of evolution has been met with extreme resistance by religions, and their antipathy for it is due to the collateral damage it does to the concepts of religious thought. For example, at exactly what point in the process did the soul evolve? Did it just appear once man became a species? When exactly did modern man become his own species for this purpose? The core concepts of religions and their view of humanity in the world are so bound up with the uptight, commonsensical thought of past peoples that religious thought cannot accept the explanations produced by scientific inquiry, lest its ideology become infiltrated and overwritten by reason-based thinking. It is this ideological cornering that has caused religions to lash out at the scientific theory of evolution for survival purposes.

Indeed, religions can never concede that the knowledge-acquisition techniques of reason-based thinking have correctly identified such an important and wide-ranging chain of causality in nature such as evolution. To do so is to admit that their relevance in the modern era is waning with the unsolved puzzles of man's identity in the universe being explained with transparent clarity by their rival. Instead, religions must hide the ball by simultaneously maintaining that evolution has not been proven to a certainty while claiming that the existence of a god has not been disproven to a certainty. The unapologetic implementation of such audacious and incoherent double standards belies the desperate state of religious thought in the modern world.

If man's origin is not special and divine relative to other life, then why are people bothering to go to houses of worship? Religions have answered the question of why other animals do not worship a god with commentary that other animals are without souls, not special, and largely scenery in the play of the lives of people. On the other hand, the wider implications of evolution are that other animals do not have gods or religions because their brains lack the capacity to imagine the concept, not because they are throwaway objects of existence in the eyes of a god. As should be clear by repetition, the casual observations of objective reality codified in religious thought have fallen prey to the same two errors repeatedly: creating arguments from ignorance and prioritizing form over substance. Such is the danger of casually perceiving complex patterns in objective reality and assuming that the naked eye will never fail to render accurate explanations.

The End of Mankind – No Current Prediction

So, the universe, life, and mankind have all come into existence. What is the end of the tale? Presently, reason-based thinking makes no prediction for the end of mankind's story. Predictions have been made of larger events that imply the demise of humanity such as the earth's sun running out of fuel and going into a supernova, which would destroy the planet. It is also hypothesized that the sun would get hotter before it began to supernova, rendering water an extinct commodity on the earth and effectively ending human life there. As for the end of the universe itself, many models have been hypothesized, but there has yet to be a reliable consensus on the issue. For all of these cataclysmic ends to mankind, the bottom line is that none is less than a billion years away, and most scenarios far exceed that time frame.

To put that amount of time in perspective, humanity has only existed on earth for about two hundred thousand years, i.e., the threat of humanity's impending doom being delivered by these events is nil. A more likely possibility for the end of humanity is the potential collision of a large meteor with the earth, obliterating the areas that it hits and destroying the ecosystem of the rest of the planet, which is not altogether unlikely but also not imminent. In other words, humanity does not have meaningful time constraints imposed on it from external sources.

If human life were to end, it is exceedingly likely that people's own actions would cause it before some external event did. The probable culprits of man's internal annihilation would be the exchange of nuclear weapons or non-military damage to the earth's ecosystem, resulting in rippling damage to the food chain and severe changes to the earth's climate. If man were to contribute to the commencement of these causal chains, his continued existence would be in serious question.

To the contrary, religions do make predictions for the end of humanity. Of course, they say little more than that a god will one day appear to end the world, and religious scholars have prophesied that day many times in human history, all of which have resulted in the unremarkable passage of time. Disturbingly, religions tend to fixate on the end of the world, and considering the logical implications of the internal workings of religious thought, it is not difficult to see why. As an extension of religious thought, the afterlife is where all of one's dreams are supposed to come true for those who have believed, all wrongs are supposed to be righted, and all discomfort is supposed to end.

In other words, religions routinely equate the extermination of humanity with the realization of true justice. From the standpoint of reason-based thinking and its associated conclusion of atheism, a perspective that links the extermination of humanity with tranquil blessings demonstrates a disturbing and macabre fetish, and it is a major reason why atheists are unsettled by religious thought. A person expecting to find a paradise in death can come dangerously close to wishing that this life were over, and without the associated baggage of religious thought to tote, those engaged in reason-based thinking do not understand such an alignment of incentives.

*   *   *

It is important to understand that The Big Bang, abiogenesis, and evolution are independent models. Each of these ideas is a different piece to a larger puzzle, and while they synergize into a storyline of the universe and man, they stand on their own merits. As stated, evolution does not explain the origin of life; it presumes that life exists and describes how life becomes diverse. Abiogenesis does not explain the origin of the universe; it explains how life could begin in a universe that already existed. Physics provides most of the reasoning for the Big Bang, chemistry is the main foundation for abiogenesis, and biology has explained evolution. Taken together, they represent science's current explanation of man, his world, and how both have come to exist. The storyline is neither perfect nor complete, but the cleverness with which man has learned to functionally catapult his senses across a staggering chasm of time by tracing patterns of causality in nature backwards represents nothing less than a marvel of intellect.

Even if scientific disciplines were in their absolute infancy and lacked explanation for any of these occurrences, reason-based thinking would still render the solutions proposed by religious thought stunningly inadequate and meaningless. How exactly is the dismissive answer "god" helpful to understanding the creation of the universe or the origin of life? After all, the word itself means little, explains less, and demonstrates a relinquishment of will to further investigate. In other words, the explanations offered by religious thought fall because they have no support of their own, not because the knowledge-acquisition techniques of reason-based thinking have sabotaged them.

12 – A Person's Place with Respect to Society

Live a good life. If there are gods and they are just, they will not care how devout you have been but will welcome you based on the virtues you have lived by. If there are gods but unjust, you should not want to worship them. If there are no gods, you will be gone but will have lived a noble life that will live on in the memories of your loved ones.
—Marcus Aurelius

Having established a new conceptual framework of objective reality and a person's place in the grand scheme, the next step is to zoom in to the next relevant sphere of interest, i.e., a person's place with respect to society, which will be captured with discussions of the concepts of morality and justice. Over the history of humanity, philosophers have spilled oceans of ink on the topic of morality, and the discussion continues to evolve today. Indeed, there will never be an end on it as long as people exist. Regardless, an exhaustive treatment of all of the philosophical considerations surrounding morality is unnecessary to deliver the practical viewpoints needed for a person to rebuild his identity.

The approach to a person's place with respect to society given here vis-à-vis morality will mimic the process of a legal system since the concepts have analogous machinery for similar reasons. By creating a moral standard, reviewing the enforcement mechanisms for it, and determining how to assess whether a person has honored it, a person's place in society will become clear from a legislative, executive, and judicial viewpoint. Even though the template of a legal system is being used as an organizational model for the discussion, bear in mind that what is legal is not always moral and vice versa. Secular law and morality are similar, but they are not identical.

Creating a Moral Standard

In legal parlance, there are concepts of rules and standards. A rule is an absolute directive, e.g., stopping at a stop sign, and a standard is a judgment call with some guidelines attached, e.g., yielding at a yield sign. Each concept has advantages and drawbacks. Rules have the advantage of certainty and ease of application: if one does not fulfill precisely what the rule says, then he has broken it. There is no ambiguity or need for interpretation. On the other hand, rules have the drawback of being rigid and inflexible, which in the moral setting translates to a disqualification of situational factors. There is no gray area with rules, and moral rules are what religions prescribe.

With the abandonment of religious thought, one does not need to live by absolute rules, which is a major upgrade for his humaneness. Rules are ideal for moral situations that have utter simplicity or a universally horrific nature such that situational factors are drowned out, but human interaction is so complex that those simple cases are rarities. Situational factors matter, and rules disqualify them by their nature. The drawback of standards is that they are more costly to apply as more information must be assessed before one can make a determination whether he or another is in breach of them. However, the advantage of standards is that they have the flexibility to handle complex situations, which is a characteristic desperately needed on the topic of morality. It is a horrific religious fiction that morality ought to be considered in an absolutist manner, devoid of nuanced consideration.

To add another layer of complexity, moral values are not static, and they emerge and die off over time for a variety of reasons. Consider the value of free speech, which is anathema to most religions. The religious concept of blasphemy precludes free speech by definition, and if humanity's morals had not evolved beyond what religions have to say, free speech would never have become an important value. As a more current example, consider changes to morality based on recent increases to human population. Centuries ago when people lived a fraction of the time that they do now and the population of the world was comparatively small, having a large family was not at all an immoral thing to do. In the present world with a burgeoning global population and strain on natural resources, having a large number of children may begin to be considered immoral.

When thinking of morality, people tend to think of specific moral values, but those can change depending on situational factors. For the present discussion, turning to moral values first represents an instance of putting the cart before the horse. Instead, a moral standard must be created, and the moral values that people recognize and use in their lives will spring from it. Is it possible to create a sturdy moral touchstone that still has the flexibility to respond to situational factors? Indeed, it is, and like the assumptions of reason-based thinking, the moral standard is likely one that a person has been using in defiance of some of his religion's instructions anyway.

The Gold Standard

"Treat others as you yourself would want to be treated, and do not treat others as you would not want to be treated." More commonly known as The Golden Rule, it has been renamed here because it is not actually a rule; it is a standard. The Gold Standard has the dual appeal of offering the range of applicability that can mold it onto the limitless contours of situational morality while simultaneously generating moral values of general applicability. Its simple effectiveness arises from the linking of one's self-interest to the interests of others as a basis for moral decision-making. By harnessing a person's empathy for himself and his own travails, the standard builds its entire foundation on one's selfish interests and then purifies that selfishness into empathy to be projected outwards onto others, which is a clever manner in which to pare the rougher edges of mankind's nature. The more that one sees himself in others or sees others as an extension of him, the more likely he is to exhibit positive moral decision-making with respect to them.

Considering the utter simplicity of the standard, its ability to redirect a person's selfish incentives into motivation to cooperate with and invest in his fellow man has charming efficiency. The Gold Standard has elemental appeal to people of all cultures and geographic locations, which is unsurprising upon due reflection. For one, the standard accomplishes a great deal in terms of creating a sensible metric of what one will consider fair in society, and without nearly universal acceptance of the standard in a population, living in a society would be impossible from a game-theoretical standpoint. If a moral standard did not exist that had its basis in mutual respect and reciprocity, then group cohesiveness could not form as the community's environment would lack the ability to offer predictable security and trust among its members in order to make any one individual's sacrifice of a portion of his personal liberty to participate in the group enticing.

As the bedrock of human civilization, the day may indeed come when civilization considers itself lucky to have survived the wanton deviance from The Gold Standard that religions have encouraged. Some religious edicts demand conduct of their members that is so contrary to the spirit of The Gold Standard that the claims of religions to otherwise honor it seem intentionally inauthentic and false. Religions prioritize gods, not people, and to the extent that religious edicts breach the spirit of The Gold Standard or specific values that it implies, they are immoral and offensive. Indeed, they are inhumane by definition as they sacrifice the decency and respect to which one's fellow man is entitled at the altar of a being they believe to be otherworldly. As will be seen in the next section when moral enforcement mechanisms are discussed, the religious version of morality and its subtle shift in purpose serve to do routine harm to moral decision-making by permitting religious believers to emotionally dissociate from human society and effectively shrug off the pressure of an otherwise powerful array of sources of moral pressure.

On the question of specific moral values generated by The Gold Standard, consider some examples. For one, it applauds charitable behavior and the general protection of the weak. If one thinks of the times that he has been low on both resources and friends, he deeply values and loves those who stuck with him and helped him to regain his footing. A person desires help and compassion for himself, and by The Gold Standard, the philosophical implication is that demonstrating that level of respect for another is a praiseworthy action, sourced in one's own empathy for his plight. Alternatively, one could instead opportunistically strip-mine the best actions and emotions of his fellow man when he is at his weakest and most vulnerable, and The Gold Standard has routine contempt for such decision-making. One would not wish to be exploited at his lowest point, and the condemnation of such impulses is an easy decision from a moral standpoint. Morally, there is nothing to respect in those who abandon or take advantage of their fellow man when he needs them the most or is without recourse to defend himself.

Another value implied by The Gold Standard is to leave people alone as long as their behavior does not result in harm to others. In other words, the incarnation of the standard in this value implies that granting privacy to others via a general indifference to behavior that does not concern them is favorable. After all, there is some aspect of everyone's life that will be offensive to someone, but being offended does not give a person the moral right to interfere with or object to his behavior. As the word is casually used, "offensiveness" is a matter of personal taste, deployed when one's sensibilities have been crossed, and its arbitrariness is endless. Proper morality does not respond to "offensiveness"; it defines it. Brutalizing those who cannot defend themselves is offensive. Betraying those who have given their trust is offensive. If a person's decision-making is not producing harm to anyone else yet still displeases someone, then his decisions are not offensive to that person; they are merely inconvenient.

As a final example, The Gold Standard is the root of man's sensation of hypocrisy. The values and judgments that one sees fit to apply to the decisions of others ought to apply equally to the person employing them, and if they do not, there ought to be a sound logical reason for the differentiation. As such, The Gold Standard necessarily implies a sense of equality and fair play among all people. To the extent that a person wishes others to comport their behavior to a higher standard than he would have applied to himself, his hypocrisy is apparent, and people do not have to activate conscious thought to feel that such self-dealing is repellant and the mark of an opportunistic person with questionable moral fiber.

With respect to the claimed monopoly by religions on the subject of morality, the most damning aspect to their claim is that a person's observance of The Gold Standard often operates as a reflex. A person knows when he has wronged someone regardless of his actual acknowledgement of the fact, and that he does not believe that there is a god watching makes no difference whatsoever to his sensing his immoral decision because The Gold Standard and its values are not rooted in divine threats. To the contrary, The Gold Standard is a concept of reciprocity entirely sourced in how people treat each other in social interactions. Many strangers live in a society, and an indispensable reason for their cooperation with and toleration of each other is their operating under the baseline assumption that systemic deviance from The Gold Standard will not occur, which has nothing to do with a god monitoring the affair.

Surely, some situations make for tough decisions that compel the individual to play an uncomfortable moral game that has no obvious winning moves. For the vast majority of the time however, people engage in countless interactions that have routine moral solutions, and their decisions and judgments occur without conscious thought. If one sees an elderly person fall in front of him, he instantly lunges to help him to his feet. If one sees a person quietly sobbing by himself in public, he tries to console him by asking him if he is alright. These decisions are thoughtless reflexes that deny the haughty claim by religions that people cannot be decent to each other without their acceptance of religious thought. In either of these situations, there is no thought of gods or infinity at the moment the person decides he wishes to help. There is only the human, the now, and the intrinsic understanding that another person needed help that the individual would have wanted for himself.

Emergency Morality – Excuses and Justifications

The Gold Standard represents the ticket that admits a person to important circles in both his family and larger society, and it serves as the glue for human society, especially with respect to non-familial interactions. For all of the incredible value and mileage that The Gold Standard provides however, it is still imperfect, and it fails when a person finds himself in an emergency situation where he or another is at significant personal risk. In such instances, he will find that the standard does not morally permit the actions he may feel he has to undertake.

Moral decisions are a function of the level of opportunity for decency that the world affords a person, and therefore, morality can be a luxury at times. The starving man will not be inclined to abide by a wealthier person's sensibilities; he simply has to eat what he can get, even if he has to steal it. No person can be morally expected to forego the basic needs for his survival in order to respect a moral standard that would kill him to maintain. This is not to say that the person who acts to protect his own life in such situations has not made an immoral decision because he has. However, his immorality in that instance is potentially excusable because of the emergency in which he found himself, especially if he is considered blameless for being in the emergency in the first place.

So, The Gold Standard requires tempering for such emergencies, which comes in the form of excuses and justifications. Borrowing again from legal parlance, an excuse is a defense for one's moral impropriety so as to claim an exemption from The Gold Standard, and a justification is a defense of a moral breach by showing that superior justice was in fact obtained by breaching the standard. In other words, an excuse is nothing about which society will be excited, but it will condone it. On the other hand, a justification will likely be applauded as a decision that has benefited society overall. These terms will come into clearer focus with examples.

Consider a destitute person who does not have the means to provide his sick child with important medicine. Upon the realization that the child is in unrelenting pain that will only worsen if he cannot procure the necessary medicine, he enters a pharmacy with a gun and robs the staff of only the medicine he needs and nothing more. While his decisions technically constitute a breach of The Gold Standard, many will likely find them excusable. He reasonably perceived significant danger to his child and was unable to responsibly purchase the item that would alleviate it, and so, he took steps to conclude his moral emergency while minimizing harm to others. Importantly for moral purposes, he did not let the potential gains of his moral breach advantageously extend beyond that which motivated it in the first place, namely, the procurement of important medicine. If his decision-making had led him to suddenly feel entitled to rob the pharmacy of other items that had not motivated his moral emergency, those decisions would not have had viable excuses and would have been subject to the ordinary application of The Gold Standard.

In situations like this, the absolute moral rules of religions have major problems finding sensible application because two important values have come into direct competition with one another. There is one value that says that a parent ought to provide for and protect his children, but there is also another value that dictates that a person not steal from others. For practical purposes, a person in this situation will make his decision based on choosing the lesser of two evils, as was described in the hypothetical scenario, and social empathy acts to diminish the moral ramifications of the breach that occurred. In religion's theoretical world of absolutes however, such an individual has been morally checkmated by his circumstance.

Now, consider a person who is sleeping at night when he hears rustling inside his home. After getting up to check on the noise, he confronts a burglar who attacks him. In the ensuing struggle, the man kills the burglar. Technically, his decision to fight the intruder will be in breach of The Gold Standard, but given the circumstances, the man's abandonment of its moral directives is not excusable but justified. He was presumably blameless in creating the predicament, and his hand was further forced by the resulting melee. While he has broken The Gold Standard, the circumstances gave him a justification for doing so, namely, the protection of his own life and possibly family. Once again, it is a dubious morality that forbids his actions, and it is likely that even religions would consider them blameless due to the obvious danger presented by the situation.

All humans understand that threats to the integrity of a person's body create exceptional circumstances and thus warrant special consideration. In the context of social interaction, The Gold Standard represents the decision-making that people ought to exhibit in any orderly social encounter. In an exigent circumstance however, society's goal of providing predictable stability and security for its members has broken down, and the emergency justification that permits the fracturing of the standard represents the acknowledgement that society has temporarily failed to uphold its end of the bargain.

In such a case, the person's previously sacrificed personal liberty is morally restored to him until the conclusion of the emergency. As with the hypothetical scenario for excuses, a person's access to a justification in the circumstance of his moral breach does not imply that he may wantonly wreak havoc on those who may have caused the emergency. His behavior will be assessed in the totality of the circumstances, and if he took excessive license with his emergency moral exemption, that in itself could be determined to be morally unacceptable.

*   *   *

So, what is this thing we call morality? What is its purpose? People instinctively feel that they want to belong to a society or group of some size, but no society ever accommodates the complete wishes of any given person in it. The individual sacrifices some aspects of his personal liberty in order to gain the protection and benefits of the group, and both the group's power and responsibility grow with the addition of another member. In other words, society is an uneasy tradeoff between personal liberty and group protection.

Morality is the concept by which people measure the presence of justice in human interaction, especially in groups like societies. There can be no justice without the existence of weights to place in its scales, and determinations of morality or immorality are just those weights. Morality is the concept that one uses to judge the praiseworthiness of another's decisions relative to him and other interested parties, and its values change as people and society do. To maintain the fiction that moral values are static outside of anything but the most universally benevolent and profane decisions is disingenuous and actually rather cruel when it has the effect of convincing a person to leave off compassion because he refuses to take into account any situational considerations. Morality progresses and regresses, and when it does, it is because the general empathy of a society has fluctuated similarly.

Another specific value implied by The Gold Standard that is worth consideration before turning attention from the terms of the moral standard to its enforcement mechanisms is that of forgiveness. People cannot always behave appropriately, and sometimes those wrongs are flagrant. Every person has some aspect of his history that he regrets in how he has treated someone, which is unavoidable. Humans can be grotesquely selfish and indifferent to the feelings of others. However, The Gold Standard allows for a value of forgiveness, and those who have wronged another and sincerely apologize by trying to correct the damage that they have done deserve forgiveness. Perhaps the granting of such forgiveness will not save the person from physical prison or the torments of his own conscience, but under the appropriate demonstration of sincere remorse, he can and ought to receive compassion from the person who was wronged by his decision-making, i.e., from whom he needs it the most. After all, any person would want such absolution for himself.

The point is that morality and The Gold Standard are not about demanding that people be perfect. The dizzying complexity of life presents too wide a variance of situations and dilemmas for people to never make a mistake, even a potentially stomach-turning one. To expect people to be perfect is to live a life destined for disappointment. Realistically, the question of the quality of a person comes down to his thoughts, motivations, and patterns, and if they are often unsavory or exploitative, then the judgment of his character is not a close call. As for the person who one ought to consider moral however, his observance of The Gold Standard is never perfect; he is just the one who deeply regrets it when it fails to be.

Moral Enforcement Mechanisms

With the lengthy discussion of the fabric of a moral code, it stands to reason that such moral law would be a waste of breath if it did not have an executive system to ensure its enforcement, which it does. One's moral decision-making actually has multiple tiers of enforcement, both internal and external, and their implicit enforcers are the people who comprise the key circles and groups with which a person identifies.

Before discussing the moral enforcement mechanisms for an atheist, a digression into understanding an important aspect of religious morality is necessary. The answers to moral questions are not always the same for religious believers and skeptics, which is not to say that they often diverge because they do not. In identical situations, they will likely reach similar solutions to the vast majority of moral quandaries. The telling differences in their respective moral codes arise in the places where their solutions do not concur, and their divergence is a function of how each views the basis for what makes human behavior moral. The key to understanding the niceties of the distinction is to realize that what religions mean by the word "moral" is not at all what atheism means by it, and before examining the moral enforcement mechanisms in society for a person who has departed religious thought, a discussion of the religious concept of sin will shed light on exactly how religions make human morality a literally inhuman affair.

Sin

In Part One, the moral structure of religious thought was not discussed, mainly because it was irrelevant to the goal of analyzing the existence of the places and beings in religious mythology. Nevertheless, the purported moral authority of religions is probably the main reason that their objective bizarreness is tolerated by the general public. In fact, religions couch everything that they say in moral terms, even actions that do not seem to have any obvious ethical connection. For example, what exactly is immoral about using sexual contraception whether married or unmarried? The connection to morality seems baffling, though many religions refuse to permit their followers to use contraceptives based on moral objections. Oddly, a very strong case could be made that not regularly using contraception is immoral in that its unnecessary riskiness increases the likelihood of unwanted pregnancies and transmission of disease.

Other peculiar appeals to morality flow from religions, and they demonstrate an important nuance to understand about their moral structure. At its core, the morality of religious thought is not about being decent or respectful to people; it is based on not offending gods. To the extent that a religion has moral imperatives that condemn actions that hurt people, this is only a coincidence. All that matters in a religion's morality is whether one's actions are offensive to its god, which is an arbitrary standard to say the least. Thus, the foundation of the moral code of religion is the concept of sin, which is a crime or offense against god. To the extent that one has hurt people or otherwise abused his fellow man without committing a sin, those actions do not enter into the person's final judgment and may even be encouraged.

With the existence of a god and religious thought in general discredited, such morality is terrifying because it is laid bare as not being grounded in any firm reasoning to control it from wildly spiraling, no matter how well-intentioned it may be. Indeed, all religions have radical members or sects that take morality down a dark lane where aggressing towards others without provocation may not only be acceptable but imperative. There are no constraints to what religious conviction makes people capable of doing to each other in the name of a god. After all, one's innate empathy for others is easily overridden by seeing them as evil, and once that empathy is destroyed, truly horrible actions can always be internally justified by the person who performs them. Despite having grabbed the title by fiat, religions have been quite successful in framing themselves as moral authorities in a world cast adrift in a tumultuous ocean of depravity, and how they create this success for themselves despite the arbitrariness of their morality is worth examination.

There are some actions so profane to humans on an innate level that one can safely presume that they are universal, e.g., murder. Murder is the premeditated killing of another person without any excuse or justification such as insanity or self-defense. To proclaim that murder is immoral and unacceptable does not constitute going out on a limb. Conversely, displaying a charitable nature to the needy is a quality of humanity so respected across cultures that it likely approaches universal acclaim. As with murder, a religion's recommendation that charity be a part of any decent person's life is likewise not news. In the venue of religious morality, religions have learned to tout obvious moral decisions as their own in order to gain credibility, which is then used to speak on any subject that they see fit, armed with their now faux-legitimized moral authority. This is a subtle trick, which purchases the right to speak on any subject from the high ground simply by implying that the same moral compass that had determined that murder was wrong has now concluded that the present circumstance also has moral implications.

Imagine if there were a religion with a moral code that did not make murder a sin. One would imagine that few would be interested in what else it had to say due to the remarkable incongruence of that omission with what humans naturally feel is proper social behavior towards others. Similarly, religions have and will continue to alter their moral codes in order to maintain relevance in populations whose morality is evolving of its own accord. If the pressure of a population against a particular religious directive becomes sufficiently strong, all that the religion needs to do is declare the problematic provision to be metaphorical, misinterpreted, or intended for an earlier time, and it will adapt to suit its audience.

Thus far, the discussion has been a theoretical exercise focusing on the hijacking of moral authority by religions in order to garner widespread respect and deference, but the practical fact is that people will tailor the moral strictures of their religions to better align with their own sense of right and wrong. Recall the discussion in Chapter 10 regarding the creation of customized religion. Morality is the main area that people will alter as they customize their religion, often in unnoticeable, internal ways, and they do so because they have their own sense of morality that likely does not completely match what their religion teaches.

Nevertheless, what is important to understand in this discussion of sin is that treatment of other people for its own sake is not the focus in religious morality. First and foremost, the approval of a god with respect to one's behavior must be achieved, and to the extent that those moral decisions do not hurt others, it is only a bonus for society. Indeed, morality as a concept is a person's metric for the quality of his decision-making in a society as well as the manner in which he will judge the decisions of others. Since religious thought looks right past human society as a faint and uninteresting flicker in existence, the appropriation of the concept by religions is a frightful mismatch.

Secular Law

As noted from the outset of the chapter, it is important to realize that secular law is not a person's morality nor does it purport to be. Secular law is a list of consequences for certain behavior that society has signaled that it either does not tolerate or that it wishes to encourage. The law is an uneasy accommodation of a countless set of competing interests that attempts to find a socially optimizing equilibrium for the stability and safety of those that it governs. In other words, secular law has slightly different goals than achieving moral decisions, and as such, secular law can sometimes betray one's sense of morality.

For example, secular law almost never requires that a person put himself at risk to save the life of another, but from a moral standpoint, such an action is almost always praiseworthy. On the other side of the coin, sometimes secular law actively demands behavior that runs contrary to what a person feels is moral. In the United States of America, laws that institutionalized discrimination on the arbitrary basis of race were met with civil disobedience for precisely that reason. Even today, so-called whistleblowers in government may find themselves betraying the letter of the law because their moral compunction makes it so they cannot bear to live with themselves if they do not.

The charter purposes of secular law and morality overlap significantly, but they are not identical. Secular law does not want to operate as a civility code or a comprehensive set of morals; its penalties are too severe and its costs of operation are too high to behave in such a manner. Secular law simply aims to create a stable society in which reasonable expectations of fairness will not fall by the wayside. In general, it represents the minimum level of acceptable behavior for a person from society's perspective. A society becomes exemplary with the extra effort, courtesy, and respect that its citizens choose to invest in it, not because such actions are legally mandated but because they are desired by the members of the populace.

Representing the circle of moral enforcers composed of society itself, secular law is one of the practical protections for the fabric of society in a populace that does not accept the existence of a god and all of his concomitant threats and promises. The executive and judicial arms of secular law, whatever form they may take, act to provide significant disincentives for behavior that aggresses on others, and if the promise of the condemnation of one's soul to eternal hell is to be considered the height of behavioral disincentives, then the guarantee of the body's loss of personal liberty in prison is a serviceable second option.

Religious believers often make the alarming assertion that nothing restrains people from tearing each other to pieces like rabid dogs loosed from their leashes without the looming threat of a god to make them think twice, which provides an unsettling glimpse into the thoughts of those who make such a remark. By espousing the position that secular law is no deterrent to malicious behavior, the implication is that the individual himself does not acknowledge the authority of secular law if and when it should come into conflict with a religious edict or divine message. In other words, the person suggests that he is capable of fracturing any secular law, regardless of the severity of the offense, by implying that divine law is the only source of one's restraint. In light of the arbitrariness of the opinions of gods, it is the religious believer who has significant potential for uncomfortably wild behavior.

Legacy and Reputation

When one does not believe that a god exists, his priorities realign, and his legacy among friends and loved ones takes on a higher value. Theoretically, legacy would mean nothing whatsoever to a religious believer because he has accepted a view of this life as only a way station towards the achievement of the next life in which the true object of his affection waits. Atheists make no such presumption, and the desire to live a life that one's family can recollect with fondness and high regard is of great significance. Due to the convergence of the religious afterlife into the physical world, an atheist does not have anything else to value beyond his eventual death.

Surely, most religious believers would agree that no one would want to live a life that casts his memory into opprobrium among his family and friends. However, they agree to that comment in defiance of their religion, not because of it. If they were loyally adhering to the implications of religious thought, all of their wishes and emotions with respect to how other people view them would mean nothing in comparison to that which they believe pleases god. Despite the theoretical inconsistency on the part of the religious in placing any value on the concept, one's legacy among his family and loved ones is a weighty enforcement mechanism for the moral convictions of both atheists and religious believers alike.

Reputation enforces moral decision-making in a similar fashion as it is the living analog to a person's legacy, and the only difference between them is that reputation implies that the person in question is still alive. As with legacies, a person with an atheistic worldview holds his reputation dear since it represents the general opinion that his family and community holds of him. With a poor reputation, he will find himself isolated from people, and without a god on which to fall back, this is a daunting prospect. Again, those who hold a religious viewpoint will surely value their reputations for practical reasons as they will have to maintain beneficial social contact with others simply to function in society. However, religious thought theoretically makes one's reputation a trivial and fleeting concept. If one were taking his religion seriously, the opinions of other humans with respect to his behavior would be a meaningless thing, fit only for those who have lost sight of their ultimate objective of pleasing and reaching their god.

That being said, reputation looms large in any person's life for practical reasons, and to ruin it with untoward behavior is to betray the human support structures that every person needs. To feel isolation from other humans on the basis of their finding one's moral decision-making and reputation to be repellant is a terrible fate, and people naturally shy away from it. Indeed, the concepts of legacy and especially reputation are not wholly distinct concerns from the last moral enforcement mechanism, the conscience.

Conscience

Without question, a person's conscience is the main enforcer of his moral behavior, mainly because he cannot ever evade its watchful eye. There are some actions that a person simply cannot tolerate doing because his conscience feels revulsion for the behavior, and to enforce its will on the person's decision-making, the conscience generates the powerful deterrents of guilt and anxiety. The concept of the conscience is a construct for the brain's social awareness and identity, and when the conscience feels that what the person is considering is wrong, it acts to restrain his decision-making.

Indeed, no other moral enforcement mechanism can operate with such violence on a person as his conscience, and if he betrays its demands, the remorse it will create is normally substantial. It is not an unusual tale that some people who commit serious crimes turn themselves in to authorities because they find that they could not bear to live with themselves if they were to have gotten away with it. As a lesser example, people routinely apologize to each other for serious breaches of trust and friendship because they know that they have been wrong. Obviously, some confounding aspects of reputation and personal companionship factor into such a decision, but the conscience takes no small part in the decision.

In order to see how the conscience operates, one must consider a situation where a person is considering a decision in which he anticipates he can make an immoral decision to his benefit with impunity from his external moral enforcement mechanisms. Safely insulated from the ramifications of secular law and damage to his legacy and reputation, the person is at his most unrestrained. Doubtlessly, breaches of morality are most likely to occur in this situation without the duplicative pressures of the other moral enforcement mechanisms, but people at such a crossroads will still be faced with the prospect of living with their exploitation of another person. If the individual has internalized his moral code into his identity, he is likely to continue his moral behavior even in the perceived absence of other moral enforcement mechanisms, and surely, this is the height of morality.

*   *   *

The survey of the moral enforcement mechanisms can be visualized in an alternative framework. Imagine concentric circles of familiarity around a person with him in the center, his family and friends in the next ring, his community members in the next ring, and lastly, society on the whole in the outer ring. With respect to the moral enforcement mechanisms, those rings may be loosely labeled from the center moving outward: the conscience, legacy, reputation, and secular law.

With the exception of the conscience, the moral enforcement mechanisms coincide with relevant groups with which a person affiliates, and it is the operation of their approval or disapproval that applies moral pressure. Humans are social animals, and the threat of being expelled from key groups that compose significant portions of their identities creates huge disincentives for immoral decision-making. Of course, the conscience as a construct for a person's social identity is the ultimate failsafe that takes into account all of these groups and one's relation to them. Indeed, the conscience is the ultimate guard of one's identity, and its sway provides a multiplier effect to the concerns of pleasing other people. By involving a trump card of a god to reign over all other moral enforcement mechanisms and relevant circles of human affiliation, religious thought only acts to undermine all of these layers of protection.

Considerations of Justice:
Intention, Foreseeability, and Reasonableness

Linked to humanity's morality is its desire for justice, i.e., the need to feel as though positive decision-making gets rewarded while negative decision-making receives punishment. Morality and justice are intimately related concepts. Indeed, the social wiring of the human brain desires them to resemble cause and effect. Continuing with the chapter-long analogy to the structure of a legal system, creating a moral standard (legislative) and locating moral enforcement mechanisms for that standard (executive) would be pointless if consideration was not given to assessing deviations from the moral standard and assigning ramifications (judicial). However, things are more complicated than simply rendering hasty verdicts, and before covering the means with which the relevant moral enforcement mechanisms can exact justice, nuanced consideration must be given to the assessment process of how one determines whether one has meaningfully complied with the spirit of the moral standard. In order to investigate these considerations, a theoretical standard for judging the morality of a person's decisions will be constructed.

When determining whether a given decision is moral, the question is one of personal responsibility, both with respect to the individual and his view of others. To begin the discussion, take a view of morality in which the ends always justify the means. If one's decision produces a net positive set of effects, then it is a praiseworthy one from a moral perspective, and an action that produces a net negative set of effects is a contemptible one. On that basis, consider the following standard of moral justice as a starting point:

A moral decision is one that produces net positive effects, taking into account all of its actual effects.

Consider a hypothetical scenario under this standard. Angela witnesses Roger crash his car into a telephone pole, which has rendered him unconscious. Smelling gasoline leaking from the car and fearing that it may explode, Angela rushes over to Roger. With the car smashed from the impact, she has a difficult time pulling him from the car, which never actually explodes as feared. Later, doctors who examine Roger find that Angela's having yanked him from the car turned a minor injury from the crash into severe and permanent spinal damage. In the end, Roger will never walk again, and his car never exploded. Therefore, Angela's actions in pulling Roger from the car were ultimately unnecessary to save his life.

Given this sequence of events, the standard above suggests that Angela's actions were not moral since they did not actually produce net positive effects. Indeed, Angela's actions have resulted in horrible, additional injury to Roger that would not have happened but for her interference, yet to suggest that Angela's actions are not praiseworthy offends human sensibilities. Her actions border on heroic in risking herself to save Roger. So, what is incongruent between the first attempt at capturing a standard of moral justice and one's innate sense of fairness in assessing a person's responsibility? The problem arises from the standard's use of actual outcomes resulting from Angela's decision instead of what she had intended to do.

What makes an action moral? What one intends to do or what actually happens? At the time that a person makes a decision, he will not have perfect knowledge of the circumstances in which he will act. In the context of the hypothetical scenario, Angela could not have known either that the car would not explode or that saving Roger would cause such damage. To hold one morally accountable after the fact for things he could not have known at the time he made his decision seems unfair. Even if it were not, a person is not in control of every aspect of what happens when he acts. Why should a later aspect of the incident, Roger's being stuck in the car, be factored into a determination of whether she made a moral decision at the moment she ran over to rescue him? At the time she made her decision, she only knew that he was in danger, and she sensed that she was endangering herself on his behalf by running to him.

The concept that is needed in the standard to remove the taint of basic unfairness in this regard is intention. What did a person intend to do when he decided to act? Was his motive benign or malicious? Suppose that Angela had seen Roger crash and had chosen to do nothing. While the events would have unfolded so as to provide Roger with a better outcome for his life than had she acted, her decision would have been based on indifference to his well-being in light of the dangerous circumstances as she had perceived them. His defying the odds and coming out of the accident without serious injury are a separate issue, arising after the fact. From her perspective at the moment she would have made her decision, he was a dead man, and while her inaction may not have been necessarily immoral, there would certainly not be anything praiseworthy about her decision to remain a bystander.

So, the first attempt at creating a standard for moral justice needs to be revised to prioritize a person's intentions over the actual results of his actions.

A moral decision is one <u>intended to produce</u> net positive effects, weighted against all of its actual effects.

Now, consider another scenario. Tom passes a homeless man, Ray, every day as he walks to work. On one especially cold day, Tom sees that Ray does not look well and asks him if he may buy him a hot breakfast to ease the chill, and Ray agrees. Seated in a diner, Ray gratefully sips coffee and chomps away at his breakfast. After drinking a few cups of coffee to warm up, Ray clutches his chest and falls over onto the table. Later, doctors determine that Ray's time spent outdoors over the years had taken a toll on his body and that he suffered from untreated high blood pressure among other ailments. By having several cups of coffee quickly, his blood pressure rose to the point where he had a massive heart attack and died.

While seemingly moral and benevolent, Tom's behavior does not receive a positive verdict when judged by the current standard. As it now sits, the standard for moral justice requires that all of the effects resulting from Tom's decision to act ought to factor into the assessment of the morality of his behavior, but should that be a part of a moral calculus? To add perspective on its arbitrary unfairness in terms of assessing one's personal responsibility, imagine that Ray had not died in the diner but instead had thanked Tom and left. Once outside the diner, Ray stumbles on a crack in the pavement and falls into traffic where he is killed by an oncoming car. Technically, Ray would not have been walking that direction at that time but for Tom's decision to take him out to eat, and Ray's tripping to his death is presently taken into consideration when assessing Ray's behavior. In legal terminology, one would say that Tom's decision to take Ray to eat was a cause-in-fact of his death in both cases, but it was not the proximate cause. The reason that Tom's actions would not be the proximate cause of Ray's death is because of the concept of foreseeability.

While a standard for moral justice ought to place some weight on the effects of a person's decision-making, it must also cut off causal chains for the purposes of the assessment. The most logical and appropriate manner in which to do so is by taking a snapshot of the person's thinking as he mulled his decision. When a person stands at a decision point in his life that has moral implications, he does not and indeed cannot take into account all of the possible ripples of causality that will result from his decision. What he considers are the chains of causality that he foresees or anticipates occurring as a result of his decision. From the discussion regarding intention and its place in moral considerations, it became clear that bringing hindsight to bear on a decision based on its actual effects is not what the concept of morality wishes to capture, and the same concern applies equally here.

If the goal is to create a standard for personal responsibility, spiraling into attenuated chains of causation is an unfair and unpredictable method, leading to results that defy what one would expect to see from a standard for moral justice. Therefore, the standard needs to be updated once again in order to take into account the concept of foreseeability.

A moral decision is one intended to produce net positive effects, <u>considering the effects of the decision actually foreseen</u>.

The first incarnation of the standard was outcome-based and externally focused, and now it has become motivation-based and internally focused. After adding the concepts of intention and foreseeability, this is no surprise, but it makes an important point about moral judgments: the actual result of one's decision-making is largely irrelevant. Morality is a measure of the praiseworthiness of one's desires and decision-making with respect to others, not necessarily the proficiency with which one executes them in the external world.

Before arriving at the final form for the standard, consider another hypothetical scenario. Imagine that Hank is a diagnosed schizophrenic. While he takes his medication, he perceives the world in a stable fashion, and he is functional in society. However, he has not taken his medication for weeks, and he suffers a psychotic break from reality. Walking outside, he hears screams coming from inside his neighbor's house, and he breaks in the door to see a man assaulting his female neighbor, Wendy. Hank attacks the man as Wendy calls the police. When the police arrive, they learn that Wendy and her boyfriend had been casually talking when Hank had kicked in the door and attacked them and that no argument had actually been taking place. In this situation, Hank had subjectively intended to make a moral decision, but his perception of the events were so warped that he deserves no praise for what he has done. As the moral standard would presently praise his behavior, its pure subjectivity needs to be tempered with an aspect of objective reasonableness.

Subjectively intending to produce net positive effects with a decision is insufficient to garner moral praise. One's intention must also be objectively reasonable. As a more likely example, consider a father who thinks that beating his daughter every night will teach her discipline and ultimately make her a successful person in life. Subjectively, he means well if he truly believes in his course of action, but his behavior is so objectively unreasonable in its method, making it likely to cause significant damage to both her mental and physical health, that his actual intentions wither in comparison. The aspect of objective reasonableness is also salient on the question of a person's taking into account the foreseeable effects of a given moral decision. If a person commits to a decision and fails to anticipate consequences that he ought to have reasonably foreseen, his decision has a quality of irresponsibility to it that likewise should not be held in high esteem.

Imagine that Sam has planned a game for his children that he calls Treasure Hunt. To start the game, Sam gives his young children a clue that leads them to a location where they will find another clue, which leads them to another location until they eventually find the treasure. His children love playing this game, and it takes Sam a long time to set up. Running low on hiding spots, Sam has hidden one clue under a rock in the median of a highway close to their house. As the kids go to collect that clue, they excitedly race across the street without looking, causing a driver to swerve to avoid hitting them. The driver then crashes, resulting in serious injury.

Generally, Sam is being a good father by investing a lot of time in keeping his children engaged in working together in a fun activity. By hiding a clue in such a busy location however, Sam has exercised very poor judgment and has disregarded or failed to understand some reasonably foreseeable dangers, both to his children and to motorists. In other words, he has taken a subjectively moral decision and spoiled it by failing to bring objective reasonableness to the table.

A moral decision is one <u>reasonably and in fact</u> intended to produce net positive effects, considering the effects of the decision actually foreseen <u>as well as any others that one ought to have reasonably foreseen</u>.

In general, people do not require theoretical musing to have a roughly accurate gut feeling about whether an action is moral. However, the moral absolutism in which religions deal is so simplistic and dismissive of any nuance with respect to assessing a person's moral decisions that it leaves people with a lot of catching up to do when it comes to considering the texture of situational morality. To have an absolute view of morality is to never have given the complexity of moral decisions or the nature of morality itself serious thought.

The circles of moral decision-making are not separate, and it is at their intersections where the difficulty lies in assessing the quality of a person's moral fiber. Many considerations must be weighed and prioritized from several perspectives, and the deep layers of complexity for which the process calls is something that religious thought prefers to avoid. To give perspective, The Gold Standard is the moral standard that generates the values and behavior that constitute the terms of the moral legislation, and the standard for moral justice looks at the totality of the circumstances in a person's thinking at the time he manifested a certain value or behavior with moral implications in order to determine if his decision-making was praiseworthy, shameful, or somewhere in between. Intention, foreseeability, and reasonableness are the core elements in the judgment of whether a person's decision is moral, and they are the reason why a person who may have technically fractured a moral value produced by The Gold Standard will not receive a negative moral judgment due to his internal thought process at the time that he did so.

*   *   *

There is no reason to try to memorize the theoretical standard just created; it is simply an academic illustration of the aspects of decision-making to which the human sense of morality responds. Besides, it will not be of much practical use in real world situations where one will almost never have the time to thoroughly assess all of the ramifications of the variety of actions he could take, and even if he did have the luxury of such time, the standard created is too vague on important details to be useful in everyday life.

The significance of massaging out the details of the considerations of moral justice is understanding that morality as a concept is not a question of the results of one's decision; it is an attempt to glimpse into the internal motivations of a person at the time he makes a decision in order to assess the extent to which he manifested care, respect, and responsibility towards other people. There are good reasons why the phrase "The ends justify the means" feels callous and ruthless from a moral perspective. Focusing entirely on external results, it misses the purpose of moral judgments, which ought to focus on capturing a person's internal motivation with respect to how he treats others. The concepts of intention, foreseeability, and reasonableness crystallize the core of moral decision-making along those lines.

Practical Justice

Before ending the lengthy discussion of morality and justice, a quick stop to canvass the manners in which a moral decision can be rewarded or punished in practicality will be reviewed. As was seen from the discussion of the moral enforcement mechanisms, there are several groups and entities with which a person identifies that stand ready to each deliver their own brand of justice based on his moral decision-making, and due to their different purposes and associations with a person, their means of creating justice take different shape.

Justice in the Venue of Secular Law

The moral enforcement mechanism of secular law mainly operates as a failsafe for the integrity of society, and as such, its legislative, enforcement, and justice systems are more concerned with forbidding malicious decisions than they are with encouraging benevolent ones, which is an asymmetry that the other moral enforcement mechanisms will not share in their approach to justice.   As has been an important caveat throughout this chapter, secular law and moral codes share substantial similarity, but they are not identical.   That theme continues here as a necessary adjunct to their differences in purpose and method.

On the question of justice, secular law generally follows a code of reciprocity where wrongs to others will exact proportionate penalties to the person who caused them. If one causes property damage to another's home, that person owes the homeowner money in the amount of the cost of repairs. If one hurts another person, then he is responsible for that person's medical bills. With respect to creating a sense of wholeness in legal remedies, secular law generally has no problem with an eye-for-an-eye approach when the matters in question only involve money, are simple, and do not imply penalties that will spiral into atrocity. At a certain level of profanity in human conduct however, secular law has policy reasons why it cannot deliver justice in the form of exact reciprocity.

A theoretical reason is that the manner in which secular law is adjudicated does not deliver sufficient levels of certainty in the decision such that the application of reciprocal punishment of the highest magnitudes is acceptable. The stakes of such punishment are so high that to inflict them upon a person whose judgment has been less than certain raises the specter of the enforcing body committing an atrocity on a person who has not deserved it. A practical reason is that secular law must enforce its sentences, and the delivery of justice as harsh as could be inferred from a premise of reciprocity is too atavistic for secular government to condone. Suffice it to say that there are some crimes for which there can be no reciprocal payback from the perspective of secular law. Their hideousness and obscenity reach into corners of the human character so disturbing that secular law cannot itself touch them without becoming infected by their inhumanity.

Positive moral decision-making will ordinarily not be addressed by secular law, which is a consequence of its purpose of insuring safety, not harmony. The machinery of secular law serves rehabilitative, punitive, and deterrent purposes in some ratio, and its purpose is limited as a result. It is debatable whether secular law is in error to only deal with disincentives to the exclusion of incentives, but as the system presently stands, the justice delivered by secular law is cold, impersonal, and mainly concentrated on correcting wrongs.

Justice in the Venue of One's Legacy and Reputation

As the social groups most interested in a person's legacy and reputation are his family, friends, and community, justice brought to bear by these groups has significant influence on his moral decision-making. In contrast to the impersonal nature of justice delivered by secular law, the people and groups who occupy the relevant realms of the moral enforcement mechanisms of one's legacy and reputation employ emotional tools to create moral justice for a person's decision-making. Also by virtue of the increased personal connection, enforcers of these moral enforcement mechanisms are the main source of a person's positive feedback for praiseworthy moral decisions.

To the extent that a person has been perceived by family and friends as having made an immoral decision, the harshest penalties available are ones tending to limit his group membership by shunning or cutting off contact. Family, friends, and community are strongly bound up in a person's identity, and if his moral decision-making is inclined to reach proportions of profanity where being limited access to these groups is a real possibility, the desolation of being abandoned by them ought to grant a person a significant moment of pause. Due to the level of personal connection between the individual and the groups in question, the methods of their moral enforcement are based on emotional leverage, and considering how important these groups are to an ordinary person's identity, they operate to impose the majority of the deterrence for a person's ignoble impulses.

With respect to praiseworthy decision-making, family, friends, and community are enabled to provide rewards that secular law simply cannot offer. As ominous as group exclusion seems when these groups are referenced, praise and love that originates from them is highly desirable, and whether it is the avoidance of shame or capturing of respect from them that motivates a person's moral decision-making, the power that they have over a person is tremendous.

Justice in the Venue of the Conscience

As the conscience operates as an internal moral enforcement mechanism, its means of delivering justice for breaches of the individual's moral code cannot be anything other than emotional. However, the conscience serves as a construct of a person's identity as well, and its influence on a person's decision-making is likely at least partly a function of having internalized the pressure exerted by the other moral enforcement mechanisms and compiled them within the self. After all, what would a person be without his family and friends? What identity could he really expect to salvage without those ideas and people?

Presumably, the highest level of morality is that which generates positive moral decision-making without the person expecting anyone to notice it since that conduct was generated outside of the monitoring capabilities of any of the other moral enforcement mechanisms to either reward or punish it. For example, charitable donations often give the donor favorable tax treatment as long as he shows proof that he has so contributed. For the person who gives to charity anonymously such that no person or agency can discover who has donated, the only reward will be internal. Unfortunately, this is the nature of morality and justice; the decisions that deserve the highest level of reward never get noticed precisely because they have been deliberately undertaken to avoid external applause from other moral enforcement mechanisms.

Conclusion

Suffice it to say that the claim by religions to maintain monopolies on morality and justice is laughable. Indeed, they have subtly polluted morality by turning a concept that was intended to be a basis for assessing the quality of human behavior in a society into a concept that determines how one can earn happiness in death. Their meddling in this state of affairs has served to upend a person's natural moral interest in others in favor of eternal salvation, and to the extent that religions peddle the audacious tale that people cannot be decent to each other without them, their duplicity is shameless. Considering their contortions of the concept of morality, it could easily be argued that people are decent to each other in a society in spite of them.

As has been shown, being afraid of the wrath of a god is only one moral enforcement mechanism, and one that is in no way worth it in that it operates to squash the rational battery of moral enforcement mechanisms, which would otherwise provide protective redundancy and realistic cause and effect. Supplanting them with a god whose morality is changeable and bizarre does not encourage humanity to develop empathy. Indeed, those who treat people well for the sole purpose of going to heaven are not using empathy at all; they are scaling the apex of self-absorption.

Almost every person in the world participates in a society in which he does not care to nor could he ever know every member. What has made people willing to bind together is the tacit expectation that the moral compunction of each member is substantially similar and that the society itself contains machinery that will give effect to moral breaches in the form of appropriate justice. While religions have encouraged the trust and placidity of the people to whom they speak, they have, intentionally or otherwise, facilitated the ravaging of indispensable social constructs as well. To the extent that religious thought has operated as to systematically pervert morality or defer justice, then its institutions owe society and its members a debt beyond calculation.

13 – A Person's Place with Respect to the Self

I have learned that success is to be measured not so much by the position that one has reached in life as by the obstacles which he has overcome while trying to succeed.
— Booker T. Washington

The last block of a person's identity to be placed onto the stack that has been constructed throughout Part Two is his place with respect to the self, most notably, his meaning in life. People can be very hardy and resilient creatures as long as they have meaning and feel driven to realize it, but if they lose meaning, they tend to shut down and enter an existential crisis as described in Chapter 9. A person's meaning constitutes his motivations to exert energy into creating action, and the discussion of rebuilding identity after the removal of religious thought could not be complete without a treatment of this all-important area. What does one value? What does he want in life? A person cannot purely reason his way out of these questions, and as the topic now turns to a person's internal world of values, the emotions will rightfully reign. If one refuses to learn about his emotions and engage them honestly, he will never know who he really is, and his search for meaning will become a fool's errand as a result.

Clarifying Meaning

Before the discussion of rebuilding identity with respect to a person's meaning in life can begin, there is final baggage from religious thought that must be discarded, which will solve the existential crisis that was discussed in Chapters 9 and 10. Religions flaunt a simplistic answer to man's quest for meaning in the form of a god and his eternal love. With the revelation that gods are ultimately phantasms that haunt man's imagination without an analog in objective reality, one would think that that might be the end of the matter and that his motives would realign naturally. To some extent, they do, but there is also a lurking danger of an incomplete withdrawal from two of religious thought's insidious assumptions about humans and existence. By dispelling them now, the road will finally be cleared for a final approach to perhaps the most important thing a person can obtain in life: meaning.

Meaning for Nature: The Consciousness Assumption

Many religious believers correctly argue that the knowledge-acquisition techniques of reason-based thinking are excellent tools to determine how nature operates but that they are incongruent to answering why nature exists or operates in the first place. From a reason-based perspective, this is a strange comment. What the knowledge-acquisition techniques of reason-based thinking aim to do is capture and mimic patterns of causality in nature and make predictions into the future if and when similar circumstances recur. In other words, the methodology of these disciplines is entirely predicated on searching for how nature works, not why.

Indeed, how would one go about answering such a question? What tools are available to make a reliable assessment of the purpose of nature? Simply put, there are none, and to the extent that faith passes itself off as a knowledge-acquisition technique to that end, the reliability of what one determines with its implementation is obviously suspect. In other words, man lacks a reliable technique with which to discover purpose in nature, assuming that it even exists.

Consider the nature of the question for a moment. What sort of information does a person seek when he uses the question word "why"? He is inquiring into motive or purpose. Why do people build houses for themselves? Why does a person have children? Why does a person go to work in the morning? The answers to these questions are obvious. Each person has experienced these motivations, and people explore each other's motives with the word "why". Similarly, why does a dog wag his tail? Why does a beaver chew through the trunks of trees? Again, the motivations of these animals are legitimate applications for the question word "why" as inquiries into the conscious motives of their actions. But why does a tree grow? Science has very definite information about exactly how a tree grows, but no one knows why. A tree has no thinking organ or general state of consciousness to lead it to create motives. A person who asks this question is really inquiring into why nature is the way that it is or why nature exists at all.

The point of this discussion and the hypothetical questions above is that the question word "why" represents a concept that man has created to inquire into the motivations and desires of other sentient beings. The reason that the inquiry "Why does the universe exist?" causes discomfort for departing religious believers when they ask it about a universe they no longer believe has a god is because they fail to recognize that they have included a subtle remnant of religious thought in the question. Considering that nature itself has no perceivable brain structure or source of conscious thought, asking why the universe exists presumes that there is a consciousness behind its creation that has a motive or purpose in creating it. In this manner, the emotional discomfort of the question arises from an intellectual error, which has been referred to here as The Consciousness Assumption.

Again, to ask why a person, animal or group of such beings has done or wants to do something is a completely understandable question and an appropriate use of the question word "why". But to ask it of nature itself is to presume that nature has a motive or purpose in its existence and operations, i.e., that it either has itself or has been constructed by a consciousness. In religious thought, imputing a consciousness to nature is axiomatic, which makes motive or purpose in nature make sense. In reason-based thinking, such a consciousness is without evidentiary support or logical necessity, and therefore there is no reason to suppose that there is any reason or meaning behind nature's existence.

When one participates in religious thought, making the assumption that the laws of nature have appropriate motivations and purpose is natural because one accepts the proposition that there is a sentient being that designed it all. Of course, believers know absolutely nothing about the purpose of nature other than what they feel at liberty to conjecture, yet they feel quite certain that such a purpose exists. Why did a hurricane kill certain people and not others? To the religious believer, it was because the storm was giving effect to a god's will, i.e., nature is the instrumentality of gods. Now that the existence of a god has been discredited along with religious thought, any inquiry into motive with respect to nature has to be discarded with it.

Meaning for Man: The Ultimate Assumption

Man has likely pondered the purpose of his existence since the time his brain became capable of having the thought. The desire to find meaning in one's life is utterly universal to the human condition. The cost of having the relatively immense power of the human brain is apparently the need of that power to have a motive or purpose before it is interested in functioning, and it searches out for that motivation constantly. The human brain craves that purpose in such a basic way that it will even manufacture it for itself if it cannot reasonably find it in reality. In all likelihood, this craving is the birthplace of most religious conviction.

For a religious believer, his god is his ultimate meaning, and to feel in his favor is his ultimate motive. Nothing else matters in the long run. Surely, this is one of the more hideous and dangerous corollaries of religious thought, namely, the proposition that nothing means anything, unless it means everything, which is what will be referred to as The Ultimate Assumption. When a person subscribes to The Ultimate Assumption, his meaning is a fixed point on the horizon, which he will never reach but will provide the emotional comfort of always being present as indeed it will as long as the person continues to accept religious thought. Unfortunately, looking into the distance at what one perceives to be his ultimate and unwavering purpose means that the people and things that one has in his life right now are given short shrift, and the disconcerting habit of training one's emotions to fixate on ultimate meaning is precisely what creates the existential crisis described in Chapter 9.

The Ultimate Assumption is a necessary implication of religious thought, in the absence of which many religious believers have a very difficult time imagining life, and the question "What are you without god?" creeps into their thoughts without a comfortable answer. As in the previous discussion regarding meaning with respect to nature, the question itself implies that ultimate meaning not only exists but is the only kind of meaning worth having, i.e., that one's personal identity is barren without a god. The logjam of the existential crisis is the result of both the intellect failing to accomplish coherence and consistency in its thoughts and the failure of the emotions to release a meaning so easy and immutable as a god. Indeed, these dual failures to recognize and expel The Ultimate Assumption represent a common mistake that has led many people to circle right back to religious thought for emotional relief even after having intellectually discredited it.

After the collapse of the mythology of religious thought, The Ultimate Assumption is an unwelcome straggler that survives because it represents an unconscious emotional habit. Logically, it must collapse with the conclusion that there is neither a god nor an infinite form of a person's consciousness, but the dependence of the emotions on it and the intellect's failure to identify it as an error associated with religious thought both conspire to create a daunting feedback loop. The good news is that recognizing from where the blowback will come operates to disengage the intellect from asking questions with no solution and enables the emotions to readjust in order to accept finite meaning as ample motivation for creating action.

*   *   *

The existential crisis and the emotional muck that it produces have been covered multiple times at this point, and the reason that they keep coming up is because they represent the seminal pitfall in attempting to leave religious thought. After all, many people can intuit their way out of religious thought; its intellectual aspect is not particularly difficult to recognize as fantastical and suspicious. However, the emotional lasso that ensnares people as a result of their religious conviction is how religions maintain their membership, and The Ultimate Assumption represents a major sticking point in religious thought that fosters that emotional dependence.

Some atheists scoff at religions as businesses that sell no product, which is untrue. In fact, religions sell the ultimate product: the meaning of life. To address The Ultimate Assumption and how its tendency to survive the collapse of religious thought results in an existential crisis and nihilistic stage of thought has been of the highest importance, and its repeated articulation in different contexts has not been an error; it has been done for emphasis. The Ultimate Assumption and its routine delivery of an existential crisis to those who leave religious thought have broken the will of many people who would not have otherwise intellectually succumbed, and the entirety of the argumentation in Part One would have been for naught without highlighting exactly how important this portion of the process is for one's emotional stabilization.

The Discovery of the Self

More than anything, leaving religious thought requires emotional maturation. So much of its appeal comes from a person's acceptance of faith, which results in the calming release of many intricate and complex thoughts. With faith, one never has to engage the dense, contemplative world of morality, and one need not be troubled by ever losing meaning in his life. Of course, religions are only addressing these issues by creating a cheap mannequin of solutions, but the emotions of calmness and certainty that result in those who buy them are very real.

However, having meaning in life is not a right; it is the greatest luxury that a person can acquire. As such, the dearness of its prize necessarily implies the difficulty of its acquisition, and for the last time, one must wander into introspective, emotional complexity in order to obtain it. To the extent that one fails to find meaning in his life, he has likely searched in the wrong place. Meaning is rarely something that one stumbles upon by chance in the external world. Once one has searched and understood himself, meaning comes of its own accord.

Mining One's Former God

In order to obtain meaning, a person must strive to meet himself for the first time without pretense, dishonesty, or shame, which is not easy to do, but before rushing headlong into the introspective work necessary to discover the self, one can avail himself of a handy shortcut. While one accepted religious thought, he believed in a god who may have seemed very real and specific, but objectively, the word itself has minimal definition. One would not bother to emote towards a being as plastic and two-dimensional as the bare bones definition of "god" implies, and while in religious thought, his personality traits were filled out by the morality that the individual chose to uphold, the care with which he believed his god had for humanity, and the general mood of his entire being whether wrathful, forgiving, or somewhere in between. This is the nature of customized religion as described in Chapter 10, and its universality arises from the linguistic hollowness of the terminology of religious thought.

The point is that the personality of one's former god ought to be used as a Rorschach inkblot in order to gain insight into the self by inspecting what the person once saw in him. The vagueness of the concept of god has allowed the brain to unwittingly project its own personality and habits onto it, and the ability to mine the personality of one's former god in order to reveal one's own values and character is a unique advantage in the attempt to discover the self due to the brain's duped compliance in the matter. As will be discussed shortly, feeling and owning one's negative traits is slippery business, and the fact that the brain has been tricked into blasting itself onto the canvass of a god hampers one's ability to lie to himself about who he is and therefore his desires and meaning in life. If one thought that his god was a vengeful, angry being and still delighted in worshiping him, the individual himself likely shares significant hatred in his own emotions for whatever reason. If one thought his god was forgiving and loving, his own thoughts and behavior likely follow a similar pattern.

The same technique can be applied to the entire cast of characters of religious thought. Depending on whether one loved or feared them, important information about the self can be harvested from their personality profiles. The reason that this method works so effectively is that the person did not know what he was doing when he created the personalities of these beings and had no reason to activate any emotional sensations that would inhibit his honesty. In other words, the information produced about the self was depersonalized and projected away, which means the person's emotional defense mechanisms stayed inactive. It is hard to impart what a boon that is, and while mining these concepts for information constitutes a big opportunity to discover one's internal values and operations, they are unlikely to produce a complete treatment such that a person's self will be sufficiently revealed. So, the investigation must be complemented with additional techniques.

Mirror Investigations

The technique of emotional discipline was discussed earlier in Part Two with an eye towards removing emotional pain and discomfort by attacking it and stripping it for information about the self. Indeed, such attempts can yield dramatic epiphanies about the self, if pursued with the proper relentlessness, but they need some modification for the present goal. In order to discover the nature of the self, a person is not going to have the roadmap of sharp emotional pain to announce the location of the solution. Instead, conundrums regarding one's meaning in life tend to produce generalized malaise instead of pain, and one loses the benefit of being driven on a clear path towards the alleviation of the sensation. So, starting with one's emotions will generally be unhelpful to the extent that they are not producing information that is reaching out for attention. Failing to have meaning in life does not produce emotional pain; it results in one's emotional apathy to feeling anything, which does not provide helpful information.

The best way to engage this process is to bounce back and forth between one's external and internal worlds to cross-reference their alignment. Many people know that they can tell a lot about a person from the people with whom he associates, but they rarely use that insight to divine information about themselves. If all of one's friends were together in a group, what would it look like? Surely, they have bonded with a person based on common traits, and the identification of those traits in them will produce insight into one's own. Likewise, with whom does a person not get along? The absence of affinity between them yields another opportunity to isolate what the self is like. The point of these exercises is that a person is often blind to how he appears to others in several ways, and if one's emotions will not trigger the needed discomfort to divulge information about the self, it must be gleaned from mirror-like sources. If the nature of the self were a room, all of these connections to other people represent keyholes with different vantage points into it, and if one glances through enough of them, he can synergize these perspectives into a coherent sketch of his essential nature.

Producing thought experiments to coax information about the self can also be a successful method to this end. What would be the last thing that a person would want to do with his life? Who would be the last person with whom he would want to spend time? Why exactly? Defining oneself by what he is not is a fruitful means of investigation when one's affirmative nature has proven evasive. Regardless of the manner in which this search is conducted, the goal is to locate external mirrors in people, places, and habits in order to determine one's nature and identify the things to which he is instinctively and thoughtlessly gravitating.

It is no coincidence that some of a person's friends may literally know him better than he knows himself. That is because his patterns of behavior are obvious to them since their view is not clouded by the thoughts and emotions that the person himself is generating in his internal world. In other words, he is distracting himself in very subtle ways that will evade his perception, and it will be a surprise only to him if he announces to his friends one day that he feels lost in life. Surely, they will have seen it coming because they will have read his body language, seen his habits, and availed themselves of his external information. A person's goal is to find ways to achieve the same perspective on his own self in order to glean from the exterior what may be closed to him from the interior.

*   *   *

While a strange topic, discovering the self is serious business. The ultimate meaning of life that religious thought once offered has sublimated into thin air but not before instilling the feeling in a person that meaning is easy and guaranteed. Nothing could be further from the truth. Having meaning in life is not easy to achieve, and to search the landscape with tired, frantic eyes looking for it is an ironic misstep. Indeed, one would be better served to close his eyes entirely in order to divine the answer. In other words, the question is not "What is the meaning of my life?"; the question is "Who am I?" If one answers the latter satisfactorily, the answer to the former will become obvious.

Death

Having covered the practical aspects of how a person reconstructs and adjusts the core aspect of meaning in his life with his departure from religious thought, there is one last aspect of a person's place with respect to the self to consider, namely, death. In religious thought, the consciousness never ends and continues forever by virtue of its true residence in the soul. As a result, the impact of death is trivialized, which is an unfortunate avoidance of what death offers to life. When one understands that his eventual death is unavoidable and without reprieve by an afterlife, the people, places, and emotions that he encounters will all shine the brighter. It is the finiteness of life that makes it worth living. Without it, one loses the perspective through which he senses that a person's time matters and that the people with whom he shares his are special.

The realization that one's emotions are fleeting creates an urgency to relish them all when one has them. When one believes he will bypass death and live without end, he has unwittingly robbed himself of piercing moments of emotional potency where he would otherwise be awash with the awareness that he may likely never again feel what he feels then. With respect to negative emotions, one's appreciation of them increases similarly, especially if he is cultivating emotional discipline. The promise of death is a gift to one's perspective on life, and while death itself is a jarring thing to witness in actuality, that it looms in the background of a person's life sharpens one's appetite for being alive.

In other words, the religious belief that death does not ever truly occur dilutes life instead of enhancing it. After all, religious thought teaches people to see their human existence as only a means to an end, namely, heaven or some version of it. Unfortunately, a worldview that looks past death does significant disservice to life. Without the concept of the soul, reason-based thinking understands the death of the body as the extinguishing of the consciousness. In that light, death is not a terrifying prospect. The termination of the brain's operation means that no sensation, awareness, or consciousness will exist. The person ceases to be, and the elements that composed his body disentangle and recycle themselves through nature.

However non-threatening that characterization may be, humanity has always feared death, and the narrative that religious thought provides to avoid that fear altogether has granted it wide appeal. For the sake of one's emotional maturation, death must be confronted and faced for what it is, i.e., the end of life. The desperate assumption that one's consciousness will somehow evade its grasp is unwarranted, unproven, and actually does a person significant harm by stealing any sense of urgency to treasure the dearest people and moments in his life while he has them.

*   *   *

With that, we have finally concluded the discussion of rebuilding identity, and it ought to have become clear along the way exactly why religious thought holds so much appeal for people: because it is easy. Life is a very simplistic chore when one is guaranteed meaning, has any puzzling nuance of morality wiped away, and is framed as being above all things and animals. Sadly, these are illusions born from illusions. They represent the stunted intellectual and emotional development that all religious believers experience because they have been delivered some of life's most cherished prizes for free, and they are cheapened by both their falseness and the effortlessness with which they have been obtained.

The intellect is a valuable and respected tool for atheists, but it tells only half the story. The emotions must be cultivated and understood as well. Indeed, the emotions are more powerful than the intellect and have the capacity to shut it down whenever they like. Constantly, people fall in love or lust with a person that they know is no good for them, but they do not care. All they care to do is look at the other person with diamonds in their eyes and feel the intoxication of the emotion. Such is religious thought. Its participants have fallen in love with a being so deeply that they do not care if it is real; they only wish to revel in their feelings. This is why emotional discipline has been given singular emphasis. One can think his way out of religious thought, but his chances are best when he learns to control his emotions from overriding his intellect's investigation into the baseline question of whether the object of their affection even exists in the first place.

PART THREE

PSYCHOLOGICAL CONSIDERATIONS

14 – Common Cognitive Errors

Get your facts first, then you can distort them as you please.
    – Mark Twain

In Parts One and Two, the concentration was on isolating an erroneous set of assumptions, extracting them from one's thinking, and filling the void that they once occupied. Now, the attention will shift to examining some of the errors that the brain had made in order to protect and maintain those assumptions once they were already in place in order to prevent such errors from recurring in the future in other venues.

The human brain is capable of amazing feats, and its power to create ideas and solve puzzles is rather unprecedented in the animal kingdom. For all of its power, the brain encounters so much data and stimuli in any given day that it simply cannot activate its highest level of analysis for everything, and it must take shortcuts in the interest of allocating its resources in a reasonably efficient manner. While the brain must take these shortcuts, it opens itself up to making cognitive errors in what it processes when it does so, and if it falls into a pattern of this behavior, it will wind up hardly thinking at all. Religious thought can create just such a cognitive rut that will encourage the brain to trick itself into bringing no meaningful analysis to bear on questions hiding in plain sight, and the only way to guard against these errors is to understand how they occur as well as to anticipate the scenarios in which they are likely to arise. For now, the discussion will mainly stick to the cognitive errors in their pure form. In the next chapter, their applications to the setting of religions and how they are employed to the advantage of those institutions will be explored.

Cognitive Errors by an Individual

The intellect has two competing goals: to deliver accurate interpretations of data and to minimize its workload. By sacrificing thoroughness for efficiency, the brain necessarily loses some of its quality control mechanisms, and glaring patterns of oversight can occur. Truly, the brain is not as efficient in its cognitive processing as people might like to think, and the ways in which it can fail are sometimes remarkable. By becoming intimately familiar with these errors however, one can learn to compensate for them by actively engaging the intellect to bring extra attention to the table in order to override the instinct to cut corners in the environments where they are likely to occur.

Cognitive Dissonance

Cognitive dissonance is a mental state where a person holds two ideas simultaneously that clash with one another, and the brain is capable of manipulating its own attitude in fascinating ways in order to relieve the discomfort. The brain craves consistency and coherence in its thoughts, and when it finds that it has arrived at a serious clash, it takes steps to remedy the problem. Suppose that Rachel's parents attend the same musical every week because they love it, and she joins them because they ask her too. Rachel gets nothing for going, but she dislikes turning her parents down for such a small request. In this situation, her brain will encounter a problem because Rachel hates performing these actions, yet she does them anyway, which creates internal stress for her as she is not being forced to go. Attempting to locate a path of least resistance, her brain has the power to change her attitude on the musical, and Rachel may actually begin to have the opinion that she enjoys it. In other words, the brain does not want to maintain internal clashes, and after examining its options, changing one's attitude towards the musical offers the easiest alternative.

One can see cognitive dissonance at work in the political sphere constantly. Suppose that Ernie has been very excited by a new politician who speaks about all of the matters closest to Ernie's heart. Ernie has spent his own money to help the politician get elected and has encouraged others to vote for him. Once in office, the politician casts a vote on a legislative issue that contradicts comments made in his campaign speeches, and Ernie is left confused. The stress here arises from the commitment that Ernie had made to get the politician elected on the basis of certain representations, juxtaposed with the failure of the politician to do what he said he would do. Especially in the political arena where people are very loyal to the political party of their choice, Ernie will likely find a way to blame the other party for the anomalous vote of his politician, effectively dismissing the possibility that the politician was simply not who he purported to be as that conclusion would render his work, time, and money an utter waste and would make him feel foolish. If the politician were to be flagrantly out of step with his campaign trail rhetoric for a prolonged period of time however, the brain's calculation on which idea to salvage may switch, and it may determine that the past investment was a sunk cost that should be accepted without suffering further manipulation from the politician.

In other words, cognitive dissonance is a situation of stress, and the brain will manufacture a way out of that stress, often by comparing its options and taking the path of least resistance. The remarkable part of the phenomenon is that the brain is not as limited in bringing its viewpoints into alignment as one would think. Indeed, it is capable of dismissing well-established facts and changing a person's attitude entirely, if those tactics represent the best way to make sense of a person's behavior or situation in light of the totality of the circumstances.

Confirmation Bias

Demonstrating a serious flaw in the brain's ability to process information with competence and accuracy, confirmation bias is probably the most common error that it can make, and the consequences of it can be hefty due to the investment that one tends to make in positions that he believes are being repeatedly confirmed as accurate.   When presented with a series of information, the brain prefers to select the bits that reinforce what it already believes, sometimes to the exclusion of information that convincingly contradicts its opinion. From the brain's perspective, contradictions entail more work and stress, and doubling down on the opinions that it has already formed demonstrates the momentum generated by certain ideas, in which the brain has found itself heavily invested.

Consider a person who has strong racial prejudices. He may casually interact with several members of the target race without incident in a given day, but upon one less-than-ideal interaction, he will likely spotlight that one and consider his opinion about the group as a whole confirmed. Of course, he will have obliviously discounted other contradictory evidence, but that will not occur to him due to the appealing feeling of confirmation bias. In other words, people want to feel like they are right, and in chasing that feeling, they sometimes sacrifice the opportunity to have opinions that accurately reflect objective reality. Actually being right is difficult, invites challenges to defend one's position, and constitutes a test of both one's debating skill and overall will. Feeling right is easier, and while the brain prefers to actually be correct in its opinions, it does not have the time or inclination to always ensure that those feelings are a proper reflection of the situation.

Consider another person who asserts that the world has been intelligently designed and that the complex efficiency of the human body demonstrates that fact. Such an argument makes use of confirmation bias in that it ignores the many failures of the human body, especially with respect to living up to the ideal of perfection. For one, the fact that the body needs things like food, water, and shelter in order to survive hardly seems perfect. Designing a body such that its intake for air is the same one as it uses to eat and drink seems dangerous and has killed people before based on choking. In other words, one who asserts intelligent design has found all of the harmonious parts of the human body and has fixated on them, thus employing a confirmation bias. In doing so, he has ignored all of the well-known flaws and errors in the body that reasonably refute his overall opinion.

More than anything, confirmation bias is an error produced by failing to force the brain to work, which is most effectively avoided by employing standards of analysis. If one rigorously employs standards of analysis to assess and interpret data, he obstructs his intellect from following an oblivious confirmatory pathway and requires that certain steps be followed in order to ensure quality control in both data analysis and opinion formation. Of course, more work will come as a result, but the process is one of fostering intellectual discipline to prevent the brain from jumping to the quick and easy conclusions that it wants. Confirmation bias is a seductive error because one genuinely feels like he is correct, but problems will arise when one attempts to defend his position to people who do not have the same prior investment in his opinions and who will reasonably find his evidence and reasoning to be lacking.

Cognitive Errors in Groups

Strange things happen to individuals when they participate and interact in groups. The group takes on a momentum of its own, and even though the individual may not agree with the group's position on a topic, he may find himself unable to resist the pressure of the group. Group pressure on an individual can even operate to change the person's mind on a topic in order to bring his opinions into alignment with those of the group. In drastic situations and depending on the dynamic of the group, the pressure may be applied with force sufficient to generate the person's obedience to perform actions he would never consider doing outside of the group setting. In all instances, the person is taking cues from the behavior of those around him, and by failing to either activate his analytical processes or withdraw from the group, he risks being swept away by an irrational current.

Conformity

An important manner for a person to gather information about an occurrence is to take non-verbal cues from other people, and while it does not produce perfect information, it is usually rather helpful. Imagine that a person walking in the park sees a woman being cradled on the ground with a knife in her stomach. He runs over to a small group that has formed around them just as the person holding her has finished saying something, and the group rises up at once with applause. Without having to be told anything, he has learned that this is likely some sort of dramatic performance, and that no one is actually in danger or hurt.

The same method of information collection takes place in groups with which a person affiliates, and unfortunate problems can occur when it is used in that setting. Unlike gleaning information from the non-verbal cues of strangers, groups have been formed for a purpose, and their agenda is a significant difference from the information produced by a randomly-emoting stranger. Indeed, groups have complex interactions based on cohesiveness, identity, and mutual affinity between its members that serve to alter a person's opinions. The pressure applied by the group is often unwitting and unintentional, but the presence of others in a group who do not object to opinions or courses of action that an individual may personally find ill-advised can operate to dull his self-confidence in his own perspective, perhaps even resulting in his opinion conforming to that of the group.

Imagine that Michelle is a young attorney sitting at a strategy meeting with other associates and partners in the firm. One partner suggests a case strategy that she has found to be unlikely to succeed due to her research on what the available evidence implies. When the partner delivers his strategy however, the room is filled with quiet nods of assent and no objections to its general thrust. Due to her relatively inferior position, she will have difficulty bucking the inertia of the group and may even have her own attitude changed with respect to the quality of the proposed strategy. Such is the nature of group conformity. The fact that one has agreed to be a member of a group acts to invest the brain in its membership and to become comfortable deferring to the judgment of its other members. People are naturally afraid to appear wrong or foolish, and the cues that they sense from the group operate to influence not only their behavior but potentially their opinions as well.

Occurring in groups by definition, conformity is alarming because well-defined groups sometimes command significant resources and decision-making capabilities. To the extent that its members have entered a stage of strong conformity, a group may commit too heavily to objectively risky decisions or may let sound opportunities slide by unnoticed. This phenomenon, known as groupthink, has led to serious errors at high levels of influence, and it will be discussed as a special instance of conformity later in this section.

Obedience

Conformity suggests that implicit group pressure has altered one's opinions and views, but obedience is the outright submission to the will of an authority figure. Conformity pressures the person to change or silence his opinion by the force of the unspoken will of the group. Obedience tends to imply an external threat of harm or ostracism, brandished by an authority figure who openly demands compliance. In other words, obedience is a stronger version of conformity. Both imply the altering of an individual's opinion due to the pressures visited upon him by associating with a group, but obedience is a phenomenon that takes place under stronger and more confrontational circumstances.

An important aspect of obedience is the perception of authority. The actual resources and authority of the person who demands obedience is not as important as the perception of his having those characteristics by the individual whose opinions or actions are being manipulated. Especially salient with respect to a person performing actions that he might not otherwise, this perception seems to operate in the individual's brain as a removal of personal responsibility for the effects of his actions. If his obedience has been achieved and results in his performing actions that might otherwise detest him, his brain will deploy two tactics in order to explain why it has acted against its own wishes. As just stated, the person may feel no responsibility for his actions as they would not have happened but for the pressure and threats of the perceived authority figure, but surprisingly, he may also attempt to reduce his cognitive dissonance by internalizing the desires of the authority figure, i.e., rewrite history to create the narrative that the individual performed the action because he actually did agree with it, not because of outside pressure.

Most people do not accept being told what to do, especially if those demands are not the terms of group membership as he understood them when he first decided to affiliate with the group. So, an environment that fosters obedience usually has to be created in order to disarm a person's will such that he prefers to prioritize the will of the authority figure over his own. Many techniques have been employed to create this environment, but one that is central is the concept of gradual escalation. In order for obedience to be achieved, the person whose obedience is demanded must not feel as though withdrawal from the group is available, or his exit may be a more appealing option. In compulsory groups such as the military, withdrawal is minimized by enforcing legal penalties, but in voluntary groups, the gradual escalation of one's commitment to the group tends to be a preferred mechanism to increase a person's psychological investment.

The escalation can come in any number of varieties like money, isolation from friends and family, or violence, and the goal of this technique is to inoculate the person against the shock of objectively huge demands for compliance from the authority figure by making increases in commitment seem marginally small, relative to the last one. Imagine a group leader that demands that a person sell his house and donate the proceeds to the group. That request would seem absurd to a new entrant who would simply prefer to exit the group rather than comply, but to a person who has already obeyed demands to donate smaller amounts of money and time to the group, it may seem like a minor increase in what he had already been convinced to contribute.

As heavy-handed as obedience may seem relative to conformity, they both produce similar effects, i.e., they operate to shape a person's opinion and outlook to match what he perceives to be the group's viewpoint. With obedience, that effect is intentional and aggressive, but with conformity, it often is neither. Their main difference is that the identity-smashing methodology of obedience can produce a level of brainwashing that may appear disturbingly alien to non-group members. Having been convinced to obey, a person loses connection with others who have not similarly had their wills broken, and the contrast between group members and outsiders becomes stark. Regardless, the ultimate difference between conformity and obedience on the question of its effect on a person's opinions and attitude is a matter of degree and not type.

Groupthink

Groupthink is a social phenomenon that can result in objectively baffling decision-making by groups. The environment that fosters groupthink always has elements of conformity, obedience, or both, and the pressure of those influences in whatever ratio they are present acts to submerge the analysis of the group into irrational waters. The ideal environment for groupthink to take root is a well-defined and homogeneous group making decisions at the unwitting expense of truly inspecting the potential costs and benefits on a critical basis. The effect of groupthink is that the decision produced tends to be a warped and poorly-considered one that sometimes fails spectacularly.

In a groupthink environment, group pressure acts to prioritize the harmony of the group over the analysis of the decision at hand, and since the people in the group likely do not sense that they are failing to accurately assess the complete contingencies and ramifications of their decision, they tend to heavily invest in it as they cannot conceive of how it will fail. For that reason, poor decisions produced by groupthink often fail in grandiose fashion because the analysis that has led to the action tends to underestimate the drawbacks or dangers of the approach. When people operate on the basis of groupthink, they tend to reach feelings of certainty because their own hunches and thinking about a situation are being reinforced by like-minded individuals without meaningful objection, creating an echo effect that the brain interprets as a thorough validation of its approach.

Like the other cognitive errors discussed thus far, groupthink operates to distort the perception of the individuals in the group by virtue of each of their brains becoming more interested in gathering non-verbal information from the other members and deferring to the group's harmonious opinion than actively attempting to solve problems. This effect makes the group gravitate towards decisions that are objectively undesirable as well as increases the likelihood that the group will overcommit. While critical and orderly disagreement tends to produce the most rational analysis for a given situation, like-minded people tend to form groups that will engage in groupthink as they prefer to avoid the helpful setting of surrounding themselves with people with whom they disagree for general social and stress-reduction purposes. As common as groupthink likely is, it does not become a dangerous thing until the group size becomes sufficiently large or if the group is in a position of major decision-making.   Only in those circumstances do the ramifications of being in error tend to ripple through large numbers of people, interactions, and ideas.

As the study of groupthink has advanced, strategies of protecting against it have been developed to counter its distorting effect.   Since groupthink is a phenomenon that bypasses critical analysis, adding a gadfly to the group who is incentivized to struggle against the ideological consensus of the other members can be a successful counter.   After all, the problem with groupthink is that it derails critical analysis due to a group's lack of interest in arguing against its homogeneous interests. With the inclusion of a vocal dissident who will resist the agenda of the group, the other members are forced to engage rational analysis in order to defeat the gadfly's arguments, which will likely air significant concerns and contingencies that the group would not have considered in his absence.

If a group has a definite leader, that person can also deliberately act to stave off the creation of a groupthink environment with a variety of strategies. A leader could require that certain people in the group, regardless of their personal beliefs, occupy the positions of gadflies and deliberately argue against the favored ideology of the group. Similarly, he could restrain the entire group from arguing in support of the conclusion that they would likely reach based on their similar viewpoints in order to manufacture the critiques necessary to achieve a critical analysis of the topic. Regardless of the tactical considerations of a leader, none are as effective as pitting people who genuinely and knowledgably disagree against each other. In that environment, the power of the group to stifle critical inquiry is minimized, and the group is less likely to arrive at poorly considered conclusions based on group pressures.

Cons and Cognitive Errors

At several points in this book, magicians have been referenced because of their expertise in playing games with cognition, but their field is unique in a different regard as well. The audiences who witness magic tricks routinely see them for what they are, namely, tricks. Even when a person is at a loss to determine how a trick has been performed, his instinct is to assume that his brain's cognition has been tricked rather than that the performer has special powers. Unfortunately, other performances that are functionally identical to magic have the presumption against authenticity reversed in their favor. Unlike magic, these fields receive the benefit of the doubt because their tricks operate without a tangible element, i.e., they are tricks involving one's thoughts. The two techniques that will be discussed here constitute the main tools of psychics, fortune tellers, and other clairvoyants. Like most magic tricks, what is remarkable about these techniques is how effective the illusions they produce are considering the simplicity of what the practitioner is really doing.

Cold Reading

In general, cold reading is a technique that creates an illusion of psychic ability in the practitioner by his utilizing probabilistic, psychological, and linguistic strategies to gain the unwitting assistance of the person being read in creating the effect. In effect, cold reading is mental fishing. The practitioner baits his hook with a comment or insinuation that he knows will have a high probability of being applicable to the person based on the person's appearance, dress, manner of speech, age, gender, etc. If the person takes the bait, he will unwittingly provide information that the practitioner will use to refine his next guess, which will evoke another information-laden reaction, and so on.

With cold reading, it is easier to see how the effect works with a sample dialogue. In the following conversation, imagine that Lynn is a 30-year old woman who is wearing a wedding ring and is seeing a practitioner who claims to be able to speak with the dead. Specifically, she has come to hear about her recently deceased father but has not mentioned this fact. Numbers appear at certain key points in the conversation for ease of reference in the later discussion.

> **Practitioner**: Before we begin, (1) I want you to understand that the messages and visuals that I get are not always clear. Many spirits communicate with me at once, and I can get confused. Now, let's begin. *pauses to channel spirits* I am hearing an older man's voice. He says that he comes around you often.
>
> **Lynn**: Um... (2) my father?
>
> **Practitioner**: What was your father's name?
>
> **Lynn**: Harry.
>
> **Practitioner**: Yes, that makes sense now. I was being shown an "H", but I didn't understand what they meant by that. (3) He says he's sorry for how he left. He's telling me that there was something unresolved between the two of you, like a fight or a misunderstanding. He's mentioning your husband.
>
> **Lynn**: I'm not sure what that could mean. He and my husband always got along.
>
> **Practitioner**: (4) He says he's sorry for how he left you. He knows that you weren't OK for a long time after that.
>
> **Lynn**: *begins to cry softly*
>
> **Practitioner**: (5) Do you have children?
>
> **Lynn**: No, but my husband and I are trying to have a child soon.

Practitioner: He wants me to mention that he sees the baby, but (6) he could be referring to a baby who has yet to be born.

Point (1) in the above conversation represents the practitioner giving himself plenty of slack for being incorrect or vague, and he primes Lynn to interpret any errors he may make as being a part of the messy work of communicating with the deceased. He concocts a fantastical story of being plagued by spirits clamoring for his attention in order to elicit her participation in helping him clarify what they tell him, and Point (2) demonstrates the payoff. The older man that the practitioner referenced could have been any ancestor in her family tree, but Lynn has narrowed that selection down by mentioning a person of obvious personal significance.

Point (3) represents the practitioner making a probabilistic gamble. Since Lynn is both a young woman and volunteered the information that her father is deceased, the practitioner is making an educated guess that Lynn feels as though she herself left some things unresolved with her dad. Point (4) demonstrates how a practitioner can downplay and pivot away from wrong guesses. He has already primed Lynn with his comments at Point (1) that he might be wrong, and most importantly, that such errors would not constitute evidence that he cannot channel the deceased. By moving on with more emotional comments of general applicability, Lynn is unlikely to dwell on the error. Point (5) is a direct question requesting information from Lynn. If she had been reluctant to volunteer this information, the practitioner would have proceeded the same way, but Lynn's speaking on the subject first allows him to improve the specificity with which he speaks about the baby. Point (6) is another coupling of the bizarreness of the channel that the practitioner has opened to the spirit realm with an improved prediction based on information helpfully submitted by Lynn.

Skilled practitioners will be able to make more specific guesses based on their abilities to profile people based on appearance, which will result in a more impressive effect. The goal is to make predictions that are actually rather generic but that sound specific. People find themselves to be unique and special, and they fail to see the patterns that they share with others. With that tunnel vision, very general guesses that are true with respect to a common pattern in many people can strike a person with surprising force because he feels he is unique, which is not to say that he is incorrect but rather that he overestimates his uniqueness.

The key to the entire game for the practitioner is to maximize the subject's willingness to help him fill in the blanks while minimizing the probability that he will ever be wrong. If he can convince the participant to play by his rules, then the effect that he is capable of producing will be rather remarkable. However, all that the practitioner is doing is allowing people to participate in their own trick by encouraging them to appropriate statements of general applicability and tailor the vagueness to suit their taste.

Again, vagueness is crucial. It operates as both the practitioner's insurance against wrong guesses as well as the needed slack for the guest to inject his own storyline into the questions. If going to a psychic or similar medium, try this simple experiment. Tell the practitioner that there is an index card with something written on it in your pocket, and request him to guess exactly what it says. Then, simply wait and listen to the excuses as to why his powers do not work that way.

Hot Reading

Contrary to the passive, non-targeted ploy of cold reading, hot reading creates its illusion by brute force. With hot reading, specific knowledge about the person to be read is discovered in advance by surreptitious means, usually by eavesdropping on a conversation a person may be having as he enters an audience for a practitioner's show. Regardless of how the information is obtained, hot reading entails the practitioner's having gained information about the subject that the subject himself does not realize he has acquired. So, the revelation of the specific details of the subject's life will appear to be impossible but for the practitioner's clairvoyance.

Hot reading is often paired with cold reading techniques. A subject who has been read with the alarming accuracy of a hot read will likely become a more compliant participant in cold reading in guiding the practitioner's questioning and commentary. Obviously, hot reading is not a technique that requires skill as cold reading does. Simply with the help of well-placed confederates or surveillance devices, hot reading is a no-brainer. In the digital age where personal information is accessible from a vast array of sources at incredible speeds, hot reading is even easier.

Similarly with cold reading and truly all illusionist methods, it is imperative for the practitioner to garner the participation of his audience on his terms. If a subject wants to start asking specific questions and demanding specific answers, the practitioner will have to deflect those attempts. If the subject continues to resist giving the practitioner control over the conversation, he will make it impossible for the desired effect to be created.

Magicians set up their stages and devices with an eye on what the audience's vantage point will be. If the audience demands to be permitted to see all vantage points of an illusion, the trick is not going to work. This is equally true of mental tricks. The practitioner wants to construct a mental stage, on which he conjures information from spirits or gods. He anticipates that his audience will be viewing the illusion from a specific vantage point, and if the subject is non-compliant in staying in that vantage point, the illusion will be exposed. If the subject desires the practitioner to submit to some reasonable experimentation of his skills, he will attempt to create disclaimers that the spirit realm does not work in that fashion or that the practitioner cannot control the information that he receives. Again, these excuses tend to work on a significant number of people because they have already been primed to believe that ordinary rules will not apply to the demonstration, i.e., that they should consent to deactivating their normal analyses and defer to the expertise of the practitioner.

*　　　*　　　*

If these tricks seem to have suspicious overlap with religious techniques, that is because they do. What is more relevant is that the people on whom these techniques succeed all share a common characteristic: these techniques work on those who want them to work. Their participation in creating the illusion may be unwitting, but most have no inclination to press the issue in terms of holding the practitioner to any standard of reasonable proof that he actually has the power that he claims. Perhaps the ultimate lesson to gather from this discussion of illusion techniques is that if the rules of a game are unclear or changeable at the discretion of the opponent, then the only winning move is not to play.

15 – Religious Thought and Reason-Based Thinking in Groups

And what are you, reader, but a Loose-Fish and a Fast-Fish, too?
— Herman Melville

Having assembled the relevant concepts regarding cognitive errors and social phenomena, the techniques that religions use to protect themselves in the practical setting can now be explored. Religious thought proposes places and beings that do not receive regular reinforcement in a person's everyday life, which means that protective measures must be put in place around its adherents in order to protect their thoughts from outside interference. Of course, touting faith as a moral virtue incentivizes a person to close his ears to non-members, but religions have also learned to employ other non-theoretical tactics in order to achieve the necessary insulation.

With the dawning of the information age and the creation of the internet, these tactics have all been done serious damage, and religions have yet to determine how to adjust to the new informational inroads that have been paved. Perhaps religious thought will find a way to adapt to these new circumstances, but how it will achieve that goal is not presently foreseeable. Regardless, religions all presently tend to follow similar patterns in how they control the thinking of their flocks, which has been a natural occurrence. After all, institutions of religious thought that do not utilize these methods eventually disintegrate in their followers as they will be unable to subdue the rational expectations of the brain.

Religion

Relative to the phenomenon of cults, religions enjoy generally widespread appeal, which allows them to give their followers more latitude in their interactions. When a religion's houses of worship are known to exist all over an area or country, many people consider their frequency to be a signal that the religion's proliferation implies its correctness, and as a result, the religion need not exert as much mental force over its followers. Of course, the conclusion that popularity implies correctness is a logical error, but obviously, religions will take their chances with respect to their followers recognizing the logical errors that they make on the question of religious thought. In any case, religious thought still requires some protective support in this environment.

Demonization of Non-Believers

In general, religions are not concerned with their followers engaging people from other religions. Often from infancy, a given religion's incarnation of religious thought is installed in an individual such that any other religious character that does not activate that indoctrination will be met with scrutiny delivered by reason-based thinking. This is not to say that religious believers do not ever move between religions but rather that the infrequency of that loss to a congregation makes the increased scope of forbidding followers to interact with people of other religions unnecessary.

The isolating tactics that religions employ to protect the numbers of their congregations are not costless, and they prefer to minimize both the number and severity of them. Due to the fact that religions tend to be rather large with a high level of perceived credibility in the public, they contain many people who are reasonable and decent, and to instruct them to cut so many potential interactions out of their lives will raise suspicion and may wind up prompting more withdrawal than had no action been taken at all. Instinctively, people desire the freedom to do as they wish within reasonable bounds, and religions have determined that the cure is worse than the disease vis-à-vis the threat of other religions leaching their members.

Non-believers are a different issue. The arguments of atheists and other similarly skeptical people threaten to attack and corrode the foundation of religious thought, and exposure to their ideas is less acceptable. However, religions are clever in this regard. Religions do not forbid their members to ever interact with non-believers; instead, they implicitly forbid them from entertaining their arguments. In this manner, religions achieve a very desirable set of outcomes. Most religions want their members to proselytize to other people, including atheists, which is an important method of maintaining a high profile and furthering the illusion that the institution has more foundational credibility than it does. By loading religious believers with the notion that atheists are either evil or horribly misled, religions split the atom of their goal to great effect. Under this strategic framing, a non-believer's comments against religious thought are disinfected and quarantined in the brain of the religious believer while simultaneously stoking the religious believer's desire to convert and save the skeptic.

In all likelihood, religions have little fear of atheists coming to a group meeting of their followers because in that setting the reinforcing pressure of the congregation can easily create an environment for conformity and the opinions of the dissenting individual can be squashed. The environment that religions fear arises when their followers are by themselves and isolated from group pressure. In that setting, a well-spoken skeptic can appeal to a religious believer's reason-based thinking and likely create significant confusion for him, which is why religions that make proselytizing a mandatory exercise for followers send them around in pairs or groups. By replicating a miniature group, the proselytizers can still enjoy mutually reinforcing conformity with respect to religious thought while maintaining the practicality of the situation. Surely, few people would be interested in opening their doors to an unsolicited stampede of religious believers. The optimal goal is for the group to be big enough such that the proselytizer has sufficient pressure holding the assumptions of religious thought in place but not so big as to overwhelm and intimidate the person whose conversion is sought.

Handling of Internal Skeptics

When a person within a religion begins to doubt its legitimacy, a unique problem arises. Ordinarily, the groupthink environment would have acted to bring the individual's opinion back into alignment, and that it has not done so means that the religion's first line of defense has failed. When a person is not satisfied with the conforming opinion of the group on an issue, active attention to the individual from a leader in the congregation will take place, and he has roughly three choices in how to handle the situation.

Depending on the severity of the religion, outright expulsion for voicing such views is an option, but rarely does this take place, however. Generally, the danger to the integrity of the group is insignificant and does not warrant such extreme action. Another option for the religious leader is discrediting the individual in front of the group. As this comes close to expelling the person, this option is also rarely exercised. These two options could only realistically occur if the individual was so intellectually defiant and aggressive towards the group that the possibility of the integrity of the group being compromised could become an issue. As people seldom summon the will to so thoroughly buck the will of a group with which they identify, these situations are rare indeed.

The most likely tactic for the religious leader is the placation of the objecting group member through explanations that bolster religious thought, especially faith. With the failure of the group to produce conformity of the dissenting individual's opinion, an authority figure for the group has now escalated the group's pressure on the individual, which represents a tactical shift from conformity towards obedience, but the group need not be present nor is there need for the authority figure to aggressively demand that the person obey. After all, the person knows who the religious leader is and what his credentials represent; the stakes of disagreeing with or flouting his comments are tacitly understood. To the extent that the individual cannot let go of his doubts, he will likely have to exit the group, and indeed, he will do so of his own accord if the pressure of obedience did not have an effect on him. To the extent that the individual does relent in his questioning and quells the concerns of the group with respect to his ideas, then he is obviously welcome back.

Initiation Rites

For good reason, religions do not instantaneously grant full membership rights to new members. As a general rule, people tend not to value things that are given to them easily, and religions have learned to provoke the investment of the individual into the group. Without requiring initiation rites, the cohesiveness of the group would be weakened as each member would sense that people can come and go as they please, having committed nothing of substance to the group. So, religions create initiation rites, through which one must pass after demonstrating certain levels of religious study and achievement. Often purely symbolic, the desirability of the rites arises from their symbolization of the member's good standing and seniority in the group, from which the individual naturally wants respect and admiration. Receiving a rite demonstrates an individual's commitment to the group and reciprocally reinforces the individual's feeling bound to the group. Like most of the practical tactics employed by religious thought to protect itself, initiation rites yield many desirable payoffs from a psychological standpoint, and their simplicity and low cost only sweeten the deal.

Initiation rites also confer responsibilities on the individual with respect to the group. On that point, the gradual escalation of commitment to the group via these rites is a valuable psychological technique. Rather than imposing all of the costs of group membership at once and overwhelming the individual, religions slowly ramp up a group member's responsibilities in lockstep with his privileges. With the gradual escalation, a person could easily find himself performing an objectively bizarre rite that he would never have considered at the beginning of his membership. What has changed in him is that he is conscious of the steps he has already taken in the previous rites, and those actions act to cause the brain to weigh the next step on the basis of its marginal cost relative to the last rite in which it had taken part instead of on its own merits. The brain is aware of its investment in the group, and unless the initiation rite at hand or the responsibility associated with its fulfillment is repellant to the individual, he will gladly accept the opportunity to acquire it.

Insulated Communities

Regardless of a person's level of devotion to his religion, he will always have to eventually go home and live his life, which will cause physical separation from the group. Luckily, religious thought and reinforcing group membership tends to separate oil from water in terms of believers scattering themselves amongst non-believers. Indeed, the populations of entire communities and towns could very well be of one religion, possibly even attending the same house of worship. In these settings, the individual has an incredible amount of pressure on him to retain his religious group membership as that identity has now conspicuously hitched itself to the other relationships in his life that may not have anything to do with his religion. In other words, all of his eggs are in one basket, and if he were to exit the religious group, the ripples of that decision will not end at the threshold of his house of worship. Indeed, they will follow him through his daily life in the community, and due to that immense pressure, there is no telling how many people in these settings wish to depart religious thought yet cannot due to the manner in which it has infiltrated every aspect of the locale.

Small, insulated communities and towns are the bastions of religious thought, and if they were to ever fall out of its control, religious thought would likely never recover. Indeed, the smothering effect of religions in these areas often acts to significantly distort objective reality for their followers. People who live in such settings are relatively unlikely to encounter arguments that disagree with religious thought due to the insularity of their community and its likely geographical isolation, and as a result, their religious belief will develop an increased level of certainty by virtue of the perceived silence of the opposition.

With disturbing frequency, such an intense level of groupthink and certainty can lead to violence against outsiders, whether geographical or ideological. When these events take place, religious thought has done the job of protecting itself too well to the point that the potency of its potion has concentrated into venom, and to the extent that a religion's followers bring violence to the equation, their aggressive zealotry ironically has the opposite effect that their religion desires, namely, group expansion. In other words, religions seek to achieve a delicate balance in the population where its perceived influence, high standing, and group integrity are maximized while avoiding the perception from outsiders that the group is extreme, unstable, and too risky an entity with which to associate.

As noted in the introduction to this chapter, the invention of the internet and other devices that dramatically increase the dissemination of arguments and information to people and places that would never have heard them at any other time in history poses a dire threat to religious thought, and religions know it. Throughout the vast majority of history, one had to speak in person to another in order to convey meaning, and the tactics of religions were well-suited to defend against that sort of penetration of ideas. With the invention of the printing press, one could memorialize ideas on paper and disseminate them in large quantities without necessarily being present to face the possibly dangerous wrath of those who would prefer that their ideas never be questioned. Now, the internet has taken another step in this progression towards the frictionless flow of information, and it has done serious damage to religions because it has enabled ideas to flow quickly and with near anonymity, i.e., the threat of danger for speaking on unpopular subjects is at a minimum.

Indeed, the most effective technique that religions have currently developed to counter this technological advancement has been to obstruct access to the internet, either by religious fiat or physical censorship of offending sites. However, that temporary levee will not hold forever, and it will be interesting to see how religious thought compensates in the coming years. One thing is clear: religious thought needs people to allow their emotions to influence or trump their intellects in order to survive, and if it cannot determine a strategy to pump emotion into dispassionate computer screens on which live conversations take place between skeptics and believers, then its arguments will not land with enough impact to be convincing, its groups will slowly disintegrate, and it itself will fall into disrepair.

Cults

From the perspective of reason-based thinking, there is no difference between a religion and a cult, aside from the number of people who participate. After all, a cult's members are still employing religious thought; that their behavior tends to be perceived as different from the followers of a religion is only a qualitative, practical observation, though it has merit. Cults are often small groups of people engaging in religious thought, but their uniqueness is that the object of their worship tends to be a living person who leads the group. Indeed, their sparse membership speaks to how humanity has internalized reason-based thinking when confronted with a new, budding religion. If a god were to manifest as a person today, it appears that just about everyone would want reasonable evidence that he was who he claimed to be.

Extreme Group Commitment

Unlike religions, cults do not have the luxury of playing it cool with their tactics. Every follower that a cult gains or loses is momentous due to their slim membership, and the intensity of the group is intentionally raised in an attempt to erase any given individual's sense of self. After all, one cannot withdraw from a group if he does not recognize an individual identity to which to return. With respect to the tactical maneuvers of religions, cults employ the same tactics, but they are high-powered in their aggression towards the individual's sense of self.

For example, the gradual escalation of commitment to a cult will likely commence innocently enough with regular attendance of group events, but they will escalate sharply. A cult member will find himself ordered to give sums of money to the organization in increasingly large amounts with the likely culmination being the person liquidating all of his assets, transferring the proceeds to the group or leader, and living on the premises of the cult's location. Aside from desiring the creation of impenetrable group integrity, cults need money, and they cannot wait for people to give it of their own accord if they wish to survive and expand. Due to these emergency circumstances, obedience is the weapon of choice in such groups instead of conformity.

Cults are ideally situated to command obedience from their followers as well because the leader of the group is often himself seen as a god or otherwise of divine lineage. If believed, then his authority speaks for itself, and members who do not comply with his wishes will be subjected to severe, dehumanizing repercussions from the group in order to break his individuality and concomitant resistance to unquestioning obedience.

Isolation from Non-Believers

Cult members often live with the group membership at all times, which means that religious thought is activated in their brains constantly. This must occur because there is no margin for error. If one person were to conspicuously leave the group or successfully defy the group leader, his actions could start a rockslide within the cult, causing its ultimate disintegration. Therefore, the doors to the exits must be perceived by the group as glued shut, the people on the outside as the enemy, and the people inside as true family.

To that end, cult leaders routinely demand that a group member be completely barred from contacting his biological family members if they cannot be assimilated into the group, which is a tactic intended to deliberately detonate the member's connection to his former identity from which he can salvage aspects of individuality. His new identity is waiting for him in the group, and sadly for him, the limited size of the group does not afford him the luxury of saving any mementos of who he once was. His devotion to the group and leader must be absolute. To permit otherwise would place the germinating seed of religious thought in the group at significant risk from withering before it sprouts.

In this manner, cults close themselves off to the world, only reaching out to occasionally grasp for a new member or allow a couple of trusted, senior members to enter society to perform essential tasks for the group such as gathering essentials or banking. Beyond that, cults live in their own world where both physical and mental intrusion from outsiders is strictly controlled. Again, religions need not concern themselves with limiting their followers' physical travels because they can take more risks with losing members of the group in order to reach for bigger rewards.

Cults must barricade the lines of communication to the outside world, which is why their members sometimes appear brainwashed and objectively insane when seen speaking outside of the cult setting. They have been forced to cut the anchor of their boat and have been drawn into a manufactured reality, and when they leave those confines, others can see how far they have drifted from shore, even though they themselves cannot. The gradual escalation of their commitment to the group has blurred their perception of that fact. It is a strange and troubling phenomenon indeed, and former cult members often recount having felt unable to resist the group's momentum. Their testimony ought to be a humbling reminder that anyone is capable of being fooled, even to unbelievable and dangerous lengths, and one's raw intelligence will not save him. Only well-reasoned standards of analysis and emotional discipline being brought to bear on what a group and its leader believe can provide that assurance.

*   *   *

Clearly, religions and cults differ, but their differences are of degree, not type. Both engage in religious thought, require group pressure on individuals in order to maintain religious thought, and employ similar tactics in order to realize that result. Their differences lie in the advantages in numbers that religions possess. Cults do not have the luxury of widespread public recognition in order to implicitly bolster their credibility nor do they have a large number of people in their membership to that same end. So, cults cannot happily skim along, quietly collecting and losing followers while only being worried about the long-term, net turnover as religions are. Instead, they are fighting for their very survival in the short-term, and the aggressiveness of their behavior towards their membership displays their desperation in this regard.

Another consideration is the inward focus of cults versus the outward focus of religions on the question of where violence, if it occurs, will be directed. When the group leader of a cult has sensed himself cornered or has otherwise been driven to the extremes of cruel irrationality, history has demonstrated his willingness to die and take his group with him by mass suicide in some instances. In other words, the violence of cults tends to be done to its own group membership. As for extremism within religions, their violence tends to be directed outwards towards both actual and perceived non-members, potentially of the same religion as the perpetrators if they do not accept the same level of zealotry in their interpretation of the religion.

Scientific Communities

Thus far, the discussion has been limited to religious thought and the environment that it requires in order to thrive. For juxtaposition purposes, the focus will now turn to the behavior of groups that have formed for the purpose of utilizing reason-based thinking, specifically professionals in disciplines like biology, mathematics, and chemistry.

Surely, these people operate in groups in that they collaborate on projects, attend lectures regarding the state of the art, and participate in peer review of results. Since they are a group of like-minded individuals, they are not immune to groupthink. Additionally, scientific group members also experience gradual escalation in their commitment to the group, generally known as attending a university. Likewise, they have initiation rites into their groups, known as graduation ceremonies upon completion of degree study. All of this may sound flip and mocking, but the point is that groups follow patterns regardless of their formation being based on the use of religious thought or reason-based thinking. As is characteristic of institutions of religious thought in nearly every topic which has been covered, they have not created any special human associations but rather have only hijacked and run aground the ordinary machinery of how people work with the wandering arbitrariness of their nature.

Utilizing reason-based thinking and peer review in the scientific community, scientific disciplines minimize the pernicious aspects of group membership that tend to create mob mentalities in religious thought. True and strident dissent is required for science to advance. Proving that one's hypothesis, methodology, and interpretation of results are sound is the only manner to garner scientific consensus.

As important as these techniques are for the management of confirmation bias and group-associated cognitive errors, the most important distinction between groups employing religious thought and reason-based thinking is that anything that any one member submits to the group in a scientific community can and must be meaningfully checked for accuracy. Due to the nature of reason-based thinking and its view of reality, a methodology and associated set of results ought to be able to endure empirical testing and logical scrutiny while also delivering explanatory force for the phenomena from which they have been gathered. With groups formed around religious thought, there is no point in the group's questioning any comment mentioned by religious authorities since faith is always going to be an acceptable basis for its approval.

The arbitrariness of faith yields no manner for a group engaged in religious thought to truly check the accuracy of what any given member thinks, and the lack of such a yardstick is why religions can so easily fragment into sects or cults. Without a convincing manner to ensure the reliability of the information being delivered, groups using religious thought have the problem that no one's opinion can ever be reasonably confirmed or defeated, and if there is an especially charismatic leader or identifiable subgroup within the religion, they may break from the group to form a new one through sheer force of will.

With groups using reason-based thinking, differences in opinion with respect to the interpretation of results or theoretical conclusions do not lead to outright exits from the group. When such disagreements inevitably occur, both sides must continue producing experimentation and building their case in order to convince the group that their perspective on the issue is preferable. Of course, the difference is that the group members recognize the knowledge-acquisition techniques of science, mathematics, and logic, and on the basis of those methodologies, they understand that the determination of who has won the debate will be based on the reasonable application of standards of analysis.

Due to the respective knowledge-acquisition techniques employed by both groups using religious thought or reason-based thinking, the former ultimately defers to the qualities of people while the latter relies on the quality of ideas. Through that lens, it is no wonder that groups formed around religious thought can be so unstable both in their coherence and cohesiveness.

*   *   *

The interaction of people in groups is problematic because a person takes shortcuts to his ordinary level of thinking when he has others around him to which to defer, and the problem is compounded when groups use religious thought. Practically, religions and cults always submit evidentiary and logical bases for their assertions to their followers, but if one finds those arguments to be insufficient or unreasonable, faith will enter the conversation. When it does, the conversation is stalemated, and no one can rationally win, which is where the arbitrary influence of group pressure, based on personalities, gut feelings, and emotions, will mix in order to decide the matter.

Of course, the social machinery of groups based on religious thought and reason-based thinking are similar because they are comprised of people who expect certain patterns in group participation. Nevertheless, they differ in how they use the machinery, and the failure of religious thought to provide any meaningful way to check its assertions causes all of the worst and most dangerous aspects of group participation to surface.

16 – Personal Conclusion

At the end of the game, the king and the pawn go into the same box.
    – Italian Proverb

At their most fundamental levels, religious thought and reason-based thinking are completely irreconcilable perspectives on how to understand objective reality. A person cannot accept one without betraying the other, yet both have sprung from the same human desire. Predictability in one's surroundings is a basic human need, and as a corollary to that need, humanity has always yearned to predict the future. In the past, man had not yet conceived scientific inquiry and was at a loss to understand anything but the most basic patterns of causality in nature. The favored strategy to coping with the stress of maintaining so much uncertainty was to largely abandon searching for causation and to generate a worldview that rendered the caprice of the physical world meaningless for the survival of the consciousness, which led to the creation of the soul. It was personal dissociation for mental health reasons, and it showcases the human brain's fascinating arsenal of tools that it can deploy to protect itself in times when it is overwhelmed.

We have concentrated our attention on the non-negotiable core of religious thought in an attempt to drill through the mystique that protects it and its institutions from ideological attack. After all, there is no need to follow their meandering skyscrapers into the clouds if the steel of their foundations is corroded and giving way. Even if every argument delivered here was considered an abject failure however, realize that all religions have several questions to answer; we have mainly focused on the first.

1) Is there a being whose consciousness is infinite and who created the universe?
2) If so, does it care about humanity?
3) If so, does it care whether humans worship it?
4) If so, which religion is the correct statement of the demands of this entity?

Religions must run the table by answering all four of these questions in order to demonstrate their legitimacy, and their conclusive failure to get past even the first is woeful. Fortunately, faith has been encouraged in their constituents, and the intellectual blank check that it produces has printed sufficient spiritual currency for religions to continue doing business in their evidentiary and logical void, even though their assertions are counterfeit. Insofar as outsiders who wish to challenge the ethos are concerned, religions have learned that one cannot be checkmated if one's king is never placed on the board.

*   *   *

For an idea so widely accepted as properly reflecting a being that exists in objective reality, gods suffer horribly when examined logically or scientifically. So, what is going on here? Why do religions enjoy such membership when their claims with respect to objective reality lack reasonable evidentiary and logical support? In total, there are three problems facing both society and individuals when it comes to the propping up of religious thought: social, intellectual, and emotional. Sadly, they are mutually reinforcing.

First, a social taboo encircles the institutions of religious thought and protects them from widespread inspection on their merits, and the deafening hush that fills a room whenever the topic is brought up for discussion is a symptom of its chilling effect on the free dissemination of ideas. Make no mistake: someone is right in this dispute, i.e., there either is a god or there is not, and the aversion that the majority of people have to getting their hands dirty in the substance of the issue is a reflection of either their intellectual inability to handle the subject or their emotional anxiety with respect to the imposing nature of its mythology. Anything worth the devotion of one's entire life is surely worth calm and incisive scrutiny on its merits before one embarks on such a pilgrimage, and to the extent that such a debate is not actively engaged due to the choking ozone produced by the high voltage of the taboo's electric current, then humanity does itself a colossal disservice. The topic needs to be addressed honestly, fairly, reasonably, and relentlessly. Indeed, the only things worth discussing are the topics that make people the most uncomfortable when they are discussed.

Taboos arise around topics that inflame the emotions, and without putting too sharp of a point on it, declining the invitation to puncture a taboo in order to solve the problems that fester beneath its surface is cowardice. It is the duty of those who have been properly educated in how to think in a linear and systematic fashion to conspicuously disintegrate the taboo that protects religious thought. Future generations will not forgive those who knew better than to bow before phantom menaces yet said nothing. And they should not. So, talk about atheism. Somewhere, someone who has never heard anyone dare to defy the invisible emperors of religious thought is waiting to be sprung from the prison of his worst fears.

Second, it is too often the case that people lack the ability to intellectually challenge the assertions of religious thought with respect to their accuracy and reliability in objective reality. To some extent, that is an understandable misfortune because a clever religious debater will know how to send an unpolished person into an epistemological tailspin where he will feel as though nothing whatsoever can be known. On the other hand, religions have sabotaged people's intellectual development in a far more pernicious way, and their duplicity in intercepting or polluting the results of reason-based thinking in order to satisfy their own agenda deserves scorn. In other words, religions have learned that if they cannot stop reason-based thinking from gaining knowledge that will cast religious thought into irrelevance, then their best alternative is to obstruct those results from reaching people in a practical sense.

Especially with respect to the scientific theory of evolution, religions constantly poison the well of education by demanding equal attention for intelligent design and relentlessly peddling the fiction that there is some intellectual competition between these two concepts. Let me be clear: there is no reasonable debate. The explanatory power of the scientific theory of evolution and its constant reaffirmation through a variety of independent evidentiary sources so completely dominates the childish and meaningless intelligent design that to even write their names in the same sentence seems distasteful. Yet people are led to believe that there is an honest controversy between them, which is unacceptable, especially when the same who slander evolution regularly avail themselves of other fruits of scientific investigation that do not similarly offend the narrative of religious thought.

Finally and most importantly, religious thought is maintained because society has failed to educate people on how to handle their emotions. The legacy of Western civilization is an intellectual one of analysis and precision, which has been a fruitful heritage indeed, but its progress has been acquired by deliberately cordoning off the emotions. In order to create methodologies with sufficient control to discover stable and reliable truths concerning objective reality, the partitioning of the intellect and emotions had to take place, and their bifurcation is precisely why the knowledge-acquisition techniques of reason-based thinking are such effective tools for their purpose. However, there is more to a person than his ability to reason on questions of fact, and each person really has two worlds in which he lives: the external realm of objective reality and the internal world of one's subjective emotions, thoughts, and identity.

A major thesis in this book has been that the intellectual dilemmas surrounding religious thought are not difficult to solve in a vacuum, and what makes the issue problematic for people is that they are using their gods and religions as emotional support systems. In fact, most religious believers do not seem to care that their arguments in support of the existence of their god and the legitimacy of religious thought in general are routinely dismissed by a well-reasoned atheist, and the reason that they do not care is because their intellects are being held hostage by their emotions, which they have never learned to properly own, manage, and control. The emotions have the power to dominate the intellect effortlessly, and when they do, a person's ability to reason in an orderly fashion becomes a near impossibility. People's acceptance of religious thought and participation in religion needs to be seen in a different light. Their intellectual errors are not the cause of their acceptance of the ideology; they are a symptom of their emotional disease.

In light of the ease with which one's emotions can subordinate his intellectual analysis, emotional discipline must emerge as the second prong of a person's educational development in the modern world. Society's willingness to offer practitioners and experts to address emotional problems after they have already overwhelmed a person is an insufficient, reactive measure on its own, and it must be complemented by a proactive approach that empowers people to correct their emotional problems before they become disabling. The continued absence of such education is a glaring societal oversight that pretends that an intellectual feast will necessarily result in the quenching of one's emotional thirst. While that can often be the case, surely it cannot always be.

The intellectual tools that humanity has developed have given people tremendous power over their surroundings, but if they are wielded by those who lack some level of mastery of their internal emotions and drives, potential calamity awaits. Consider exactly what religions ultimately want for mankind. Throughout human history, religious leaders have predicted the end of the world, and their followers have rejoiced at the thought of that end being realized. Take a moment to allow that to sink in. Religious believers yearn for the end of all things because that is when they have been told that all of their dreams will come true and when ultimate and perfect justice will be wrought on mankind. The linking of the concept of death with intimate passions of reuniting with a lost love is horrific and disturbing. No other animal on the planet would suffer such reckless lunacy from its community, and to the extent that humanity does, it is playing with fire. In this peculiar time in history where the receding pall of superstition is temporarily in eclipse with the advancement of reason-based thinking, those who close their eyes in bliss at hearing the longing whisper of the annihilation of humanity now exist in the same time and place with scientific products that could actually realize that result in the wrong hands.

Religions deserve to be completely routed on all of the explanations of human existence that they claim for their relevance and legitimacy in order for there to be no mistake about who has the superior argument. Intellectually, their claims with respect to beings existing in objective reality have been routinely exposed as poorly-reasoned and fraught with emotional appeals. Emotionally, they have encouraged people to seize short-term escapism to their long-term detriment. Morally, they have enabled people to abuse and disrespect their fellow man with impunity from their moral enforcement mechanisms by implicitly prioritizing their egomaniacal desire for salvation in death over the benefits of mutual cooperation in life. First and foremost however, truth is not on the side of religious thought, and if man is not willing to grab and desperately consume truth whenever he is able to distill it from the confounding brew of existence, then we are undone.

*   *   *

In the modern age, one's religion is all about personal convenience. The gods of religious believers appear and vanish with impish delight as they limbo around the rays of light shot through the black box in which they operate, and their blessings take suspicious shape. Consider a religious believer who survives a spectacular car wreck but needs months of rehabilitation and surgeries to repair his body. If gods are in such control over the world, why are they given credit for delivering such feeble protection to their followers and none of the blame for overseeing the fact that there was ever a car accident in the first place? The refusal of religious believers to recognize absurdity of this order in their beliefs demonstrates a conspiracy of their emotional desires with the easy failure of their intellects in finding confirmation bias.

Indeed, a simple proposal can lay bare the depths of religious conviction. Many times, I have offered a religious opponent to be my slave until I die and in return I will be his slave forever in the afterlife. No one has ever taken the deal. Why not? His finite servitude would be a blink in comparison to my interminable captivity. They do not take the deal because it represents an inconvenience for them, and they are utilizing their religions for the opposite purpose. After all, every religious believer in the world would be completely bankrupt and impoverished if they believed anything that they claim, but to give all of one's money to the poor and entirely put his faith in his god to protect him constitutes a major inconvenience. Instead, they customize their religions to their liking, handsomely omitting insinuations that the gates of heaven swing closed to those who hoarded money and resources that others desperately needed during their lives.

Deep down, religious believers possess a simmering fear of both the world and themselves, which is compounded by the fact that they have adopted an ideology that frustrates attempts to properly understand either. As a result, they cannot commit to their beliefs in the way that they know is most logical. If one truly believed his religion, he would have his eyes sewn shut as the ultimate gesture of surrender before a god who craves nothing more. Instead, the fear of religious believers distastefully masquerades as deep, intimate love, and that it bubbles to the surface to be spouted forth as incoherent homage to a disarrayed god ought not to confuse one about their emotional turmoil. After all, there can be no deeper horror than to have no idea who you are, and no one knows himself less than he who fails to recognize his own signature on the mental portrait of a god that he himself has painted.

Stripped of the convenient justifications of religious thought, let the religious finally be laid bare to see what they really are. If they hold prejudices for their fellow man on arbitrary bases, they do not deserve to feel as though their malice has some eternal justification or birthright. If they delight in mocking others with tales of their perceived salvation, they do not deserve to see themselves as virtuous. If they implant the code of their religion into secular law, they do not deserve to see their actions as anything more than the impressment of others into their religion against their will. I do not believe that the majority of religious believers who presently do these things would do so if they truly understood the nature of their behavior, and to the extent that their convenient ideology enables their base metals to pollute the aqueducts of their nature, their emotional turmoil perpetuates itself through ironic absurdity.

Speaking of convenience, the true appeal of religions is the manner in which they purport to solve the most confounding problems of the human condition. Framing deeply complex areas like morality and personal meaning as simple and clear-cut, religious thought traps people in a childlike state where nuanced consideration is forfeited for the false embrace of certainty. Considering the complexity of morality, the changeability of personal meaning, and the general gyrations of life, the certainty with which the religious hold their opinions on such overwhelming topics is the best indication that they are wrong. Life is a messy thing, fraught with no-win scenarios and fundamental unfairness, and slicing through its knottiest cords with simplistic answers has appeal. However, a solution offered without showing the work and reasoning employed in its determination receives no credit, and the charming siren's call of easy knowledge is always an illusion.

The price of the convenient solutions of religious thought is paid in its dehumanizing and ghoulish perspectives on the nature of people, which are internalized by its adherents. In many religions, a person is defective by virtue of simply being born, which can only be remedied with one's initiation into a religion. Such a view of mankind is slavish and detestable. Could there be a system of belief worthy of more contempt from mankind than one that appears to have nothing but contempt for mankind? How could one be truly said to have free will when he perceives the infinite penalty of hell on the table beside it? How could one be expected to love a being that he must simultaneously subserviently fear? What is just about meeting finite crimes with infinite penalties? Why do bad things happen to good or innocent people with a benevolent and omnipotent god watching over them? How many flagrant contradictions and contemptuous commentaries about the nature of people is one expected to endure? Nothing makes sense in religious thought, and the people who are seduced by its convenient solutions have accepted a Trojan Horse within their intellectual gates only to find it filled with looters and thieves.

What is religion? It is an insurance company that has the extremely profitable advantage of underwriting policies, the coverage of which only commences at death. It is a corporation with shareholders who provide it with endless funds and never request a say in how the organization is being run. It is a carnival that one attends to be dazzled by the oddities and high-velocity logical carousel, designed to simultaneously entertain and disorient all those who buy a ticket. It is a spiritual casino where the house has rigged the games to never lose and has convinced its guests to play forever. It is a Hollywood blockbuster where the only way one is going to be able to enjoy the show is to suspend all disbelief. Yet, it persists, and it does so because it offers people easy convenience.

If written properly, this book has delivered the message that nothing worth doing is ever convenient. The challenges of conquering one's own emotional fear and intellectual ignorance are not easy, and if they were, there would not be any reason to speak of them. The glory in life lies in the nobility of one's intentions and the quality of his effort, and if one's will to exert effort is sandblasted off his persona and repainted with a complacent finish, he has not been successful in obtaining this high honor. What makes a person extraordinary is his willingness to embrace the inconvenient and to feel fortunate to have the opportunity. The things that come easy are never valued, and to the extent that one accepts the convenient in his life, he ushers personal growth, development, and reward out the door in order to accommodate it.

*   *   *

The fact is that god is simply an idea. For all of the human brain's creative power, it tragically lacks an objective reference to definitively determine which places and beings that it conceives are proper reflections of objective reality and which are not. Human imagination has conjured countless entities that no one believes exist, and no one particularly cares either because these entities do not come with the uniquely interest-piquing skill set of omnipotence and extreme interest in the human race. Some examples of these beings are unicorns, werewolves, leprechauns, and vampires. Almost universally, people recognize these creatures as fantastical and not sourced in objective reality, but when the emotional stakes are raised, people have come to believe in entities that are no different from any in this list from an evidentiary or logical standpoint. Some examples of such beings are ghosts, gods, angels, and demons.

The only difference between these two groups is that the entities on the latter list are linked to a never-ending afterlife. In their respective mythologies, a werewolf could torment a person's body just as viciously as a god, but at least when a werewolf has bled him dry, the pain will end. In other words, the actual existence of werewolves and their threat to humanity have finite stakes. When it comes to gods, infinity hangs in the balance, and people have been averse to taking a risk on being wrong in that regard. Overwhelmed by the perceived costliness of an error that may have infinite ramifications, humanity has for too long been cowed into obedience. Gods are only an idea and a meritless one based on a reasonable assessment of the evidence, and if there is such a thing as a god who would harm a person for not believing that he exists under such circumstances, one ought to consider it an honor to be forever banished from his sight.

Reason-based thinking provides the necessary stability and reliability in its conclusions with respect to objective reality to shake off these specters from past civilizations. Without emotions clouding the analysis, one can see plainly that there is no such thing as theology; there is only mythology, and some of it has not yet fallen out of favor culturally. Werewolves, gods, leprechauns, angels, vampires, and demons are all notes in the same song, drearily playing in the heads of people for centuries and beyond. There is nothing special about any of them, i.e., they are all born from the same human impulse to dramatize and personify one's fears and hopes.

Religious thought perverts a person's rational thinking and teaches him that it is acceptable to cherry pick those aspects of any given outlook on the world that suits him. What the religious do not understand is that their items of modern convenience were built using a methodology, the assumptions of which render believing in gods a preposterous notion. Every time they turn the ignition to their cars and drive them, they are themselves unwitting testaments to the non-existence of gods. Every time they make a phone call, they are silently telling the person on the other end of the line that neither of them has a soul. Every time they simply drop a glass and cringe in anticipation that it will inextricably hit the floor, their reflexes betray their religious indoctrination by implying that they suspect that gods will not arbitrarily stop this chain of causality from being actualized. That they do not realize the implications of their actions is disappointing because the solutions to the puzzle are dangling all around them with every step they take.

To the extent that one wishes to withdraw from scientific knowledge and the fruits of its investigation in order to fully realize his religious convictions, at least that would be respectable from the standpoint of intellectual consistency. The discomfort that the religious feel in the modern world arises from the fact that they are attempting to hold together intellectual magnets of the same polarity, i.e., differing sets of assumptions of the world that both want to explain the same phenomena on their terms. When they inevitably repel each other, the force acts to tear a person apart from the inside when they are both present.

*   *   *

As I have written and spoken about atheism, I have been surprised by the number of religious believers who are energized by hearing its arguments, which is not to say that they all wind up eventually agreeing with me because they do not. Yet, many have seemed excited to hear that they are not alone in sensing that something simply does not add up about religions and gods, and the reason that these things do not add up is because they do not want to be calculated. Their mysteriousness is not an accident; it is deliberate. Religions encourage people to live in a state of intellectual resignation by teaching them to believe in things that they do not understand, and that is a contemptible thing. There is no honor in encouraging people to be afraid. There is nothing to respect about teaching people to cower before a rumor, especially when the supremacy of gods is appropriated by men who use it for their own profit and power. If there is a god who desires such weakness in men, I cannot imagine who would want to be in his blessings if his benevolence takes the shape of our servitude.

Reason-based thinking never sought to do anything but develop rigorous methods of discovering reliable truths about objective reality, but in looking out to examine the world, it inadvertently gained insight into our own identities. All that we have is each other, and scientific inquiry has unintentionally given us the tools to remember that. By squinting through high-powered telescopes to examine the disheartening distances between cosmic bodies, the intimate proximity of our own becomes precious. By bearing witness to the rudderless violence of nature, man's capacity for compassion is respected. By listening to the deafening silence emanating from other worlds, the opportunity to hear even bloodshot rage expressed is a relief.

When certain truths of the universe have been hidden from man, it has often been because he lacked the necessary perspective to understand them. It is quite understandable that people once believed that the earth never moved, was flat, and that the sun orbited it. Casual, unrefined perception would lead to such conclusions. However, man's senses betrayed him in these observations because they had not been checked for accuracy by a rigorous, analytical methodology. Gods, demons, and souls are concepts that ascended to dominance at the same time in human history, and the same principles and thinking that have permitted man to see the true nature of his planet as a globe similarly reveal these other beings as vagaries of perception.

The worldview delivered by the assumptions of reason-based thinking holds exquisite clarity that has harnessed the intellectual power of the brain in order to permit its imagination to run free but not wild. Reason-based thinking lays bare ideas and practitioners who are unapologetically fraudulent and unforgivably exploitative of the well-intentioned and credulous, and it returns our most tender and valuable emotions to us where they rightfully belong. With reason-based thinking, no longer does anything come between a person and his loved ones; one can give his entire self to them and vice versa. Indeed, what other result could be expected from such a convergence in identity? Life matters, and only a fool would spend his daydreaming of the inevitability that it will one day be over for him. In religious thought, The Ultimate Assumption is the culprit that robs people of such awareness and causes people to linger on death in their thoughts, and the obvious trouble with that approach is that when people fixate on death, they miss out on life.

In light of the state of the world and the atrocities that people have seen fit to visit upon each other, one ought to feel tremendous relief to hear the news that there is not in fact a fickle and self-absorbed immortal overseeing this state of affairs. Humanity's problems can only be solved by humans, and the sooner that more people accept that perspective, the sooner creative solutions can be devised and implemented. The rampant injustices that riddle society will never be corrected by gods, and their permanence is assured if humanity has a sensation that they someday will be. Nevertheless, reason-based thinking and its conclusion of atheism cannot save civilization; they only have the power to convince people that no one is coming to do it for them.

Anyone can read the news and lose heart by seeing the worst of mankind, which is largely because news organizations have learned that their readership increases with tales of brutality, intrigue, and other morbid sensationalism. Sadly, their opportunistic exploitation distorts the nature of humanity itself and warps it into a depressing caricature that implies that humanity's doom marches ever closer with each day of corruption, aggression, and misery. Without question, people can be despicable and wretched things, but humanity's best elements are far more numerous than these institutions make them seem. That the voices of these best elements do not rise into violent and entertaining cacophony ought not to mislead one about their frequency in the population.

The best deeds go quietly unnoticed. The most moral person will never get the attention he deserves, and humanity continues into the future nevertheless. The future does not belong to those who terrify man and make him wail upwards in desperation to the silent indifference of the night sky. The future does not belong to those who chill the flames of education in order to selfishly buy more time to clutch the melting pearls of their god. The future does not belong to those who wrack man's spirit with self-hatred. The future belongs to those who come to the aid of their fellow man to clear the cynical obstructions erected in front of him by less scrupulous men. The future belongs to those who enable the liberation of mankind from the sad, invisible shackles of its own creation. The future belongs to those who fling their good names into the fire in defiance of the illegitimate authority of religion, expecting that whenever the tumbling dice of history finally come to rest that they will no longer be counted villains.

Whenever it may be that the ideas of religious thought are ushered into obsolescence, it will not be a dramatic, instantaneous event. Their grip over the brains of people who have never heard them questioned is strong, and most do not want to be rid of them. To defeat these ideas will take courage, determination, and transparency. Technically, the dams of religious thought were blown to pieces a few hundred years ago with the dawn of reason-based thinking. That there are people who do not realize that that intellectual event took place speaks to how crucial it is to protect proper education and fight for it; its lessons were not cheaply bought by our ancestors.

No one knows what course humanity will take into the future, but if there must be a period on the end of our sentence, let it come in a world where the flagships of religion have been thwarted from circumnavigating the intellects of man on the trade winds of his emotions. Religions have seen their day on this planet, and if their goal has been to bring peace to mankind, then they have failed in that objective conclusively. As an investigative methodology, religious thought has yielded no item, instrument, or lesson that has helped to advance society. So, let it go. What are you without god? You are a part of all things, unique only in how your elements have arranged themselves. You are a force equipped with a rare gem in the universe: compassion. You are a person endowed with the glory of action and the torch of reason to light his way. You are a brain that has finally come home to itself.

In the end, life is a strange game, the object of which is not to win but simply to play. So, play well. Be hungry and ravenous for life. Find the people and things that evoke your passion. Release yourself from the fruitless burden of hatred. Be willing to both succeed and fail stupendously. Relish the chance to conquer fear. Earn the prizes of intellectual and emotional discipline. Cherish those who are there for you when the chips are down. Tell people that you love them when you feel it. Decide to be a part of this world. And always remember: to the one who understands that both his revels and his heartaches will always end, peace comes of course.

Acknowledgements

My parents have stuck with me through my eccentricities, always trusting that I knew what I was doing, and for that, I am endlessly grateful. I also thank Raynetta and my cousin, Jen, for being interested in and supportive of my writing before many people were. Truthfully, I am indebted to my entire family from the Smarts to the Deitches to the Krzeminskis. I hope I have made you all proud with the delivery of this final product. You mean the world to me.

As a departing religious believer who had never read a book on atheism, it was very helpful to become a part of an online community that shared ideas and engaged questions of newer skeptics in order for them to develop and stabilize their reasoning. Some people who demonstrate exceptional qualities in both knowledge and patience in this regard are Donovan Badrock (@MrOzAtheist), Melissa (@Mel_in_Canada), and Joe (@JoeUnseen). I respect the time and effort that they have exerted to assist newer atheists who are both intellectually and emotionally vulnerable.

Special scientific acknowledgement goes to Brendan Moyle whose expertise in biology enlightened me on issues surrounding the state of the art. I thank Heather for her incredible support for this project and my work. While this debate can see unpleasant acrimony, Derek Vester has demonstrated that disagreements can happen calmly and with class, which is too rare of an experience. Finally, I would like to acknowledge Jared Riley (@BoyGenius001), Anonymous (@IRaiseUFacts), Dean (@TheDudeinSF), and Archana Sharma (@archie229) for their significant and sincerely appreciated support.

About the Author

Christopher Krzeminski is 31 years old. He holds a B.A. in Mathematics from Duke University in Durham, NC and a J.D. from The University of Alabama School of Law in Tuscaloosa, AL. He currently resides in New Jersey.

He may be contacted for questions or comments by email at chris.krzeminski1@gmail.com or on Twitter @marco_iO9 where he writes under the pseudonym, Marco the Atheist.

CPSIA information can be obtained at www.ICGtesting.com
Printed in the USA
LVOW01s1446251013

358633LV00011B/497/P